Migration, Minorities and Citizenship

General Editors: **Zig Layton-Henry**, Professor of Politics, University of Warwick; and **Danièle Joly**, Professor, Director, Centre for Research in Ethnic Relations, University of Warwick

Titles include:

Rutvica Andrijasevic
MIGRATION, AGENCY AND CITIZENSHIP IN SEX TRAFFICKING

Muhammad Anwar, Patrick Roach and Ranjit Sondhi (*editors*)
FROM LEGISLATION TO INTEGRATION?
Race Relations in Britain

James A. Beckford, Danièle Joly and Farhad Khosrokhavar
MUSLIMS IN PRISON
Challenge and Change in Britain and France

Gideon Calder, Phillip Cole, Jonathan Seglow
CITIZENSHIP ACQUISITION AND NATIONAL BELONGING
Migration, Membership and the Liberal Democratic State

Thomas Faist and Andreas Ette (*editors*)
THE EUROPEANIZATION OF NATIONAL POLICIES AND POLITICS OF IMMIGRATION
Between Autonomy and the European Union

Thomas Faist and Peter Kivisto (*editors*)
DUAL CITIZENSHIP IN GLOBAL PERSPECTIVE
From Unitary to Multiple Citizenship

Adrian Favell
PHILOSOPHIES OF INTEGRATION
Immigration and the Idea of Citizenship in France and Britain

Martin Geiger and Antoine Pécoud (*editors*)
THE POLITICS OF INTERNATIONAL MIGRATION MANAGEMENT

Agata Górny and Paulo Ruspini (*editors*)
MIGRATION IN THE NEW EUROPE
East-West Revisited

James Hampshire
CITIZENSHIP AND BELONGING
Immigration and the Politics of Democratic Governance in Postwar Britain

John R. Hinnells (*editor*)
RELIGIOUS RECONSTRUCTION IN THE SOUTH ASIAN DIASPORAS
From One Generation to Another

Ayhan Kaya
ISLAM, MIGRATION AND INTEGRATION
The Age of Securitization

Zig Layton-Henry and Czarina Wilpert (*editors*)
CHALLENGING RACISM IN BRITAIN AND GERMANY

Marie Macey and Alan H. Carling
ETHNIC, RACIAL AND RELIGIOUS INEQUALITIES
The Perils of Subjectivity

Georg Menz and Alexander Caviedes (*editors*)
LABOUR MIGRATION IN EUROPE

Huub Dijstelbloem and Albert Meijer (*editors*)
MIGRATION AND THE NEW TECHNOLOGICAL BORDERS IN EUROPE

Jørgen S. Nielsen
TOWARDS A EUROPEAN ISLAM

Pontus Odmalm
MIGRATION POLICIES AND POLITICAL PARTICIPATION
Inclusion or Intrusion in Western Europe?

Prodromos Panayiotopoulos
ETHNICITY, MIGRATION AND ENTERPRISE

Aspasia Papadopoulou-Kourkoula
TRANSIT MIGRATION
The Missing Link Between Emigration and Settlement

Jan Rath (*editor*)
IMMIGRANT BUSINESSES
The Economic, Political and Social Environment

Carl-Ulrik Schierup (*editor*)
SCRAMBLE FOR THE BALKANS
Nationalism, Globalism and the Political Economy of Reconstruction

Vicki Squire
THE EXCLUSIONARY POLITICS OF ASYLUM

Maarten Vink
LIMITS OF EUROPEAN CITIZENSHIP
European Integration and Domestic Immigration Policies

Östen Wahlbeck
KURDISH DIASPORAS
A Comparative Study of Kurdish Refugee Communities

Lucy Williams
GLOBAL MARRIAGE
Cross-Border Marriage Migration in Global Context

Migration, Minorities and Citizenship
Series Standing Order ISBN 978–0–333–71047–0 (hardback) and 978–0–333–80338–7
(paperback)
(*outside North America only*)

You can receive future titles in this series as they are published by placing a standing order.
Please contact your bookseller or, in case of difficulty, write to us at the address below with
your name and address, the title of the series and the ISBN quoted above.

Customer Services Department, Macmillan Distribution Ltd, Houndmills, Basingstoke,
Hampshire RG21 6XS, England

Ethnic, Racial and Religious Inequalities

The Perils of Subjectivity

Marie Macey
University of Bradford, UK

and

Alan Carling
University of Bradford, UK

palgrave
macmillan

First published 2011 by
PALGRAVE MACMILLAN

Palgrave Macmillan in the UK is an imprint of Macmillan Publishers Limited, registered in England, company number 785998, of Houndmills, Basingstoke, Hampshire RG21 6XS.

Palgrave Macmillan in the US is a division of St Martin's Press LLC, 175 Fifth Avenue, New York, NY 10010.

Palgrave Macmillan is the global academic imprint of the above companies and has companies and representatives throughout the world.

Palgrave® and Macmillan® are registered trademarks in the United States, the United Kingdom, Europe and other countries

ISBN 978–0–230–24763–5 hardback

This book is printed on paper suitable for recycling and made from fully managed and sustained forest sources. Logging, pulping and manufacturing processes are expected to conform to the environmental regulations of the country of origin.

A catalogue record for this book is available from the British Library.

A catalog record for this book is available from the Library of Congress.

10 9 8 7 6 5 4 3 2 1
20 19 18 17 16 15 14 13 12 11

Printed and bound in Great Britain by
CPI Antony Rowe, Chippenham and Eastbourne

*This book is dedicated to our friend and colleague
Ian Vine (1942–2010), a tireless champion
of democracy and human rights*

Contents

Preface

Migration, diversity and inequality

The root of social diversity in most Western European countries lies in their recruitment of labour from colonies and former colonies to fill gaps in the labour market following the Second World War (WWII). The issue is not one of scale, for migration over this period pales into insignificance relative to that of previous eras (Casanova, 2007). It is, rather, a question of the extent of difference in both cultural and religious terms between the post-war settlers and the European societies that they have made home.

It is also a matter of inequality – which is traceable to the use of labour from outside Europe to do the jobs that Europeans were no longer willing to do. This meant that settlers – whether migrant workers (as in Germany) or citizens (as in Britain) – were usually located at the bottom end of the labour market. This disadvantaged position was exacerbated by widespread (institutionalised) racism which interacted with socio-economic positioning to establish a pattern of inequality that has generally remained stubbornly resistant to change to the present day.

Secularisation and the turn to religion

For most of the post-WWII incomers, religion was, and is, an important part of identity. But for large numbers of the natives of Western European societies, religious observance has been in steady decline. The process of secularisation, that is, is clearly observable – at least in terms of practice, if not self-identification through, for example, Census results in Britain. And whilst there is considerable variation by country, Western Europe can be regarded as secular by any objective measure (Norris and Inglehart, 2007).

Notwithstanding this, in recent years there has been the widespread assertion of a global resurgence in religion such as to predict the death of secularisation (Kepel, 1994; Esposito et al., 2002; Berger, 2007). Certainly, there has been a 'turn towards religion' in public and official discourse, which is reflected in many areas of debate, policy and legislation.

At one level, these trends are evidently contradictory. On the one hand, there has been a continued movement of secularisation, and of further disengagement from organised (or institutionalised) religion within the state and civil society. On the other hand, there has been a renewed recognition of the importance of religion as a focus of personal identity, and – for good or ill – as a source of social action, extending at the extreme to terrorism (Awan, 2007).

But the renewed focus on religion by many states, including, but not only, Western European ones, predates by some margin the recent (ab)use of religion to justify violence. In Britain it was linked to growing concern about ethno-religious inequality and social exclusion and the development of broader conceptions of human rights. It was also linked to changing demands at the grassroots level and the shift in identity politics from a focus on racial equality to one on religious equality (Malik, 2009).

Whatever the reasons, or combination of reasons, there seems, nonetheless, to be a common concern among Western democratic states to address the 'question of religion' in new ways against the backdrop of a widely shared conviction that some of the older ways are inadequate to the new circumstances (Sané, 2007). In particular, the post-Enlightenment location of religion in the private sphere is now challenged by a multicultural ideology that demands its inclusion in the public arena. Indeed, to the extent that government policies, including legislation, now place religion on an equal footing with other equality issues (of race, gender, sexuality, disability and age), religion is already firmly located in the public arena. And this has far-reaching implications for the operation of secular, liberal democratic states.

The purpose of this book

The purpose of this book is to explore some of the issues raised by this new landscape of religion in its international context, with special reference to the experience of Britain. We are interested in both sides of the equation – what changes have been taking place in the religious allegiances or practices of the population 'on the ground', and what policies have been adopted to deal with these new developments. And underpinning this, to ask about the role of religion in relation to minority ethnic inequality.

Our research has brought home to us an important problem in the sphere of ethnicity and religion. This is in addition to the inherent difficulty of separating religion and ethnicity in research terms to establish, for instance, whether discrimination is based on religion or ethnicity, or, indeed on race in the sense of physical differences. This is the extent of the discrepancy that exists between what is *believed* to be the case and what is *actually* the case about the social correlates of religious faith.

This discrepancy applies not just to incidental details of the broad picture, but to such key features as the real extent of religious observance and the incidence of injustice suffered by religious minorities. And it applies not just to the beliefs entertained by some religious or campaigning groups, but to those of many academics and politicians, as well as the general public. The relevance of this finding is that where a discrepancy exists between a social phenomenon and the beliefs held about it by influential social actors, policy can go awry. For example, legislation may be passed to address social problems which are assumed by policy-makers to loom much larger than they actually do. And generally speaking, it seems to us to be preferable to base policy and practice on the facts of the matter (insofar as these are available), rather than on unfounded presuppositions. This is because, as Miles notes: 'As has been said on countless occasions concerning the unity of theory and practice, if the analysis is wrong, then it is likely that the political strategy will not achieve the intended objectives' (1989: 5). Miles' cautionary note applies directly to one of the key issues addressed in this book, that is, the concern to enhance equality between minorities and majorities.

But another of our key concerns in this book is to balance investigation of the harms that may be done to minority ethnic groups on the basis of religion with the question of the harms that both institutionalised religion and its cultural interpretations may inflict on others. These include both believers (of the same and different faiths) and non-believers, and in the book we have concentrated particularly on women and non-heterosexuals. This is not to suggest that these are the only areas of concern within a wider focus on equalities, but it is to propose that in both cases, religion plays a powerful role in legitimising discrimination against them. And this raises two fundamental questions in relation to the (re)introduction of religion into the public sphere. The first concerns the conflict between the widespread religious condemnation of homosexuality and legislation designed to protect the rights of lesbian, gay, bisexual and transexual (LGBT) individuals. The second concerns the potential impact on women of the erosion of the 'secular spaces' which Patel and Siddiqui (2010) claim are an essential precondition of women's struggle for freedom in the personal and public spheres (a point made by Sahgal as early as 1992).

Moreover, the potential effects of these issues are not restricted to minorities within either (or both) majorities or minorities but have implications for wider society at a number of different levels. For example,

Patel and Siddiqui (2010) suggest that the British government's recon-struction of ethnic minorities as faith communities has reinforced the power of (frequently self-styled) community leaders whose agendas are authoritarian/fundamentalist and separatist. This fits uneasily with the focus on cohesion which has been an increasing concern of many Western societies over recent years.

At a different level, religion can be viewed as part of the multicul-tural challenge to Enlightenment thinking and, indeed, to the hegem-ony of Western definitions of modernity itself (Eisenstadt, 2000). And whilst, within a liberal democratic framework, this is a legitimate – and probably necessary – matter for debate (Habermas, 2010), our research suggests that, far from this debate taking place, there is, instead, the dominance of a multicultural and inequalities ideology which amounts to a 'conspiracy of silence' that acts to prevent genuine debate. This is probably linked to what Taylor calls 'the massive subjective turn of modern culture' (1991: 26) and what Berger (2002) refers to as the cul-tural revolution that sought to turn sociology into an instrument of ideological advocacy. The implications of these changes for both the academic enterprise and liberal democracy itself need no rehearsing.

The orientation, and limitations, of this book

This is not a theological work, so that we will not usually be concerned with the contents of religious doctrine, experience or thought, though we are interested in the social effects of some religious beliefs. Nor is it a philosophical work, so that we are not usually concerned to examine abstract concepts in great detail. Our focus, as sociologists, is mainly empirical rather than theoretical, though we are concerned with some of the leading concepts through which the relationship of religion to the polity has been addressed – such as 'multiculturalism', 'secularism' and 'cohesion'.

This book may be read in conjunction with two other works on related topics: *Multiculturalism, Religion and Women* (Macey, 2009) and *The Power of Belief?* (Macey et al., 2010). The latter report was commissioned by a prominent equality and human rights organisation, and contains an extensive review of the recent literature on religion and equality in Britain. It is available at http://bradscholars.brad.ac.uk/. The situation in Northern Ireland is beyond the remit of the current work because it raises distinctive issues concerning a minority religious population's status as a 'national minority' and because of the geographical limita-tion of the main literature search.

Acknowledgements

Alan thanks his partner, Beryl Spink, for her unstinting support and valued comments during an intensive writing process. Both authors thank Sheila Furness for her collaboration in earlier research that has informed the approach taken in this book.

1

Landscapes of Religion or Belief

What is religion?

The premise of this book is that religion is an important topic because what goes by the name 'religion' is important in the lives of many people, and that religious understandings exist in their own right. They cannot be treated as derived manifestations – the ideological reflexes – of cultural or social phenomena defined at other levels.

However, it may not be easy to say exactly what 'religion' involves. The law demands an answer to this question, by granting religion(s) a special legal status in a number of jurisdictions, including Britain and the US (Dennett, 2006). Purdam et al. observe, however, that 'despite its legal recognition, there is no unproblematic definition of religion – either in law or in academic studies' (2007: 147). (See also Weller et al., 2001, and Hepple and Choudhary, 2001.) They nevertheless assert that 'In its broadest sense, religion is a set of recognisable values, practices, and beliefs' (Purdam et al., 2007: 147). This definition would seem to use too broad a brush, since it makes no reference to any distinguishing features of the religious worldview, involving such concepts as the sacred, the holy, the divine or the transcendental. Bruce addresses this issue with the following definition: 'religion...consists of beliefs, actions, and institutions which assume the existence of supernatural entities with powers of action, or impersonal powers or processes possessed of moral purpose' (1995: ix). Dennett has taken a similar line, viewing religions as 'social systems whose participants avow belief in a supernatural agent or agents whose approval is to be sought' (2006: 9). 'With its reference to an ultimate, transcendental source of meaning and authority', adds Aldridge, 'religion has a unique character that sets it apart from secular belief systems' (2006: 153).

The difficulty with these definitions is that they seem to exclude movements of faith or belief that would commonly be included within the purview of 'religion'. Thus the Baha'i faith, which originates historically from within the Islamic tradition, is humanistic, non-scriptural and non-ecclesiastical. It does not therefore exhibit Aldridge's 'authority', expressed through either texts or institutions. Likewise, the origins of Jainism predate both Islam and Christianity, but it has evolved to become atheistic in belief and emphasises norms of personal conduct – such as non-violence and vegetarianism – more than orientation to the transcendental. Quakerism is an outgrowth of the Christian tradition that does not (at least in some variants or interpretations) require a belief in a supra-individual divinity. It can be described as 'post-Christian' rather than Christian, and would be similarly difficult to accommodate within Bruce's or Dennett's or Aldridge's concepts of religion. Buddhism will be excluded by any definition that refers to a supernatural deity. And we have not even begun to ask how 'religion' relates to a (more general) category such as 'spirituality', or whether (or in what senses) the so-called New Religious Movements (NRMs) or New Age Spirituality/ies are indeed religious (see Hick, 2010, for a detailed analysis of this).

Haugh (1990: 2) comments: 'Literally thousands of scholars have attempted to define religion, always with less than satisfying results. No matter how carefully they "define" religion, other experts will eagerly indicate what the definition has left out.' It seems almost impossible to find the right balance between definitions that are too broad (and fail to pick out what is distinctive about religions) and those that are too narrow (and mistake features of particular religions for features of religion as a whole). One definition that appears in a number of dictionaries and websites, including the BBC's, is:

> Religion can be explained as a set of beliefs concerning the cause, nature, and purpose of the universe, especially when considered as the creation of a superhuman agency or agencies, usually involving devotional and ritual observances, and often containing a moral code governing the conduct of human affairs. (www.bbc.co.uk/religion/religions)

This tries to square the circle between the general and the particular by introducing careful words of qualification: 'especially', 'usually', 'often'. Nevertheless, it excludes Buddhism once again, by referring to the 'purpose' of the universe, which Buddhism would deny. But if the reference to 'purpose' were left out of the definition (to allow Buddhism its place as a religion), the whole of natural science would be included within the ambit of the definition, since science certainly tries to explain both the 'cause' and the 'nature' of the universe. So the definition is either too broad (by including science) or too narrow (by excluding Buddhism).

It may be, indeed, that there is no essence shared between all the phenomena that count properly as religious, so that the attempt at definition can never succeed. Max Weber (1963) wisely postponed the question of definition at the start of his great work on *The Sociology of Religion* and had not returned to the question by the end of his unfinished writing on the topic. We will not pursue this issue further, but adopt the declarative approach, and simply name the traditions of thought and action we have in mind.

More specifically, we will take our lead from the answers given by respondents who are asked to indicate their own religious identity. This approach is made much easier for the UK in recent years because of the inclusion of a question on religion for the first time in the 2001 Census, which generated the following results. Just over 42 million UK respondents gave Christianity as their religious identity – nearly 72% of the whole population – followed in order of responses by Islam (1.6 million), Hinduism (559,000), Sikhism (336,000), Judaism (267,000) and Buddhism (152,000). Smaller numbers were recorded in England and Wales for Spiritualism (32,000), Paganism (31,000), Jainism (15,000), Wicca (7,000), Bahai'ism (5,000), Rastafarianism (5,000) and Zoroastrianism (4,000). These named religions and their associated traditions are therefore what we regard as 'religion' for the purposes of this book. In the UK context, we will sometimes use the term 'minority religions' to designate all the non-Christian religious traditions. A large number of people (just over three million) identify with these minority religions, but these represent a small proportion of the population – a little over 5%. To put this in perspective, about three times as many respondents (just over nine million, or 15% of the population) identified themselves as having 'No Religion'. These figures are set out in detail in the Statistical Appendix (Tables 1 and 2).

The social impact of religion

If it is difficult to define what religion is, it is even more difficult to evaluate its overall impact on society. It is perhaps where religions make the appeal to some form of 'higher power' (and 'higher authority') that they become among the most potent of social institutions, with immense potential for both good and ill. Religion can provide people with strength and hope, but it can also be used to mobilise them to divide and to kill (Afshar, 1989; Al Sadaawi, 1991; Lutz, 1991; Rath et al., 1991; Rex, 1991; Turner, 1991; Macey, 1992; Allen and Macey, 1994).

Historically, the scale of influence of religion can be appreciated by the fact that it was responsible for creating much of the social world that we know today (Allen and Macey, 1994). This includes what is often thought of as *Christian* Europe, whose culture has, in reality, been profoundly influenced by both Islam and Judaism (Dummett, 1991; Turner, 1991; Modood, 1992). As an example of their influence, religious institutions have played a central role in the direct provision of education, health and social welfare in Britain. This lessened over time, as the state assumed responsibility for these areas, but well into the twentieth century, the Anglican and Nonconformist churches continued to provide important welfare support at times of economic crisis. And the faith sector continues to make a huge contribution to welfare provision across all areas, including community development, health and social care, post-compulsory education, criminal justice, asylum and refugee services, welfare-to-work, job creation, the rural economy, the arts and cultural life. In fact, the Church of England is the largest voluntary organisation in Britain (Yorkshire Churches, 2002; Furbey et al., 2006; Annette and Creasy, 2007; Grieve et al., 2007; Jochum et al., 2007; Smith and Lowndes, 2007; Church of England, 2008; Davis, 2008). The Anglican Church's high level of service provision, which involves millions of volunteers, is motivated and sustained by what the Commission on Urban Life and Faith (CULF) (2007) and Davis (2008) describe as 'spiritual capital' and Furbey et al. (2008) refer to as 'faith as social capital'. Additionally, there is little doubt that the development of public social policy in Britain was significantly influenced by Christian social thought (Farnell et al., 1994), so that religion has continued to play a role – albeit less overtly – in an apparently secular context. These findings for Britain can be replicated in many other national contexts, particularly the US.

However, a balanced assessment cannot ignore the fact that religion is not only a source of stability and social cohesion, but is often implicated in conflict, including warfare. This is particularly the case in situations of ethnic diversity, as Wirsing (1981) and Turner (1991) point out and as both historical and contemporary reality illustrate all too clearly. Some of the principal religious traditions are sometimes seen as antithetical to human rights and, indeed, as being responsible for some of the worst cases of their abuse in human history (Hitchens, 2007). A number of atheistic writers, including Grayling (2004), Dawkins (2006), Dennett (2006), Harris (2006) and Hitchens (2007), have recently followed up this line of argument with swingeing criticisms of religious belief as a matter of 'blind faith' that is contrary to reason, and opposed in principle both to science and to the Enlightenment discourse from which ideas of human rights derive.

Other writers have opposed the view that religion and secularism must be seen as 'binary opposites' (Dinham et al., 2009; see also Sandercock, 2006, and Baker, 2007). McTernan asserts that:

> In each faith tradition we see an affirmation of life that extends beyond the physical boundaries of their own communities. ... In each tradition ... there is clearly a seminal presence of the right of the individual both to seek truth and to dissent – principles right at the heart of the Universal Declaration of Human Rights. (2003: 148)

Furbey (2008) has argued that all the major world faiths preach the equality and unity of human beings in ways that do not differ from secular human rights thinking. It follows from this view that those who commit rights violations in the name of religion are acting in a profoundly *anti*-religious way. However, it is worth noting that McTernan, who is a Catholic priest with long experience of conflict resolution, also recognises the potential pitfalls of the religious mentality:

> Whatever the psychological, social and political factors that trigger violence in fringe and mainstream religious bodies, the religious mind-set is itself an important factor that needs to be acknowledged and understood if durable solutions are to be found for many current conflicts. (2003: 40)

And Harries, who is a former Anglican bishop, makes a related observation, even if he perhaps generalises too freely about religion in the process:

> There is a particular danger in religion, one that is more fraught with evil than even nationalism. For all religions claim to mediate the absolute. It is easy to topple over the brink and identify that absolute with the final human structures through which that absolute is disclosed to human beings. (2002: 78)

It is similarly tricky to evaluate the historical evidence concerning the role of religion in social conflict. Martin (1997) and Al Sadaawi (1991) note the use to which religion is put by states that are pursuing nationalistic projects or operating authoritarian regimes, and Rex (1991) emphasises its power as a mobilising force. But Martin concludes, nevertheless, that the historical evidence does not support the attribution of a general or central role to religion in conflict. And we have seen above that a fair-minded assessment must also take account of the positive social role played in many contexts by religiously motivated individuals, not least in the areas of social support and social welfare. And though some writers view religion as inherently conservative (Crockett and Voas, 2003), it has also played a key role in various liberation movements, from Gandhi (Hinduism) to Martin Luther King (Christianity).

It is not the purpose of this book to evaluate all these claims and counter-claims in detail, or to address, let alone to resolve, all the issues between religion and science, or between religious and secular worldviews. These issues are well covered elsewhere: see, for example, Midgley (2004) and Furbey (2009) for recent general discussions on the relation between science and religion, Hick (2010) on religion and neuroscience, and Rawls (1999), Parekh (2005) and Modood (2007) on some of the implications for policy. The following basic points will hopefully prove useful, nevertheless, for the subsequent discussion.

First, it will be evident that most of the questions about the role of religion are bivalent. Thus, most religious traditions carry the potentiality for *both* good *and* ill in social terms. Religions typically conflict with science in *some* respects but not always in others. And there is at least a tension, but not necessarily a contradiction, between some religious views and the Enlightenment agenda of equality and human rights. This last relationship with equality and human rights is made more complicated by the fact that religious traditions are rarely in historical practice the monoliths that they are sometimes represented to be. Significant variations of praxis tend to produce a number of branches or interpretations of each religious tradition. As a result of this tendency, differences are liable to occur *within each religious tradition* (and not just between different religious traditions) in the extent to which the religion clashes with equality and human rights. It is particularly important for the argument of this book to distinguish those branches of each tradition that are, roughly speaking, more friendly towards equality and human rights from those branches that are less friendly.

Second, it is striking that the case made by atheists against religious worldviews tends to be (as one would expect) cognitive and rationalist (or materialist) – revolving around such questions as the evidence for religious beliefs that the atheists view simply as incredible. The title of one of Dawkins' books speaks characteristically of *The God Delusion* (2006) in this respect, since it suggests that adherence to a religion involves a straightforward cognitive mistake – a personal or psychological inability to see the external world as it truly is. Setting to one side the question of whether or not this rationalist frame of reference is the appropriate terrain on which to contest the issues between religion and science, it is clear that this way of posing the question tends to leave out of account the emotional aspects of religious observance, and their social resonance. As Durkheim (1915) recognised so clearly, this is an important part of the social reality of religion, and a contributing factor, no doubt, to the longevity of religious traditions. And Marx (1957 [1844]) had already spoken famously of religion as the '*sigh* of the oppressed creature', 'the *heart* of a heartless world' and the '*spirit* of a spiritless situation', choosing words that underline its human appeal (emphasis added). We would note in passing, however, that these (social scientific) accounts fail to note that 'Much in the great world faiths is far from comforting, much is profoundly challenging, and much is, by implication, socially revolutionary' (Hick, 2010: 12).

It is not without irony that a writer such as Dawkins (2003) appears to acknowledge this emotional impact of religion when he suggests that the awe of the natural world, or wonder at the process of evolution, could form the functional equivalent in human terms for love of God. And it is apparent more generally that strong emotions are driving writers such as Dawkins or Hitchens, and not just a detached appraisal of religious arguments. The point for us here is that both religion and science have behavioural and emotional aspects – neither is a purely cognitive activity concerned solely with 'belief'.

Third, we are nevertheless committed to science in the form we take it to have in social science. We are especially keen to examine certain claims made about the social dimensions of religion in the light of the evidence for or against those claims. Our approach is to be distinguished mainly from the recently fashionable trends of postmodernism, which serve to deny the very possibility of social science in our intended sense. We assume, however, that our approach is not incompatible with religious belief itself, so that our presentation below is not party to the argument between religion and science. We assume, that is, that the issues between religion and science are not such as to rule out the possibility of a social scientific approach to religious phenomena, where certain issues at least can be resolved by an appeal to the sociological facts (in so far as these can be established). In this, and regardless of our personal views, we are merely following a distinguished line of religious believers or non-believers from many different traditions of faith or belief who have contributed to the study of the topics considered below.

The social dimensions of religion: identity, belief and practice

Purdam et al. (2007) have cited identity, belief and practice as distinct dimensions of religious experience. (They also include 'Religious Orientation' as a fourth dimension, but this is omitted here because it is not very clearly defined.) These three dimensions do not always go together, which means that the religious landscape of any society needs to be described with reference to all three dimensions.

First, a staple of the theoretical literature is that *identities* are not singular, but plural, and that the expression of these different aspects of identity depends upon the social context. This view has been emphasised recently in relation to religion by Sen (2006) and emerges from a number of other studies, such as those by Burris and Jackson (2000), Hopkins and Khani-Hopkins (2004), Sellick (2004), Hopkins (2006) and Modood (2007). Focus group research, too, has stressed '[the] need to recognise that people have "multiple" identities – they are never just black or female or gay or disabled, for example' (Equal Opportunities Commission [EOC], 2003: 9). Peach says that 'identity is nested and contingent' (2006: 354) and Ansari states that it is 'complex, diverse and equivocal' (2002: 32). This does not mean that every aspect of identity is equally in play in every social context; it merely means that their comparative salience is the subject of investigation. However, a number of studies suggest that some adherents have increasingly prioritised the Muslim religious identity in recent years, particularly young men (Jacobsen, 1998; Macey, 1999b; Dwyer, 2000; Archer, 2001; Mirza et al., 2007).

Second, the issue of *belief* is seen as a way of measuring religiosity (Glock and Stark, 1965) since believers are expected to accept the doctrines espoused by institutionalised religion. The term 'belief' will be used in two distinct senses in this book, however. On the one hand, 'belief' refers to the cognitive aspects of a religious tradition, as in 'the doctrines of the faith'. On the other hand, 'belief' is used to refer to non-religious philosophical systems or worldviews as a whole. The composite phrase 'religion or belief' (sometimes 'religion/belief') is used in a related sense to designate the largest possible range of worldviews, including, for example, atheist or agnostic views. This usage follows the terminology of British law. At other places below, the term 'religion' is used to cover both religion *and* belief. This is in the interests of economy of expression, where the intended contrast is between all ethical/philosophical worldviews and some other aspect of social life. Thus the term 'racial, ethnic and religious identity' is preferred to a term such as 'racial and ethnic identity, and identity of religion or belief'. It is hoped that it will be clear in context which senses of the terms 'religion' and 'belief' are intended.

Third, Purdam et al. define religious *practice* as 'specific religious activities that believers are expected to perform, such as worship, prayer, participation in special sacraments, and fasting' (2007: 154). They also refer to Glock and Stark's stress on the frequency and variation of practice, as well as its meaning and significance for participants.

If we take each of these dimensions separately, we can see that problems are liable to arise in each case about how individuals are to be classified according to their religion. As far as *identity* is concerned, how often, or how strongly, or in which contexts, must one identify with a religion in order to qualify? How much priority must be given to religion, compared with other aspects of identity? And is the test merely subjective, so that every declaration of religious identity must be accepted at face value, or is some objective test of allegiance required, such as participation in a rite of passage, like baptism or confirmation in the Christian tradition? Purdam et al. (2007: 154) have distinguished in this sense between religious 'community', which involves a looser form of identification, and religious 'membership', which requires a stricter test.

It is here that the connection between religious and ethnic identities enters the picture. Put at its simplest, the generally agreed definition of ethnicity in the social sciences centres on the shared cultural characteristics of human groups, including factors such as language, customs and, more problematically, a sense of shared history, nationality or community, formed by narratives of common descent, bonds of mutual relationships and common circumstances or fate. Anderson (1991) has pointed out that these features of ethnicity can be either real or imagined, but they create powerful historical forces in either guise. Since these shared cultural characteristics often include religion, with the shared history being in part a history *of* religion, religious allegiance often forms part of ethnicity. Religious identity would be seen as necessary to ethnic identity in such cases. Conversely, there are instances in which ethnic identity (in the shape of common descent) is regarded as necessary to religious identity, as, for example, the Orthodox insistence on the inheritance of Jewish identity through the female line.

In addition, religions typically have long histories of give and take with their social environments, and are often carried sociologically by popular customs and beliefs as much as by elite discourses and practices. It follows that the traditions are likely to be experienced as whole cloth, with the religious and the cultural elements closely interwoven.

It may take an analytical effort, imposed from outside the lived experience, to distinguish the two, so that religious and ethnic identities may not be separated clearly in the minds of those who possess them. In a recent consultation, Gurharpal Singh has, for example, argued strongly for the inherent linkage between ethnicity and religion in the Sikh case (cited in Woodhead, 2009).

This picture is complicated further by the issue of racial identities, which cut across both religious and ethnic identities. 'Race' is now distinguished from 'ethnicity' in social sciences by referring only to physical characteristics such as skin colour, rather than cultural characteristics (see Mason, 2000, for a clear exposition of this distinction). But these physical features may carry (positive or negative) social valuations in given social circumstances, which can lead in turn to shared experiences by those subject to these valuations, and an associated sense of community. So the distinction between 'ethnicity' and 'race' is not always easy to draw in practice. Indeed, it has become common to use classifications that mix racial and ethnic criteria, such as 'Asian', 'black' and 'white', in order to cover the relevant social distinctions, even at the most highly aggregated levels of analysis. The term 'Black or Minority Ethnic' (BME) is often used for similar reasons. It follows that it is preferable to think generally of a composite *communal identity*, which has racial *and* ethnic *and* religious components. The phrase 'RER identity' will be used on occasion below to mark this social reality. It also follows that religious groups in any given historical situation may vary a good deal in their ethnic and/or racial composition, depending on factors such as their histories of settlement, and patterns of socialisation, recruitment or conversion. Since the 2001 Census asked questions about both religion and ethnicity/race, it has become possible for the first time to offer an extensive map of these variations in the UK context. The full figures are presented in the Statistical Appendix, but the broad picture is as follows.

Looking first at the racial/ethnic composition of religious groups, the Census found that the Christian and Jewish and No Religion groups are almost entirely white. (See Statistical Appendix, Figure 1.) The Hindus and Sikhs in Britain are largely of South Asian origin and of Indian ethnicity, although some people of Indian heritage came to Britain from East Africa following mass expulsions (especially those orchestrated by Idi Amin in 1972). Such migrants brought with them levels of social capital that may help to account for some of their families' subsequent attainment.

The Muslims from the Indian subcontinent originate mainly in Bangladesh and Pakistan. Muslims as a whole in Britain are, however, more heterogeneous than many other religious groups, with a third having an ethnicity other than South Asian. Buddhists are also a diverse religious group from the viewpoint of race/ethnicity, with 39% white and 51% 'other ethnicity' (which includes Chinese).

Taking the opposite tack, and looking at the religious composition of racial/ethnic groups, the black-Caribbean and white groupings are largely Christian by self-identification (over 80%), and with similar proportions answering 'No Religion' (15% or more). (See Statistical Appendix, Figure 2.) The black African group has a much lower proportion of 'No Religion' than the black-Caribbean group, and a significant Muslim component (22%). The Indian group is the most mixed by religion, containing Hindus, Sikhs, Muslims and Christians. By contrast, members of the Bangladeshi and Pakistani groups are almost exclusively Muslim (98% in both cases).

The variations in these relationships indicate the dangers of essentialising the characteristics of either ethnic or religious groups, and of using religious and ethnic descriptions as substitutes for one another. In some circumstances, it may be reasonable to marry the two, by assuming that Pakistani or Bangladeshi respondents are Muslim, for example. But it is generally less reasonable to treat South Asians as Muslims, or *vice versa*. The broad conclusion is that it is always necessary to bear in mind the distinctive, and potentially independent, contributions to a person's communal identity made by the distinct aspects of race, ethnicity and religion. This 'hyphen-group' perspective on communal identity is further reinforced by studies of social inequality, as covered in Chapter 2.

The dimension of religious *belief* raises its own uncertainties of classification: must the assertion of the relevant beliefs demonstrate knowledge and understanding, or will rote recitation suffice? Which beliefs is it necessary to endorse in any case, in order to establish allegiance to a particular religion? And how much doubt (if any) can be entertained simultaneously about these beliefs? This issue of classification, which arises in the first instance as a somewhat technical matter, cuts quite deeply into the structure of religious institutions. It raises questions concerning both the content of belief – what is the essential core, the credal heart, of a given religion? – and the authority to decide – who says?

As we have seen above, the existence of either scriptural or institutional authority cannot be made into a defining characteristic of religions in general. But many religions nevertheless exhibit both forms of authority – indeed, in sociological terms they can be said to be constituted by this dual source of authority where it exists. It is not uncommon for religious texts to be arranged, for example, in a hierarchy of authority, with those at the top of the hierarchy most central to the tradition. This pattern applies to the Bible in the Catholic tradition compared with, say, the catechism, or to the *Qur'an* compared to the *hadith* in Islam.

And since religious traditions develop over time, and respond to new circumstances (and, indeed, to new knowledge and to new technologies), the list of 'authoritative' (or potentially authoritative) texts continues to grow to some degree, even if they do not seek to challenge the most definitive statements of the faith. There is, for example, the practice of *Qiyās* ('deduction by analogy') within Islam, or the *Responsa* tradition ('questions and answers') within Judaism, which have historically extended the reach of faith to new fields. But the existence in practice of a variety of texts, with a variety of claims to authority, inevitably produces a boundary problem for each religious tradition: what is essential to the faith – the *sine qua non* of adherence to the tradition – and what is merely incidental (or perhaps 'desirable but not essential') for the true believer? Where these boundaries of faith are drawn, and how much leeway is allowed for new developments, are factors that tend to separate historically the 'orthodox' from the 'modernising' tendencies within each tradition.

A similar point applies to religious authority, which can be institutionalised and/or attained in a variety of different ways. The authority can be concentrated or dispersed in operation; personal or collegiate in location; 'authoritarian' or 'liberal' in tone; educational or intellectual, bureaucratic or charismatic (or even commercial) in origin, and so forth. The important implication here is that, given these typical structures, religions are inevitably *sites of contestation*, concerned with both doctrine and the location of the authority to determine the doctrine. As a result, there may be no neutral answer to the question of what comprises the core of belief for a given religious tradition, and what lies in its penumbra. To draw the lines of faith at one place rather than another may favour one interpretation of doctrine over another and accede in effect to one source of authority within the tradition at the expense of another.

The fact that the law recognises religions for certain purposes makes these boundary issues directly relevant to practitioners. The Chartered Institute of Personnel and Development (CIPD) has asked, for example, 'if…a Christian is [legally] protected if he or she has been baptised but does not attend church' and whether it is 'necessary to have made a conscious decision to be an Atheist, having considered the issues [in order to establish oneself as an Atheist]' (2003: 6, 2).

The answers will evidently depend on what the courts decide, but in order to do so, the courts will be drawn inevitably into a process of adjudicating the different interpretations and authorities within each religious (and non-religious) tradition. It is not obvious that they are generally well-equipped to perform this task. At a deeper level, the argument above suggests that this cannot be done in a neutral way, and the courts – and thus the power of the state – may be enlisted, in effect, on one side of internal religious disputes rather than another. This is not to argue that the state should avoid protecting religions; it is to point out a probable consequence of it doing so.

The boundary issue also applies to religious *practices*, which may be extended from religious rituals or sacraments in the strict sense (whether or not these are performed at designated places of worship) to many other aspects of attitude and/or behaviour that may be said to constitute 'a religious way of life'. Purdam et al.'s definition of practice given above may be too narrow in this respect, since it speaks of religious sacraments but not the whole of life. The significance and scope of religion to a person's existence can plainly vary, depending on how many, and which, of life's activities fall under its distinctive sway. But how much does each religion demand of its adherents by way of minimal commitment, say, in their daily lives? Once again, different sources of authority within the same religious tradition may put forward different positions on this question and invoke different texts to support them. So it may not be easy to decide what constitutes the appropriate test for religious adherence on the dimension of practice. This point was made memorably by one Western Buddhist respondent to a religious survey who said: 'To the question "Are you a Buddhist?" all less than Buddha must say "to some extent yes, to some extent no"' (Weller, 2004: 10).

If the uncertainties on these three dimensions are considered together, it can be seen that there is an even greater uncertainty – a compound uncertainty, so to speak – about where the boundaries of each tradition are to be drawn in terms of a *combination* of identity, belief and practice. At one end of the composite spectrum are those who say they belong to a religion, but who do not avow its (allegedly) characteristic beliefs or follow any of its (conventionally recognised) practices. At the other end of the spectrum there is, well, Buddha.

The fact that religious identity, belief and practice are not always aligned can produce quite different impressions of the religious landscape of a given country, depending on which aspect is emphasised, and how it is measured. This choice of measure impacts in turn on questions such as secularisation, and affects the judgement that is made about changes in the religious landscape over time, as we consider next.

How Christian is Britain? The Census question and the issue of secularisation

When it was decided to include a Census question on religion for the first time in 2001 'the approach adopted ... was a deliberate decision to use a measure [for religion] based on identity rather than practice' (Office for National Statistics [ONS], 2006: 2). In England and Wales, the question asked was 'What is your religion?' For Scotland and Northern Ireland, the equivalent question was 'What religion, religious denomination or body do you belong to?' (ONS, 2006: 17). As indicated above, a large majority of the UK population – nearly 72% – answered 'Christian' to one of these questions.

However, this finding of the extent of Christian identification is sharply at odds with the evidence regarding Christian religious practice or Christian belief. If church attendance is adopted as a measure of Christian practice, for example, then religious activity shows a steep, progressive decline over time (Brierley, 2000; 2005; 2006a,b; 2008; Bruce, 2002; 2006; ONS, 2003; Crockett and Voas, 2006; Voas and Bruce, 2006). This is coupled with the diminishing – albeit still substantial – role of the Christian religion in law-making, education, culture, welfare service provision and, perhaps, individual consciousness. One of the reports from the organisation Christian Research on decreasing church attendance is dramatically entitled *Pulling out of the Nosedive* (Brierley, 2006a). The research shows that attendance declines with each successive age cohort, does not seem to be a response to the allegedly distinctive experience of WWII or the 1960s, and there is some evidence of decline by generation among immigrant families of both Christian and non-Christian religion (Coleman et al., 2004; Crockett and Voas, 2006).

This evidence is consistent with the view that Britain is experiencing a general process of secularisation, a process that is linked in the sociological literature with Enlightenment thinking and modernisation. It is defined as a long-term tendency by which religious thinking, practice and institutions lose their significance, so that religion 'ceases to be significant in the working of the social system' (Wilson, 1982: 150). Secularisation in the West is seen to be highly advanced and to operate at the socio-structural, cultural and individual levels (Berger, 1967). Most of the key figures of modern social thought generally believed that religion would cease to be significant with the advent of industrial society – Auguste Comte, Herbert Spencer, Emile Durkheim, Max Weber, Karl Marx, Sigmund Freud (discussed in Bruce, 1992, and Aldridge, 2000). The 'death of religion' has been the dominant approach throughout most of the twentieth century, as crystallised in the observation by C. Wright Mills that 'In due course, the sacred shall disappear altogether, except, possibly, in the private realm' (1959: 32–3).

This viewpoint seems to be borne out by the most recent Church Census in England, which covers all the Christian denominations and found that just 6.3% of the population were attending church on the appointed Sunday – 8 May 2005 (Brierley, 2006a). There is thus an astonishing discrepancy – of greater than an order of magnitude in percentage terms – between this figure and the findings of the UK Census mentioned above. Viewed from the perspective of (self-reported) identity, Britain can be characterised as 'a majority Christian country'; viewed from the perspective of religious activity (as measured by Church attendance) Christianity is the preserve of a very small minority – an active interest affecting less than one in fifteen of the population. How can these findings be reconciled?

An initial issue involves the wording of the Census question itself. Voas and Bruce (2004) have suggested that the question in England and Wales encouraged a 'Christian' response as a statement of a national (or ethnic) identity rather than a religious identity. The British Social Attitudes (BSA) survey was conducted in the same year as the Census, using a different question 'Do you regard yourself as belonging to a particular religion?' and produced a much lower 'Christian' total – 54% rather than 72% (Voas and Bruce, 2004; ONS, 2006: 4). Davie has pointed to the central uncertainty, asking 'what the 72% who declared themselves to be Christian really meant. Did they mean they were not secular? Or did they mean they were not Muslim (or indeed any other world faith)?' (2004: 58). It seems clear, then, that the form of words does make a difference to the response, and that the context does matter: what appears to be a statement of religious identity may carry a different meaning in the micro-context of completing a Census return.

Alternatively, it may be that the Census question for England and Wales was interpreted by respondents as a question about religious upbringing or background rather than current allegiance (Scottish Executive, 2005). A careful comparison of the findings for England and Wales with those for Scotland, and some other survey data, suggests that this did indeed occur in a number of cases (Macey et al., 2010). This analysis suggests that the BSA survey figure (of 54%) provides a more accurate indication of Christian self-identification than the National Census result in England and Wales. The comparable figure for Scotland is 69%.

This conclusion brings the figures for Christian self-identification and Christian practice slightly closer together, but it still leaves a huge difference to explain. The key to this explanation is that the various surveys are measuring *different dimensions of religion*, so that the divergent figures are picking up different aspects of a more complex social reality. What these results mean for 'Christianity' in the UK depends on the judgements that are made about how religion is measured with respect to these dimensions, and where the threshold values for minimum Christian compliance are set.

It is clear, for example, that the Church Census figure of 6.5% underestimates Christian churchgoing in England, since it excludes those who happened to be absent on the appointed Sunday. Brierley (2005) gives a figure of 8% for 'regular churchgoers' in 2000, representing a decline of over a quarter from the 1980 figure of 11%. The 2005 Church Census also recorded a figure of 8% for those attending church at least quarterly. This rises sharply, however, to 14.5% of the English population who attend church at least once a year – a rise caused mainly by those who attend just at Christmas (Brierley, 2006b). Thus, if church attendance is made the litmus test of Christian practice, there is still a considerable range in the estimated proportion of practising Christians – between 8% and 14.5%, depending on the threshold chosen for 'minimal Christian practice': should this involve attendance at least four times a year or at least once a year? And it might be questioned whether church attendance is in any case the only relevant test of Christian practice. There will be devout Christians who are prevented from attending church through personal circumstances, such as illness or disability. Or there might be a more relaxed general test for Christian practice, such as 'praying or reading the Bible, but not going to church' (Brierley, 2006a: 152), which would include those who are absent by choice as well as circumstance.

Even though the question of where to draw the line remains a matter of judgement, it seems reasonable nonetheless to accept the figure of 14.5% for the proportion of practising Christians. This estimate takes a conservative view, in the sense that it tends to maximise the figure for Christian participation, and it includes very large numbers of individuals who attend church just once a year, usually at Christmas.

This test of practice is not a particularly demanding one, but it still leaves out of account at least 40% of the population – over twenty million individuals in England and Wales – who identify with Christianity but are not practising according to this test. This is the group whom Brierley (2005) has described as 'nominal' or 'notional' Christians. In a succession of important publications, Davie (1994; 2001; 2002; 2004; 2005; 2006) has focused debate on these 'believers but not belongers', who 'retain some sort of belief in God (or a life force), but rarely attend a place of worship' (2004: 55).

The first implication of Davie's work is that the secularisation thesis may be overstated, since the decline in church attendances may not imply a commensurate decline in religious faith. But the clue to the second implication is provided by her reference to 'life force' in the quotation above. As Davie has acknowledged, the severing of ties with organised religion can lead to doctrinal 'drift', in which the content of religious beliefs becomes diffused:

> those who cease to go to church for a wide variety of reasons…lose, as a result, the discipline that comes with regular attendance and participation in liturgy. What seems to occur thereafter is a drifting away from the credal or historic statements of faith (and in Britain, this usually means Christian faith) towards forms of belief with a stronger emphasis on immanence rather than transcendence, on the God within rather than the God without – in other words, towards patterns that fit more easily into a culture dominated by consumption. (2002: 332)

This underlines how the dimensions of religious practice and belief are tied together in practice, even if they are separable analytically. But it also raises a significant boundary issue in relation to belief: at what point in the attenuation of specifically Christian beliefs do the 'believers but not belongers' cross the line from the Christian religion to some more general spiritual – rather than religious – approach? Once again, it is a matter of judgement where the threshold of 'minimal Christian belief' is to be located, but it seems reasonable to say that belief in a 'life force' is insufficient to qualify as a variety of Christian understanding, counting rather as a more general spiritual consciousness.

Relatively little information is available about the precise distribution of religious and/or spiritual views among the Christian-identified population, so it remains difficult to be sure how many individuals fall on the Christian side of the line in relation to belief, and how many are on the spiritual – non-Christian – side. Brierley (2005) presents some data suggesting that spiritual views outnumber religious (Christian) views in the population at large. One authority has claimed moreover that:

> Surveys [other than the UK Census]…show that something quite extraordinary is happening. In Britain, let alone other European countries (especially in the north), the number of people believing in a personal God [of Christian tradition] has become considerably smaller than the number of people believing in the God within or some sort of spirit or life force. (Heelas, in Brierley 2006b: 0.4)

If this is so, then a conservative (religion-maximising) assumption would be that at most half of those with an acknowledged Christian identity (who are assumed to believe in some form of God) are also Christian believers (in the sense of believing in a recognisably Christian God). This would imply that Christian believers form up to 27% or 36% of the population, depending on whether the BSA figure or the UK Census figure is taken as the baseline for Christian identification. This range is consistent with the figure of 31% of British respondents who said they believed in a 'personal God' in the 1999–2000 European Values Survey, compared with the 40% who believed in a 'spirit or life force' (Weller, 2008: 51; and see Bruce, 2006, for comparable estimates).

To complete the picture of Britain's landscape of religion/belief, the same questions about identity, practice and belief need to be asked first in relation to the minority religions, and second in relation to secular belief systems.

Identity, belief and practice: the minority religions

Just as there are individuals of Christian identity or background who are more or less 'Christian' in their religious beliefs and practices, so Ameli et al. (2004) and Brown (2000a) refer to 'cultural and secular' or to 'nominal' and 'sociological' Muslims respectively, and Graham (2003) distinguishes similarly between 'secular' and 'religious' Jews. Modood et al. (1997) found that 95% of Muslims, 89% of Hindus and 86% of Sikhs defined religion as 'very' or 'fairly' important in their lives, relative to 46% of Anglicans and 69% of Catholics. The 2001 Citizenship Survey found a similar gradient for the importance of religion compared with other aspects of personal identity, with 67% of Muslim, 61% of Sikh, 51% of Hindu and just 21% of Christian respondents who 'said that their religion said something important about them' (ONS, 2006).

The 2005 Citizenship Survey found that 79% of Muslims were 'actively practising', compared with 73% of Hindus, 74% of Sikhs, 54% of 'Other Religions' and just 38% of Christians (Kitchen et al., 2006). These proportions are lower in each case than the figures given by Modood for those who attach personal importance to their religious allegiance. This suggests the existence of a gap between identity and practice for the minority religions, just as in the Christian case. The figures indicate that the gap may be narrower for the minority religions than for Christianity, but it is difficult to be sure how comparable the different surveys are. Zubaida (2004) puts the total for practising Muslims throughout Europe much lower (at around 30%, with 70% as 'secular or cultural Muslims'). Mirza et al. (2007) note that their Muslim respondents vary in the extent to which they observe religious prohibitions on alcohol, for example, or interest-bearing mortgages. A survey conducted by Channel 4 Dispatches (2006) found that although 89% of Muslim respondents rated religion as 'very' or 'fairly' important, 48% of the same sample never attended mosque. Again, it is a matter of judgement (and potential controversy) as to what constitutes 'minimal practice' for the Islamic religion, but the figures are nonetheless suggestive. And there are some general indications of a declining trend of observance in non-Christian religions, as there is in the Christian case (O'Beirne, 2004; Zubaida, 2004; Channel 4 Dispatches, 2006; Mirza et al., 2007).

Overall, it seems fair to conclude that minority religions experience pressures similar to those affecting the Christian faith, including the pressures of secularisation (and Davie's 'consumerism'). It may be that the disjunction between these dimensions is not as marked (or as far advanced) as in the Christian case, but the quality and coverage of the evidence is insufficient for confidence on this point. A conservative (religion-maximising) estimate for the proportion of practising members among those identifying themselves with minority religions is about 80%. This implies that about 4% of the British population practises a minority religion (given that 5% identify with one of the minority religious traditions according to the Census data).

Identity, belief and practice: the alternatives to organised religion

Issues of identity, belief and practice do not arise only for organised religions. A person can take steps to identify explicitly as a Humanist by, for example, becoming a member of the British Humanist Association.

The 2005 Citizenship Survey suggested that there is no distinction between a practising and a non-practising Atheist by categorising all those of 'No Religion' as 'not actively practising' (Kitchen et al., 2006). Yet recent publications have raised interesting issues about Humanist or Atheistic identification, practice and belief (Belden and Grayling, 2005; Dennett, 2006; Grayling, 2007). These include proposals to change the self-chosen designation of Atheists. Dennett (2006) has suggested 'brights', whereas Grayling (2007) prefers 'naturalists'. The idea, presumably, is to enhance the visibility of Atheists and to reinforce their sense of identity.

Kemp (2003) discusses 'New Age' allegiances similarly, and Brierley (2008) provides a statistical digest of NRMs, which have also been covered by Barker (2001), and alternative forms of spirituality, covered by Heelas (2001) and Heelas and Woodhead (2005). Generally speaking, however, there is a dearth of research information on the alternatives to organised religion that is somewhat surprising, given the proportional sizes of the groups concerned.

And the Census is not as helpful in this respect as might be hoped. Just as there is an issue in understanding the 'Christian' response to surveys, there is an issue about what 'No Religion' means. Does it imply a rejection of organised religion, or a rejection of belief in God, or, alternatively, an acceptance of a 'spiritual' view, which is regarded as distinct from 'religion' as such? And where should Agnostics place their tick? Since different respondents may approach the question in a variety of different ways, it becomes very difficult to assign a precise meaning to the results of the surveys. It may be noted, for example, that whereas 15% of Census respondents said that they had 'No Religion', the figure for the contemporaneous BSA survey was much higher – 40% (ONS, 2006). The most recent report from the Pew Global Attitudes Project (2008) found that a majority of British respondents (57%) saw religion as being either 'not at all important' in their lives (34%) or 'not too important' (23%).

There is a humorous episode that throws an unexpected light on some of the issues involved. Following an Internet campaign, just over 390,000 adults (0.7% of the population) defined themselves as Jedi Knights in the 2001 Census (www.statistics.gov.uk; Weiss, 2004 [Weller, 2008, misreports this number as just over 39,000 rather than the correct figure of 390,000, although he does have the correct percentage – 0.7%]). The authorities classified these respondents, no doubt sensibly, as having 'No Religion'. But notice that these figures make 'Jedi

Knights' as numerous as all but the Muslims and the Hindus among the minority religious groups. If the definition of religion or belief is confined to identity, and the answers given to the Census question are regarded as sufficient to determine identity, then it would become very difficult to refuse consideration to the Jedi Knights as a substantial 'group of religion or belief' on this basis. This demonstrates the problem of relying, as the Census does, on identity alone for the ascription of religion or belief. It seems clear that this decision by the Census authorities, coupled with the wording of the question as it applied in England and Wales, led to a dramatic overestimation of the Christian presence in contemporary Britain, and a corresponding underestimation of the alternatives to organised religion.

As Weller (2008) has argued, the religious landscape in the UK is best considered in tri-partite terms, as including (a) a Christian component, (b) a plurality of organised minority religions and (c) a set of alternatives to organised religion. Weller describes the latter as 'secular', but this designation does not do justice to the range of viewpoints involved. It seems better to characterise the alternatives to organised religion in terms of *an alternative spectrum of spiritual, agnostic or secular practice and belief.* This designation embraces those who:

- Adopt spiritual beliefs, leanings and/or practices which lie outside the organisational and theological frameworks of the major faith traditions (including 'believers but not belongers' whose beliefs are 'spiritual' rather than 'religious');
- Hold agnostic views of a kind that do not serve to align them with any specific system of religious, spiritual or secular practice or belief;
- Reject religious and spiritual belief systems, and may identify themselves explicitly with a secular belief system, such as Humanism or Atheism;
- Have no religious or spiritual views (or any comparable non-religious outlook).

This spectrum almost certainly includes a majority of the population in England, and it may account for as many as two-thirds. Occupants of this alternative spectrum may still, however, identify themselves as 'Christian' (especially by heritage and/or upbringing) in various social contexts or for various social purposes (such as answering the Census question about religion).

Britain's landscape of religion or belief

Pulling all these findings together, a reasonable estimate for the distribution of religion or belief emerges for Britain as follows:

Christianity

- Christian Believers: at most 27%–36%, including
- Practising Christians (attending church at least once a year): 15%

Minority Religions

- Practising Members: 4%

Alternative Spectrum

- Spiritual (post-Christian) Believers: at least 27%–36%
- No Religion: at least 15%

An estimate for the 'religious population' (in the sense of those having a connection with organised religion in terms of practice and/or belief) is therefore up to just over two-fifths at the very most. Depending on the definitions used, the proportion actually practising any religion is probably no more than a fifth. The majority of the population almost certainly occupy one of the positions in the alternative spectrum, although the precise distribution of views within this broad spectrum remains uncertain.

It should be emphasised that these estimates rely on very relaxed definitions of what it means to practise or to believe in Christianity and make the statistical assumptions most favourable to the totals for organised religion. It should be noted, on the other hand, that the best estimates for Christian practice come from the Church Census, which took place in England alone, so that the estimates will extend to Britain as a whole only if it can be assumed that the patterns of Christian attendance in Scotland and Wales are sufficiently similar to those in England. And no assumptions are made for estimation purposes about those who did not answer the Census question on religion, who included almost 8% of UK respondents. Although the broad outlines of the religious landscape are reasonably clear, many of the details remain shrouded in uncertainty.

Trends and counter-trends in religion or belief

A balanced appraisal of the currently available evidence bears out the secularisation thesis to a greater extent than appears to be the case from the Census data considered at face value. But it does not follow that the process of secularisation is bound to continue, because a number of counter-trends are also evident. Mirza et al. (2007) found that belief is systematically more intense among younger than older cohorts of Muslims, and the dramatic reduction in the number of observant Christians does not apply uniformly. A notable exception is the Pentecostal tradition generally and the more recent West African movements in particular (Hunt and Lightly, 2001; Hunt, 2002; Christian Research, 2005). Martin (2001) estimates that there are at least 250 million Pentecostals worldwide and possibly many more, because of the growth in countries such as China where reliable information is scarce. Berger (2007) argues that the two most dynamic religious movements are resurgent Islam and popular Protestantism, notably Pentecostalism. Vulliamy (2006) notes that migration from Eastern Europe is helping to revive inner-city Catholic churches in some areas of Britain. Smith (2000) records the growth of a number of new religious groups in Newham (East London) – Hindu, Muslim and Sikh, as well as Pentecostal Christian. Indeed, 94 out of the 171 religious groups studied (especially the Pentecostal churches) had been founded since 1971, which suggests that the secularisation process is far from consistent over time. Similarly, Hunt and Lightly (2001) and Hunt (2002) describe one Nigerian church, established in London in 1994, that had developed 50 congregations in England with a combined membership of approximately 170,000.

Davie has described the conservative Evangelical church as 'the success story of late twentieth century churchgoing' (2006: 28). This is reflected in the growing Evangelical presence among Anglican ordinands (Gilliat-Ray, 2001), which has reversed earlier predictions of a trend towards a liberal ministry (Towler and Coxon, 1979). And Brierley (2006a) estimates that 100,000 people started to attend church through Alpha courses in the years from 1998 to 2005.

Kaufmann (2007a,b) has contributed another element to the debate by linking secularisation with demographic factors. He investigated the three Abrahamic faiths in Europe, North America and Israel, and found consistently higher birth rates among religious than non-religious families, and among conservative families of each tradition than non-conservative families. Projecting these trends forward for Europe, he concludes that 'by 2045, the proportion of secular people will have peaked, and de-secularisation will begin, albeit gently' (Kaufmann, 2007a: 7). A recent issue of *Religious Trends* has also attempted to predict the future balance of numbers between different faith groups (Brierley, 2008).

Although the credibility of Kaufmann's and Brierley's detailed predictions is dependent on more information becoming available about religious mobility (see the discussions in Kaufmann and Voas, 2007, and Moore et al., 2008), these contributions reinforce the argument that there is nothing inevitable about secularisation. And the balance between the more orthodox and the more liberal tendencies within each tradition is a matter of general public concern, as we will argue below. It is not just an internal issue for the traditions themselves.

Overall, the recent turn to religion has led to some notable reassessments from prominent scholars. Peter Berger (1967) was cited above as an early exponent of the view that secularisation is a consequence of modernity. But thirty years later he was writing about the 'resurgence' of religion, and, whilst noting that western and central Europe were exceptions to the global trend, felt able to suggest that 'this means that a whole body of literature by historians and social scientists loosely labelled "secularization theory" is essentially mistaken' (Berger, 1999, cited in Norris and Inglehart, 2007: 32). More recently he has reiterated this position, stating that it is religious pluralism, rather than secularism, that follows from modernity: 'The contemporary world, far from being secularized, is characterized by a veritable explosion of passionate religion' (2007: 21); 'Simply put, [secularisation theory] has been empirically falsified' (2007: 20).

Other writers, too, have challenged the secularisation thesis. In 1990, Stark published an article entitled 'Secularization, RIP', and in 2000, Stark and Finke stated: 'After nearly three centuries of utterly failed prophesies and misrepresentations of both present and past, it seems time to carry the secularization doctrine to the graveyard of failed theories' (2000: 79).

There is little doubt that these obituaries for secularisation are premature. As we have seen above, secularisation is alive and well in Britain, both as a current fact and as an historical tendency. This finding is borne out by a careful survey of the international scene carried out by Norris and Inglehart. They conclude that:

> The existing evidence in Western Europe consistently and unequivocally shows two things: traditional religious beliefs and involvement in institutionalized religion (1) vary considerably from one country to another and (2) have steadily declined throughout Western Europe, particularly since the 1960s.

and that:

> Regular churchgoing also dropped during the last two decades in affluent English-speaking nations such as Canada and Australia. (2007: 34, 35)

Discussing the question of whether the US is an exception to the European trend, or whether Europe is an exception to the American trend, they conclude that:

> the United States remains one of the most religious in the club of rich countries, alongside Ireland and Italy. ... Nevertheless, the accumulated evidence suggests that secular tendencies in the United States may have strengthened, at least during the last decade, narrowing the gap with the less religious societies that dominate Western Europe. Public displays of religiosity by politicians and the salience of religious issues in an increasingly diverse population should not be confused with a broad-based religious revival within society. There is little evidence of the latter. (2007: 40)

This conclusion points in the same direction as a number of other arguments considered in this book. What has been called 'the re-emergence of religion as a social force' (as part of the title of a conference held in Cambridge, UK, in 2010) may be described more accurately as 'the re-emergence of religion as a political force'. It is perhaps not surprising that the latter has occurred in the wake of 9/11, religiously claimed bombings in Europe and Asia and international conflict in Afghanistan, Iraq, the Middle East and elsewhere. But the increased volume of discussion of religion in political circles, in the media and culture more generally and in academic research should not be taken to indicate an increase in religiosity in everyday life. We are confident of this conclusion regarding the United Kingdom, and the broad sample of other post-industrial countries covered by Norris and Inglehart's research. The situation may well be different in other parts of the world, but we would have to be convinced of any such countertrend by systematic empirical work that respected the complex social character of religious allegiance and practice.

Religious identity and the peril of subjectivity

We will leave this chapter with two general observations, both concerned with the idea of 'religious identity'.

First, there is a *performative* aspect to a religious identity that may not be present in the same way for other dimensions of personal identity. It is not enough simply to say that one belongs to a religion in order to do so. It is necessary also to believe certain propositions, and to act in certain ways in certain contexts – to *possess* the faith and also to *demonstrate* it. Contrast this, say, with age. A person's age is given by the time that has elapsed since their date of birth. The demonstration of one's age requires at most the presentation of evidence about one's date of birth; it does not require a person to say anything in particular, or to believe anything in particular or to do anything in particular. There are, of course, numerous social constructions placed upon age, and it is in virtue of these constructions that issues of rights, equality and justice arise that bring 'age' within the purview of politics and law. But the identification itself exists independently of the social construction.

By contrast, religious identification is determined by its social construction: one *is* a certain age, but one must *act* a certain religion (or belief). It is beyond the scope of this book to investigate all the ways in which religious identity differs from (or resembles) identities of age, gender, disability, sexual orientation, race, ethnicity or social class. The point here is a precautionary one. The fact that all these dimensions of identity are brought into the same frame of reference – especially for the purposes of law, say, or by using similar sociological language to describe them – does not mean that they all operate in the same way. There may be something genuinely different about religion or belief in the field of identity politics. It is, for example, the only dimension on which the equality laws appear to protect social organisations as well as individuals.

A second and related point arises directly from recent research, and especially from the experience following on from the inclusion of a 'question on religion' in the British Censuses of 2001. Roughly speaking, this and other sources have increased enormously the *quantity* of information that has become available about the social correlates of religion. It is less obvious, however, that it has increased the *quality* of information to the same degree. Indeed, as we have seen, the data can give a positively misleading impression, especially where it takes a superficial – too easy – view of what constitutes religious identity. Such is the peril of subjectivity, that a person's declaration of their religious identity in some context be regarded as sufficient to establish their practical allegiance to a faith. The latter requires a more objective test. This is not an argument for ignoring the existing data as a source of understanding – far from it, the data remains indispensible. But it does underline the need for great care in interpreting the data. Britain is not a majority Christian country, under any conventional understanding of the term. In everyday life, most members of the population are either opposed to religion, or indifferent to it, or uncertain about it, or else prefer to follow an individual and spiritual path to (what Christians call) salvation.

2
Religion and Culture Make a Difference

Religious inequality

In this book, 'religious inequality' (or 'inequality of religion or belief') is used as a descriptive term to denote any variation in circumstances between members of groups defined by religion or belief. We focus especially on inequalities that exert major effects on the life chances of individuals. An unequal situation does not necessarily imply unequal or unfair treatment, since the latter judgement will depend on what has brought about the unequal situation. Religious inequalities may, nevertheless, point up areas of potential concern regarding injustices of religion or belief such as prejudice, hate crime or discrimination, which are covered in more detail in the next chapter. We argue in this chapter that it is necessary to achieve a balanced view of the extent and causes of religious inequality in order to provide the foundation for appropriate policy initiatives.

The focus in this chapter lies mainly on the minority (non-Christian) religions, for three main reasons. First, concerns about inequality – and unequal treatment – have arisen mainly in relation to these religions, especially Islam. Second, as argued in the previous chapter, it is sometimes difficult to know what meaning to attach to findings based on 'Christian' self-identifications, especially in relation to Census data. Third, where Christian self-identifiers provide a large proportion of the respondents (as in the Census data once again), the average figures for any variable of interest are heavily influenced by the 'Christian' totals for technical reasons. As a result, the statistics are unlikely to reveal distinctive inequalities in the situation of the Christian population.

One of the main themes of this book is the emergence of religion as a dimension of the equalities agenda in its own right, as distinct from race on the one hand and ethnicity on the other. This point is reflected in the fact that much of the information about religious inequality has been inferred in the past from data drawn up in categories relating to race and/or ethnicity.

The extent of these inequalities related to race (and to some aspects of ethnicity) had already been well established by the 1980s, either in general terms (Brown and Gay, 1985) or in specific fields. This literature, which extends to the present, has been covered in detail elsewhere (Modood et al., 1997; Macey, 2009), but some of the main findings are summarised here as significant features of the context within which the issue of religious inequality has arisen.

The current disadvantaged position of BME groups can be traced back to their initial (post-WWII) settlement in Britain in response to recruitment drives in the Caribbean and the Indian subcontinent. For not only was no provision made for their arrival in terms of, for example, housing, but they were confronted by deeply entrenched (institutional) racism on all dimensions of 'social wealth' – *health* (Gordon and Newnham, 1986), including *mental illness* (Burke, 1988); *housing conditions* (Association of Metropolitan Authorities, 1985; Brown and Gay, 1985; Greater London Action for Race Equality, 1987); *education* (All Faiths for One Race, 1982; Department of Education and Science [DES] [the *Swann Report*], 1983; All London Teachers against Racism and Fascism, 1984; Troyna and Williams, 1986; Troyna, 1993); *employment* (Allen et al., 1977; Association of Metropolitan Authorities, 1985; London Association of Community Relations Councils, 1985; Newnham, 1986; Brennan and McGeevor, 1987; Gifford et al., 1989); *social services and social security* (Gordon and Newnham, 1985; Connelly, 1987; Rooney, 1988); and the *criminal justice system* (Home Office, 1981; Gilroy, 1982; Commission for Racial Equality [CRE], 1987; Pilger, 1988; Tompson, 1989).

Nor was this position subject to rapid improvement. Brown and Gay's national research in 1985 showed that there had been no overall change in the geographical or economic position of black Britons since they first arrived as immigrant workers in the 1950s and 1960s. And in 1990, Allen and Macey observed that the position of many of their children had actually worsened, partly due to the economic situation, and despite the implementation of three Race Relations Acts (in 1965, 1968 and 1976).

More recent work has confirmed that these inequalities are stubbornly persistent, and members of minority ethnic groups remain, on the whole, in more deprived positions than their white counterparts on many indices of social wealth. They continue to experience worse *employment* prospects, for example, and are paid less. Bangladeshi men have the highest unemployment rate, at 20% – four times that of white men (ONS, 2002) – and Pell (2007) has emphasised the sixteen-point gap in economic participation rates between the BME and white populations, which are 60% and 76% respectively. However, this headline figure glosses considerable variation in the rates for different groups, which are discussed further below. These findings are supported by a careful analysis of the Census data for 1991 and 2001 from Clark and Drinkwater, who conclude that 'in spite of increasing employment rates for most ethnic minorities, large employment deficits remained in 2001, even for those ethnic groups whose employment rates had risen' (2007: 45). The results, nevertheless, varied between groups: 'for Indian and Chinese men, there is very little "problem" as far as employment penalties are concerned, while for Pakistani, Bangladeshi and Black men, these are severe' (Clark and Drinkwater, 2007: 47).

In relation to *earnings*, Berthoud (2000) refers to an 'ethnic deficit/penalty' in male weekly pay, showing that when such factors as education and age are controlled for, there remains an ethnic penalty of 7% for Indians, 24% for Caribbeans, 36% for Bangladeshis and Pakistanis and 40% for Africans. Clark and Drinkwater concur that 'earnings penalties are a fact of life for ethnic minorities in the UK labour market' (2007: 47). Platt (2007b) points to the gendered nature of pay differentials, demonstrating substantial pay gaps not only between men and women, and between majority and minority ethnicities, but also between minority men and women, with an average weekly pay gap for minority women of 20% – over three times as high as that suffered by minority men, at 6%. The EOC's (2007) statutory investigation into Bangladeshi, Pakistani and black-Caribbean women and work in Britain identifies five 'employment gaps': low participation rates, unemployment, lack of progression to senior levels, the pay gap and occupational segregation.

On other dimensions, too, gaps remain between members of majorities and minorities, though clearly some of these are linked to employment and earnings – or social class status – and the differences in provision that are correlated with this, as in the 'postcode lottery' (Janes and Mooney, 2002). These include *poverty*, with over half of Pakistani, Bangladeshi and black African children growing up in poverty (Platt, 2002; 2007a,b,c). In *health*, there are disparities in health status, lifestyle and access to services on the basis of ethnicity/religion (Heath Education Authority, 2000), as well as differential treatment (CRE, 2004; Scottish Health Survey [Bromley et al., 2005]; Social

Exclusion Unit, 2005). And both the provision and use of *health and social services* vary by ethnic religious and racial group (Chambra et al., 1998; Ahmad et al., 2000; Atkin et al., 2002; Katbamna et al., 2002; Chahal and Ullah, 2004). Minorities are over-represented in the *mental health system* (Nazroo, 1997; Sproston and Nazroo, 2002; Sproston and Mindell, 2006; Healthcare Commission, 2007). In *housing* there is relative overcrowding, poor conditions and poor neighbourhoods (Sellick, 2004; Beckford et al., 2006), as covered in greater detail below. In *education*, while gaps remain between majority and minority ethnic groups, these vary by both gender and ethnicity/religion, with some minorities (such as Indians and the Chinese) doing as well as, or better than, their white counterparts, while Pakistanis are underachieving, though girls are beginning to catch up (Abbas, 2002; 2003; Equal Opportunities Commission, 2007; T. Phillips, 2007).

In the *criminal justice system*, there are a number of areas of concern: on the one hand, black and Asian people are over-represented as far as being stopped and searched by the police and receiving custodial sentences when charged with offences (Jones and Singer, 2008); they are also more likely than white people to be the victims of *racially motivated violence*, including homicide (Jones and Singer, 2008; Institute of Race Relations, 2008; 2009). On the other hand, they remain under-represented in employment in the criminal justice system, particularly at the higher levels.

Overall, then, there is clear evidence of inequalities related to race and ethnicity, covering a broad range of social indicators and types of service provision. The evidence also reveals the differentiation between race and ethnicity, where the situations of members of the same racially identified groups vary according to their ethnicity.

Since religion is correlated with both race and ethnicity, it has always been possible to infer the existence of religious inequality from the data available on race and ethnicity. But it is only in the past fifteen years that studies have begun to make explicit reference to religion. And it is even more recently that larger-scale or more comprehensive studies have appeared, using quantitative or qualitative methods that are more sophisticated and/or more reliable in their conclusions. These 'pioneer studies' help to provide a clearer picture of the distinctive profile of religious inequality, and form the main focus of attention below.

Religious disadvantage

Following Weller et al. (2001), the term 'religious disadvantage' (or 'disadvantage of religion or belief') will be used to denote the position of particular groups of religion (or belief) that are treated less favourably than other groups through lack of equal recognition in official or institutional contexts, including the law. There are a number of clear-cut examples of religious disadvantage in Britain.

The most significant examples are the constitutional ones. The Church of England is the established church in England, and in Scotland the (Presbyterian) Church of Scotland is the national church. The Church in Wales, which belongs to the Anglican Communion, is, however, disestablished. Given its position as the established church, the law of succession to the Crown privileges Anglicanism, and the House of Lords includes only Anglican representatives of religion by right. In these respects, all non-Anglican religions suffer disadvantage in Britain (and non-Presbyterian groups similarly in the Scottish context).

There are a number of ways in which non-religious believers experience disadvantage. As a result of the 1996 Education Act, members of the alternative spectrum of belief (who make up the majority of the population) do not have their views reflected in the school curriculum, since the teaching of non-Christian beliefs tends to comprise 'world faiths' (i.e. religions), rather than agnostic or secular belief systems. Secularists tend not to be represented on such decision-making bodies as School Boards of Governors, and in some publicly funded initiatives such as the Inter-faith Network (which if truly inclusive would become a 'Network of Faith or Belief'). Humanist weddings are not recognised in England and Wales. The Charities Act 2006 (which applies only to England and Wales) defines a charity in part by reference to purposes that include the advancement of religion if it is for the public benefit (Jahangir, 2008), but it excludes the similar advancement of secular belief systems. The decision by the BBC to exclude secular speakers from its radio programme 'Thought for the Day' offers a minor example of this kind of disadvantage.

More broadly, provision is less frequently made for non-Christian denominations (and for non-religious belief systems) than for their Christian counterparts in connection with hospital and prison chaplaincies and facilities for the practice of faith within these institutions. A national survey of multi-faith chaplaincy arrangements in hospitals in England and Wales showed that the majority of full- and part-time chaplains were Christian (93.3% and 91.4% respectively); 6.7% of full-time chaplains were Muslim, and of the remaining 8.6% part-time chaplains few were from non-Christian faith groups (Sheikh et al., 2004). A similar situation applies in Scotland, where most chaplains have been appointed and employed historically by the Church of Scotland's

Board of National Mission (Levison, 2005). Nevertheless, it should be emphasised that the Muslim share of hospital chaplains is higher than their overall share of the population, so that any verdict of proven disadvantage needs to be approached with caution. The NHS has issued guidance on meeting the religious and spiritual needs of patients and staff in hospitals which requires the provision of suitable 'spaces', accessible 24 hours a day (Department of Health [DoH], 2003). Spalek and Wilson (2002) looked at religious provision in prison with respect to access to imams. Because the penal system is basically oriented towards Christianity, particularly the Church of England, imams are placed in a relationship of dependency with Anglican chaplains and are marginalised from decision-making mechanisms.

Since religious disadvantage (in the sense used here) by definition involves unequal treatment on the grounds of religion or belief, it creates a *prima facie* case for the existence of religious injustice. The remedy for this injustice is also clear-cut, at least in principle: give equal recognition in official contexts to all varieties of both religion and belief. What this might imply in practical terms is discussed in Chapters 3 and 6. It is, however, worth noting at this stage that the principle of equal advantage leaves open a wide range of measures. It is consistent, for example, with secularism, which gives no recognition to any religion or belief system. This chapter returns to the discussion of the social and economic dimensions of religious inequality.

Religion, economic activity and social class

Brown's (2000b) investigation into the economic activity of South Asians in Britain is the most prominent early example of a study in which religion is made an explicit variable, and which, significantly, predates the 2001 Census. The study is based on the 1994 National Survey of Ethnic Minorities, with a large sample (N = 3,795). This is, however, a 'pioneer study' not only in the chronological sense, but because Brown's findings set the agenda for subsequent research, in three respects especially.

First, Brown's findings show that 'neither ethnic nor religious group boundaries alone capture the labour market participation among South Asians. Thus, among Indian men, Sikhs experience more than double the unemployment of Hindus, while among Muslims, Pakistanis and Bangladeshis record more than double the unemployment level of Indians' (2000b: 1047). This finding has been borne out by more recent work, with unemployment rates among Muslim men of working age (between 16 and 64) ranging from nearly 30% for black African Muslims to between 15% and 20% for Bangladeshi, Pakistani and white British Muslims, down to just over 10% for Indian Muslims. Unemployment rates for Muslim women show a similar range and pattern by ethnicity (ONS, 2006).

These results give credence to the idea that 'hyphen-groups' of joint racial, ethnic and religious composition might form the most appropriate units of socio-economic analysis, since it is 'Indian Muslims', say, rather than 'Indians' or 'Muslims' who have a distinctive profile of activity. There is an interesting pattern here, reminiscent of the consequences of the earlier trend to distinguish 'ethnicity' more explicitly from 'race', which was noted above. When 'religion' is treated as distinct from both ethnicity and race, it appears that religious background differentiates the social outcomes for those of the same ethnic/racial groups. Conversely, ethnicity and/or race differentiate the social outcomes for those of the same religious background. This reinforces the case for treating communal (RER) identity as composed of race *and* ethnicity *and* religion, since it seems that all three elements must be addressed in order to generate an adequate picture of social inequality: in particular, religion does make a difference.

Second, Brown comments: 'whilst it is relatively straightforward to demonstrate differences between religious groups in economic activity, it is harder to establish causality' (2000b: 1058) and 'proof of religious discrimination is difficult to establish in the absence of hard statistics' (2000b: 1037). This may either be because religion acts as a proxy for other factors relating to culture of origin, or because it has operated historically by contributing 'indirectly to differences in factor endowments of migrants entering Britain' (Brown 2000b: 1059). This underlines the point made at the beginning of the chapter, that the issue of religious inequality is distinct from the issue of religious injustice. Brown's conclusion on the issue of discrimination is worth quoting in full because of its broad relevance:

A more direct effect [of religious affiliation] may be at work in the form of religious discrimination. The relatively disadvantaged position of Muslims, in particular, may tie in with the view (discussed earlier) that Muslims (and Islam) are increasingly experiencing a negative profile within the British media and society at large. However, the revealing of a relatively advantaged Indian Muslim minority would seem to challenge this thesis (though there may be differences between Indian, Pakistani and Bangladeshi Muslims in the expression of their faith that might have a bearing on their identification as

Muslim and exposure to discrimination). Finally, a direct effect may operate through attitudinal and aspirational differences between religious groups that impinge on, and may affect the 'success' of, labour market participation. (2000b: 1059)

This quotation makes the third point that can be gleaned from Brown's work. In general, religious inequalities are likely to be caused by a combination of (a) factors internal to a group and/or its members (including cultural values and economic endowments) and (b) factors in the external social environment of the group and/or its members (including religious, racial and/or ethnic discrimination). The relative contributions of these different factors will vary from case to case.

Lindley (2002) conducted a similar analysis on the same data set, but using slightly different statistical techniques. Her conclusions, perhaps unsurprisingly, were in broad agreement with Brown's. She did, however, undertake a specific analysis on the position of Muslims, which concluded that 'Muslims do experience some unexplainable employment penalty, relative to other non-white religions, over and above all other characteristics (including ethnic differences and language fluency)' (2002: 438). This is consistent with the operation of direct or indirect discrimination in the employment relationship, but the results also suggest that 'Muslims appear to be less assimilated and/or have less transferable human capital than other non-whites' (2002: 439). This bears out the general conclusion reported in the previous paragraph on the need to combine internal with external factors.

Social class – or 'socio-economic status' as it has become known more recently – is important because of the ways in which class positions provide resources that affect not only employment opportunities but also a wide range of other life chances. Census data shows clearly how class differentiation not only varies between religious groups but depends also on ethnicity and gender. Thus, both men and women from Jewish and Buddhist groups have substantially higher proportions of middle-class (managerial and professional) occupations than the population at large. Jewish men and women have very low representation among working-class occupations (semi-routine and routine). There are more Buddhist men and women in such working-class occupations, but still fewer proportionately than the national averages.

By contrast, Muslim and Sikh men and women are less likely to have middle-class occupations, and more likely to have working-class ones. There is, however, some variation by ethnicity within religion, with Indian Muslim men having a somewhat more favourable employment profile than Pakistani Muslim men (in terms of the conventional ranking of social class positions), who in turn have a more favourable profile than Bangladeshi Muslim men. Interestingly, Muslim women's employment profiles show less ethnic variation than Muslim men's, which suggests that ethnicity makes less difference to women's employment than to men's employment (ONS, 2006). Detailed information on these class differences by religion is given in the Statistical Appendix (Table 3). Importantly, the results given for Jewish and Buddhist groups demonstrate that minority religious status per se is not necessarily associated with social deprivation in Britain.

Khattab's (2009) study sheds further light on the relationship between religion and social class by introducing educational achievement as an intervening variable. The study is based on a sub-sample of the Census data for England and Wales, but it still has a huge sample size (N = 250,000). The study compares educational achievement with relative occupational status for a series of groups, taking the (majority) Christian White British (CWB) group as the reference group. The findings create an interesting and complex picture of the situations of different groups, as follows:

(a) Above-average educational qualifications and higher occupational status than the level of qualifications would predict: Jewish White British; Non-Religious White British and Other White British.
(b) Above-average educational qualifications and the same occupational status as education would predict: Hindu Indians.
(c) Above-average educational qualifications and lower occupational status than education would predict: Christian Black Caribbeans; Christian Black Africans.
(d) Below-average educational qualifications and the same occupational status as education would predict: Muslim Indians.
(e) Below-average educational qualifications and lower occupational status than education would predict: Muslim Bangladeshis; Muslim Pakistanis; Muslim Whites; Sikh Indians.

It can be seen that the groups are differentiated sharply in terms of educational qualifications, in ways that mirror some, but not all, of the general correlations between religion and social class. The White Jewish, No Religion, Hindu Indian and Black Christian groups have higher qualifications than average, whilst the Muslim and Sikh groups have lower than average. The picture changes, however, when it comes to *converting* these qualifications into an employment status corresponding with the level of qualifications. Here the White Jewish and White No Religion groups achieve a higher occupational status than their qualifications would lead one to expect (relative to the majority reference group). These groups are *under-qualified* for their class positions. By contrast, the Black Christian, Sikh and Muslim groups (apart from the Indian Muslims) are *over-qualified* for their class positions, and have not converted their education into occupational status as one might anticipate. The two Indian groups (of Hindus and Muslims respectively) convert qualifications into occupational position in a manner that is very similar to the reference group, but at two different educational levels.

This pattern of findings certainly reinforces the 'RER' perspective once again, since it shows the contributory effects of race *and* ethnicity *and* religion on the fate of group members. But these findings also highlight the difficulties in inferring causal linkages from statistical correlations. It is tempting to think that both Sikhs and (non-Indian) Muslims suffer from religious and/or racial discrimination in employment, which helps to explain why they are unable to gain the jobs to which they are suited by their educational qualifications. A similar inference would suggest that black Christians face racial discrimination in the labour market. But the same argument would also imply that Indians do not face any discrimination in access to employment (whether they are Muslims or Hindus) and that, for example, there is positive discrimination *in favour of* white Atheists (those of 'No Religion') in Britain. Since the latter inferences appear unlikely, there is reason to doubt the previous inferences as well, because they are derived from analogous reasoning. The very different social positions of those who are not easily distinguishable in terms of appearance, such as Indians (Christians, Hindus and Sikhs) relative to Bangladeshis and Pakistanis (Muslims), may give pause for thought about the causal influence of ethnic or religious discrimination. Or consider the possible causes of the position of white Muslims. Does (something about) their religious identity lead to below-average qualifications and/or lower occupational achievement for this group? Alternatively, are those whites who become Muslims more likely to do so because of these deficits? Or is there some independent factor that is correlated with the identity and which causes the deficits? The data by itself cannot decide between these possibilities. As we will argue in the next chapter, determining the incidence of discrimination requires methods that are directed specifically at the justice issue, as opposed to the inequality issue.

The furthest one can go at this stage is to follow the findings of both Brown and Lindley and conclude that it is a combination of external factors (including the possibility of racial, ethnic and religious discrimination and the effects of local labour market conditions) and internal factors (including Brown's 'attitudinal and aspirational differences' and a range of cultural differences) that are responsible for the observed patterns. Clark and Drinkwater (2007) make a similar point whilst discussing the 'explained' and 'unexplained' effects in their models, where the residual (unexplained) terms include the possible effects of discrimination. On the other hand, Khattab says that 'it is probably not the colour of skin, although it is still important, but the meaning and values that the dominant group attaches to the skills and who possesses them [that makes the difference to occupational achievement]' (2009: 12). This comment seems to exclude the influence of the skills differentials themselves, as opposed to the *perception* of these differentials, in achieving higher occupational status. It thus downplays the possible effects of the internal factors (skills as indicated by qualifications) in favour of external factors (quasi-racist perceptions by 'the dominant group').

It should be emphasised that these results concerning average profiles are compatible with a full range of variation of class positions within each religious group. Minority religious communities have all been established long enough in Britain for class differentiation to have developed within them. And some of these differences may be founded on the differential possession of social and/or economic capital at the time of their settlement in Britain, acquired in varied countries and (urban or rural) regions of origin. The position of the Ugandan Asians has already been mentioned in this respect, and the point is underlined in the quotation from Brown above: migration can exert social effects long after the process of physical relocation has taken place.

It follows that there are issues of economic inequality *within* each ethno-religious community as well as between a given community and the rest of society. It would be very helpful to be able to pursue this analysis into the highest reaches of the class system, for example, and to investigate the ownership of property and businesses as well as employment status. Sadly, there is relatively little research evidence on this issue. It is reported, however, that fewer than 3% of FTSE 100 directors were from minority ethnic backgrounds in 2004 (Clark and Drinkwater, 2007). This figure can be read in two ways. On the one hand, this proportion is considerably less than the minority ethnic representation in the population at large (8%); on the other hand, there clearly are a number of high net worth individuals in Britain from these backgrounds. Ansari (2002) reports that there are over 5,000 Muslim millionaires in Britain, with combined liquid assets above £3.6 billion.

The other difficulty with estimating the economic position of members of some ethno-religious communities lies in the effect of established communal or kin-related practices for the redistribution of resources. Bolognani (2007a) and Ballard (2004) discuss the transnational dispersion of funds – to relatives in the region of origin, for example – and the importance of a cash economy among Pakistani Muslims, both of which must be taken into account to estimate their overall economic position. It is clear, nevertheless, that there is a full range of variations of wealth or social status within each of the religious groups, so that there are many wealthy Muslims and numerous socially disadvantaged Jews.

We emerge from this section with three points that are essential to a balanced view of the relationship between religion and equality:

1. Hyphen-groups of combined racial, ethnic and religious identity are often the salient entities of social action or empirical comparison;
2. Injustice is distinct from inequality;
3. Religious inequalities are caused in general by a combination of factors external to and factors internal to religious communities.

In the next section, we consider two examples of what can go wrong in policy terms if these essential points are not taken to heart.

60/76 and *Moving on Up?* – a cautionary tale

In 2007, Gordon Pell, who was then the Chief Executive of Retail Markets for the Royal Bank of Scotland, presented a report into minority ethnic employment from a prestigious body called the Business Commission on Race Equality in the Workplace. He had been selected by the Prime Minister, Gordon Brown, to chair this Commission on behalf of the UK's National Employment Panel and to 'advise Government on policies and practical measures to increase the recruitment, retention and progression of ethnic minorities in the private sector' (Pell, 2007: 7).

In the Foreword to the report, Pell explained that:

We have entitled this report '60/76' because it is important to get one striking fact into as many minds as possible. 76% of white people in the working age group have a job; only 60% of working age people from ethnic minorities are in employment. This gap has remained largely unchanged for a generation. It is unjust, socially divisive, and bad for the economy. (2007: 3)

The report goes on:

> Britain takes itself to be one of the most tolerant and open-minded countries in the world, and among the most economically efficient. But we will never live up to this ideal whilst the ethnic minority employment gap persists. It is unfair; it foments social strife; it excludes productive talent from the workplace; and it is not going to go away on its own. (2007: 5)

The report accordingly recommends that the government establish the long-term goal of 'eradicating the ethnic minority employment gap [of sixteen percentage points] within twenty-five years' (Pell, 2007: 21). A number of quite forceful legislative and administrative measures are then recommended as ways of closing this gap, which enlist the powers of state to improve the performance of both the public and the private sectors. An action plan is established, with detailed quarterly targets running from the year of the report up to 2015, under the ultimate supervision of the Chancellor of the Exchequer.

The premises of this strategy are evidently (a) that the sixteen-point gap is caused largely by factors in the social environment of ethnic minorities, especially labour market discrimination ('it is unjust'; 'it is unfair') and (b) that the state and private employers acting together in a concerted fashion have the power between them to close the gap.

Each of these assumptions is highly questionable. In the first place, it transpires that there is not 'one striking fact' about the employment gap that needs to be lodged in 'as many minds as possible', but two striking facts. This is because the employment gap is very different for men and for women. For men, it is not sixteen points, but eleven points; for women, it is no less than twice that figure, at twenty-two points (figures estimated from the data given at Pell, 2007: 56). The headline figure of sixteen points emerges as the average of these two very different percentages. And the reason for the difference between the genders is that the employment rates for Pakistani and Bangladeshi women are both 24%, which represents an employment gap of no less than 49% compared to the corresponding figure for white women (which is 73%), and 38% compared with Indian women (whose employment rate is 62%). Since it is reasonable to assume that Pakistani and Bangladeshi women have Muslim religious backgrounds, it is clear that there is a significant component of religious inequality within the ethnic minority employment gap for women.

The purpose here is not to challenge the goal of eliminating the employment gap for women – far from it – but rather to appeal for a higher level of sociological awareness regarding its achievement. In particular, the elimination of the gap implies a three-fold increase in the employment rates of the Pakistani and Bangladeshi women concerned, from about one-quarter to about three-quarters. This would require a substantial shift in a range of attitudes and practices within their communities. Clark and Drinkwater's conclusion on this issue of women's employment, under the heading 'religion matters', is worth citing in full:

> Our regression models suggested that religion is an additional source of variation in labour market behaviour. In particular, there is some evidence that, controlling for other factors, Muslims have lower employment rates than individuals with another, or no, religion. Quantifying this is problematical for some of Britain's ethnic groups simply because ethnicity and religion are highly correlated. Cultural attitudes and norms may underlie some of the low employment rates, especially for Pakistani and Bangladeshi women, but separating the influences of ethnicity and religion is extremely difficult, both conceptually and empirically. It is also true that it may be tradition, rather than religious belief per se, that influences attitudes to female labour force participation and childcare. (2007: 48)

Given that the causes for the lower employment rates involve a combination of (a) external circumstances (including RER and gender discrimination) with (b) individual choices conditioned by religion and/or culture, any policy aimed at increasing participation rates would need to address both sides of the question. Insofar as the causes are internal to the ethno-religious communities concerned, it is beyond the power of external employers to bring such changes into being, however formidable they may be as economic organisations. Moreover, the campaign to close the gap would at some point encounter religious opposition (or at least opposition phrased in religious terms), and it might be inconsistent in some respects with other aspects of government policy such as multiculturalism or community cohesion (or so the argument would go, at any rate). It is thus unrealistic to announce a government programme to eliminate inequality that rides roughshod over all these social factors and political considerations.

As a second point, it is interesting to note that Pell proposes to commission direct research into the extent of employment discrimination – 'Benchmark Discrimination Testing'. This is indeed essential to create an accurate picture of the minority ethnic employment position, but Pell's recommendations overlook the fact that the appropriate target for the gap-closing campaign *depends on the results of this research,* which has yet to be undertaken. The report therefore jumps the gun by announcing the target as '60/76', since the gap caused by external labour market discrimination is almost certainly much smaller than the sixteen-point discrepancy – up to a third of the gap may be accounted for by the situation of Pakistani and Bangladeshi women alone. In short, the Pell Commission has misidentified the target for policy (since it has been chosen in advance of the facts) and mistaken the means of reaching it (since closing the gap is beyond the power of the measures it proposes).

The important conclusion for the purposes of this book is that these failings in policy can be traced back directly to faults in the underlying model implicit in the work of the Commission: a one-sided focus on the external (environmental) factors at the expense of internal (communal) factors, coupled with the habit of conflating inequality with injustice. Both these faults are characteristic of what may be termed an 'ideological' stance in this field, as opposed to an analytical stance.

The same points are illustrated by the statutory investigation into Bangladeshi, Pakistani and black-Caribbean women and work in England, Scotland and Wales conducted by the EOC, and published under the title *Moving on Up?* The researchers actually stated at the outset that they were determined to 'move away' from cultural, ethnic or religious influences to focus on workplace discrimination (EOC, 2007: 4). This is to endorse explicitly the focus on external factors at the expense of internal factors that is characteristic of the *Pell Report.* Subsequently, however, the authors list under 'work based discrimination', such factors as lack of language skills, overseas qualifications and lack of support for family and childcare responsibilities. These factors are all related (in various ways and to varying extents) to circumstances internal to community life, including migration histories and family roles. This research adds other elements to the inventory of problematic assumptions, by relying entirely on *perceptions,* rather than evidence, of discrimination, as well as including many 'barriers to employment' which apply to both majority *and* minority women, and so may be the consequences of gender discrimination rather than ethno-religious discrimination.

These two studies from official bodies display what we will call in this book 'conceptual inflation'. Conceptual inflation stretches the application of value-laden concepts such as injustice or discrimination beyond their proper spheres of reference. This typically has the effect of misrepresenting the incidence of social harms or wrongs, by exaggerating some and masking others. We will see in Chapter 3 that the examples of conceptual inflation in these two sources are not isolated instances – the problem recurs throughout the contemporary literature on religion and equality.

The localisation of minority religions

One of the main findings from the 2001 Census is the extent to which the minority religious (non-Christian) populations are localised in particular areas of the country. These populations tend to live in particular towns or cities in which members of their own group are represented much more frequently than their average throughout the country, and to live in neighbourhoods within these cities in which members of their own group are represented much more frequently than their average throughout the city as a whole. A similar point even applies at a national level, to the constituent nations of the UK.

These facts of social separation do not in themselves constitute an issue of inequality, but they are connected with the concerns of this book in several ways. First, the social and economic prospects for members of minority religions will depend in part on the areas in which they live. Second, the levels of social separation condition (though they do not determine) the prospects for social interaction and cultural exchange between different religious traditions, and the corresponding dynamics for the formation of ethno-religious communities (Carling, 2008). Third, the social, political and administrative implications of religious diversity are experienced much more directly in some parts of the country than in others.

In terms of Britain as a whole, the overwhelming majority of the minority religious population – over 95% – is resident in England (2,940,000), compared with much smaller numbers in Scotland (95,000), Wales (44,000) and Northern Ireland (5,000). In terms of urban areas, London is unique in the range and size of its minority religious population, with a total of 1,250,000 – no less than 40% of Britain's entire minority religious population. This population is otherwise heavily concentrated in a few English urban areas outside London – and by no means always those with the largest populations (ONS, 2006). These provincial centres include Birmingham (196,000), Bradford and Leicester (both 86,000), Luton (35,000), Slough (33,000) and Blackburn (28,000). Minority religious proportions range in these cases from 17% of the local population (London) up to 31% (Leicester). By contrast, there are no other local authority areas where the proportion rises above 15%. The detailed figures are set out in the Statistical Appendix (Table 4), but it is only a slight exaggeration to say that the issues raised by minority religions are (in numerical terms at least) issues primarily for London and a handful of provincial English cities. This point has potentially far-reaching implications for policy in the field of religion. To give just one example: Coles and Bonney (2003) consider the pressures imposed on the education system as a result of geographical concentration.

Analysing the residential distribution of specific religions shows, moreover, that some minority religions tend to be concentrated even more heavily in particular places. (See Statistical Appendix, Figure 3.) The non-Christian religious populations of Blackburn and Bradford are largely Muslim, for example (over 85%). In both these cases, it is known that the Muslim population comes not only from one country – Pakistan – but also from one particular area of that country, with migrants linked to each other by close ties of kinship. For example, at least 70% of the Pakistani Muslim population of Bradford originates from the Mirpur region of Azad Kashmir, and some sources put this closer to 90% (Moss, 2006). (For a description of this region, see Ballard, 2002.)

Scotland and Wales, London, Leicester and Slough are, by contrast, much more heterogeneous in their minority religious composition, although Muslims form the largest grouping in every case except Leicester. Luton and Birmingham fall between these two poles. This difference in composition underlines the geographical concentrations of particular minority religions: there are more Muslims in Bradford (75,000) than in the whole of Scotland, Wales and Northern Ireland combined (66,000). And 56% of the Jewish population of the UK resides in London (ONS, 2006).

There are, of course, understandable reasons why members of ethnic and religious minorities tend to be found in some areas of the country more than others. Ballard (1994) has discussed the process of 'chain migration' by which immigrants follow in the path of relatives or other contacts who have already settled in particular locations. Simpson (2005) has written similarly of the process by which ethno-religious communities are formed, offering support to established migrants and hospitality to newcomers. The presence of existing communities and facilities for worship adds a specifically religious ingredient to this mixture of factors (Lewis, 2002), and transcontinental kin marriage is another powerful force promoting consolidation in specific places.

In terms of the effects of residential separation on economic opportunities, it is noteworthy that some minority religious populations are located in areas with relatively poor economic performance, such as those parts of Lancashire or Yorkshire that are experiencing the transition from industrial economies. A similar point applies at the local level if members of religious minorities seek employment within their own ethnic communities (Alam and Husband, 2006), are constrained by lack of local opportunities, or have a tradition of not travelling outside the locality for work or education (Bolliver, 2006). Clark and Drinkwater have emphasised 'the importance of the local area' for economic outcomes and identified a corresponding range of 'neighbourhood effects'. They note that 'individuals who express a preference for living in areas with a majority of people of the same ethnic group have unemployment rates of up to 20 percentage points higher' (2007: 50). And they conclude that:

> The tendency of some ethnic groups in the UK to exhibit 'oppositional identities' has also been noted by Battu et al. (2003) and such attitudes may reduce interactions with other groups and hence limit labour market opportunities. Of course, a desire to isolate oneself from other ethnic groups may be borne of experiences of discrimination or victimisation. (2007: 50)

The concerns raised here about the effects of residential separation within towns and cities are related to the issues of 'parallel lives' and 'community cohesion', which received much attention in the wake of the disturbances that took place in the cities of Burnley, Oldham and Bradford in 2001 – the so-called Northern Riots. (These are covered in more detail in Chapter 4.)

There has been a corresponding, and often lively, academic debate about the extent of residential separation (sometimes called 'segregation') in the city of Bradford, and its trend over time (Johnston et al., 2002; 2005; Simpson, 2002; 2004; 2005; Poulsen, 2005; Carling, 2008). It has now been established that the degree of minority ethnic residential separation in Bradford, and some similar places in Britain, is high by international comparison, and approaches the level found for some of the most racially segregated cities in the US. Moreover, there is good evidence that the degree of separation in Bradford increased during the 1990s (Carling, 2008), contrary to the claim made by Simpson (2004).

Residential separation is matched, or sometimes exceeded, by educational separation, that is, a tendency for children and young people from different ethnic communities to be educated at different schools

(Burgess and Wilson, 2003; Miller 2004; Burgess et al., 2005; Johnston et al., 2006a,b; Osler, 2007). The concern here is that young people from different ethnic and religious backgrounds can grow up lacking regular contacts with members of other groups, even when living in close proximity to them. Special measures have consequently been put in place to facilitate such contacts, such as Bradford's Linking Schools project, which was evaluated very positively by Raw (2006), and was included as an example of good practice in *What Works in Community Cohesion?* (DCLG, 2007b).

The academic debate about community separation has been conducted largely in categories of race and/or ethnicity rather than religion per se, because of the constraints imposed by the available data. D. Phillips (2006) and her colleagues (Phillips et al., 2002; 2005) have, however, provided some direct evidence of religious self-separation in the West Yorkshire region – that is, families or individuals choosing to live in certain areas in order to enjoy proximity to co-religionists. The general conclusion is that patterns of separation are caused by a combination of factors that are internal to communities (such as relative preferences for closeness with those of shared culture and/or religion) and factors that are external to communities (such as the experience or apprehension of hostility or discrimination). These factors may even be combined, as suggested by Clark and Drinkwater in the quotation above. It should be emphasised, however, that preferences for co-association may not be absolute and do not necessarily exclude a simultaneous desire for inter-cultural (or inter-religious) contacts under appropriate circumstances. Self-separation need not, therefore, imply self-seclusion (Carling, 2008).

The first large-scale study of residential patterns to make the religion variable explicit was conducted by Peach (2006) in relation to London, based on Census data. Taking the main religious groups as a whole, it found that Sikhs and Jews are highly separated residentially. Hindus are moderately separated; Muslims have low separation and Christians have very low separation.

However, the low Muslim result, which suggests that Muslims are dispersed relatively evenly throughout London, turns out to be a consequence of the fact that the various Muslim populations of different ethnicity are highly separated *from each other* (in different parts of London), as well as from the general population and from other ethno-religious groups. 'Despite some strong linkages, such as [that between] the Indian and Pakistani Muslims…,' Peach (2006: 364) reports that '[the] residential pattern of Muslim groups in London is largely fragmented along ethnic lines' and that 'the Ummah exists spiritually, but is not manifested in residential terms'. He concludes that 'there is not a single Muslim community but a community of communities' (2006: 368).

This finding reinforces the hyphen-group perspective once again, since it suggests that the operative social units regarding choice of residence combine elements of both religion *and* ethnicity. It should be emphasised, however, that social class remains the strongest determinant of residential location, because of the way that class factors affect access to housing markets, and the Peach analysis does not take these factors into account. Since class is known to be associated with religion, part of the findings for religious separation in London will reflect social class constraints rather than ethno-religious preferences (but see Carling, 2008, for the demonstration that ethnicity has effects on residential separation in Bradford that are independent of social class).

The provision of religious buildings

It was mentioned above that the existence of facilities for worship is one of the factors attracting migrants to particular locales. Religious buildings are perhaps the most striking symbols of the religious character of a neighbourhood, and one aspect of Britain's Christian heritage is its dominance of the British skyline. The issue of discrimination against minority faiths in relation to planning permission for religious buildings has attracted considerable attention in recent years (Nye, 2001; Weller et al., 2001; Edge, 2002; Gale and Naylor, 2002; Gale, 2004; 2005). Beckford et al. summarise the position by saying that planning processes surrounding the religious buildings of Hindus, Muslims and Sikhs 'have frequently been problematic' (2006: 54). If such discrimination were proven, it would count as an example of religious disadvantage in the sense defined above.

However, according to Vertovek and Peach (1997) there were at least 839 mosques and a further 950 Muslim organisations in Britain by the mid-1990s. McLoughlin refers to 'the pervasive Islamisation of the inner city' in Bradford (2005: 1046), noting that the majority of Bradford's Muslims live within the five square miles of the city centre, an area that contains 44 mosques. There are currently 143 Hindu *mandirs* in Britain: 121 in England, 3 in Northern Ireland, 4 in Scotland and 15 in Wales (National Council of Hindu Temples, UK, 2008). Singh says that the modern *gurdwara* movement in Britain now embraces 250 Sikh institutions, including the £17 million building opened in Southall in 2003.

He calls this 'the premier symbol of Sikh presence in Britain, one of the new, emerging, "cathedrals" of multicultural Britain' (Singh, 2006: 147). In 2001, there were 202 *gurdwaras* in England and Wales (5 in Wales), 11 in Scotland and 1 in Northern Ireland (Weller, 2003). Notwithstanding this, the apparently positive situation in Britain with respect to religious buildings may have been affected by the politics around international and national terrorism, as events in Dudley in the Midlands seem to suggest. There, in 2007, planning permission for a new mosque was refused following a sustained public campaign largely orchestrated by the UK Independence Party (UKIP) and the British National Party (BNP), both of which play on public ignorance and fears in relation to migration, asylum seekers and refugees (Reeves et al., 2009).

Whether or not planning processes in Britain have been 'problematic' in the past and, indeed, continue to be so in some cases, the significant number of religious buildings stands in stark contrast to the situation in France, for example, where it was not until the 1990s that any real change in attitudes towards minority religious buildings took place (de Galembert, 2005). Opposition to religious buildings in various parts of Western Europe is frequently couched in terms of fears of 'Islamisation', as in Switzerland, which has recently banned the building of minarets (BBC News, 2009), and in Germany, despite its strong record of approving the building of mosques (Spiegel International, 2008). Dzi (2009) comments that religious buildings signify the message 'We are part of this society and we will stay here', but religious buildings can also be said to symbolise the assertion by minority faiths of their right to representation in the public domain. This has wider implications than the creation of spiritual and social spaces, and some authors see it as a challenge to the Enlightenment distinction between the public and private domains, or, indeed, to the prevailing definitions of modernity itself (Eisenstadt, 2000), as discussed in Chapter 5.

Religion and housing

Poor housing conditions form one aspect of inequality which has often been associated with BME status, as noted above. In the light of this long-standing finding, and the results reported above, it can be inferred that there will be associations between minority religious status and housing deprivation. As in other fields, however, it is only relatively recently that research on housing has taken explicit account of religion, driven partly by government concerns with managing diversity and neighbourhood renewal/regeneration (Sellick, 2004).

The Census provides information on housing tenure by religion, set out in the Statistical Appendix (Figure 4). Sikhs, Jews and Hindus were most likely to own their own home, followed by Buddhists and Muslims (ONS, 2004; Graham et al., 2007). Muslims were the most likely to live in social rented accommodation: in 2001, 28% of Muslim households were in social rented accommodation, compared to less than 10% of Hindu, Sikh or Jewish households. Buddhists were the most likely to be living in private rented accommodation (24%). A very small percentage of all households live rent-free (2%), but Muslim households were twice as likely as others to do so (4%). This data as a whole runs counter to the stereotypes of Muslim owner-occupation.

There is a correlation between ethno-religious groups and the affluence of their residential locations that, as expected, mirrors the findings for social class. Hindus tend to live in more affluent locations; Sikhs are more likely to live in middle-class areas than Muslims, who tend to occupy poorer housing (Beckford et al., 2006). Muslims form 10% of the population resident in the most deprived decile of residential neighbourhoods (an over-representation of more than three times), and there is a less pronounced tendency for Hindus and Sikhs to share this residential deprivation (ONS, 2003). A similar variation was found in a study of BME housing in Wales conducted by the Welsh Assembly (2005): the least disadvantaged were Indian and Chinese residents and the most disadvantaged were black-Caribbeans, Pakistanis and Bangladeshis (who in the latter two cases can be assumed to be mostly Muslim).

The number of rooms in a house relative to the number of occupants is commonly used to determine housing deprivation. Of all households, 40% Muslim, 26% Hindu and 22% Sikh experience housing deprivation of this type (Beckford et al., 2006). In 2001, just 6% of Christian households experienced overcrowding. The high proportions for Muslim, Sikh and Hindu households in these totals are to some extent a reflection of their larger family sizes – their average numbers being 3.8, 3.6 and 3.2 people respectively, compared with 2.3 people among Christian, Buddhist and Jewish households (ONS, 2006).

However, overcrowding can be seen as a Eurocentric measure of deprivation, which does not take into account lifestyle preferences and the financial and familial advantages of living as extended families. The need for larger housing to accommodate extended and inter-generational families was raised by Hindu and Muslim respondents to the consultation for the *Weller Report* (Weller et al., 2001). Beckford et al. (2006) also note the issue of *shar'ia* compliance in relation to the acquisition and management of properties as a directly religious factor in Muslim housing needs.

At the same time, a careful study conducted by Sellick for the Housing Corporation brought to light another dimension of the issue, that 'the 15% of Muslim one person households reflect not only the independent status of high achieving independent professionals, but also the marginality of ex-offenders and the mentally ill' (2004: 5). Sellick's considered view on the housing situation of Muslims could stand as a conclusion on the housing situation of the minority religions more generally:

> [this] report has...highlighted the diversity within the...population and the need for sensitivity to the differences borne not only of religion but also of socio-economic position, age, gender, locality and transnational commitments. (2004: 4–5).

Once again, it is not religious identity by itself that is the key to policy in this field, but religion read in conjunction with a variety of other aspects of personal identity and social situation.

Religion, health and disability

The Census provided systematic evidence for the first time on certain aspects of the relationship between health, religious identity and gender. The broad findings, which are given in greater detail in the Statistical Appendix (Figure 5), show that Jewish men and women have the best health of any group. The Christian, Buddhist and No Religion populations fare slightly worse, with women's health in each category being slightly better than men's. On the other hand, the health of women with Muslim, Sikh, Hindu or 'Other Religious' identities is worse than that of their male co-religionists, and – with the exception of Hindus – worse for both genders than for the general population. The differences reported by the Census are striking: Muslims are almost twice as likely to suffer from long-term illness or disability as Jews (about 23% compared to about 12%).

It is interesting that these results follow a similar pattern to the social class differences by religion, so that it is not at all clear to what extent the health statistics are expressing class differences rather than religious differences. And it is also noteworthy that there is a deficit in women's long-term health or disability compared to men's for all the minority religions, including Judaism, with Buddhism being the lone exception.

As in other examples, the religious inequalities are clear, but the explanations for them are harder to determine, and a review of the published literature in this area does not take the discussion much further forward. On the one hand, the research highlights the numerous ways in which religious beliefs and/or practices can impact on either the incidence or the treatment of health or disability, and on the well-being of those with health conditions. This impact can be either positive or negative, which implies a corresponding 'religious' effect on inequalities of health or disability.

On the other hand, this field of research is characterised by its fragmentation. There are a considerable number of studies, but they tend to involve small sample sizes, often confined to one city or health authority, and to focus on very specific topics within the overall field: an example is the study by Heim et al. (2004) of the alcohol consumption of 174 Indian, Chinese and Pakistani men in Glasgow aged 16–25. These small-scale individual studies are not generally placed within a systematic framework of theory and evidence. A flavour at most is given here of the connections between religion, health and disability revealed by this literature; fuller information is contained in the review by Macey et al. (2010).

Religious individuals often demonstrate their faith via charitable acts or social works, and religious orders continue to be involved in health care provision in Britain (Farnell et al., 2003). There is some research on the relationship between religiosity and psychological well-being, with modestly positive conclusions (Koenig, 1998; Maltby et al., 1999; McCullough and Larson, 1999; Koenig et al., 2001; Coleman et al., 2004; Francis et al., 2008). The relationship between ethnicity and mental health has been a long-standing concern, prompted by the over-representation of BME individuals in this sphere. This has been blamed on racism in psychiatry, though alternative models are now being considered (Singh and Burns, 2008). However, a survey by King et al. (2006) of 4,000 BME adults found no difference in the prevalence of common mental disorders (CMDs) between religious and non-religious people.

One of the main ways in which religion affects health and disability is where either a religious prescription or a cultural stigma attaches to a particular social activity. If the activity has negative consequences for health, then the religious or cultural prohibition will have positive consequences for health, so long as the prohibition is observed. If, however, the prohibition is not observed and health deteriorates as a consequence, then the stigma attached to the condition may lead to denial and make health care more difficult. There are a number of studies tracing the incidence of such effects in relation to activities such as drinking, drug-taking or smoking (Khan, 1997; Bush et al.,

2003; Douds et al., 2003; Heim et al., 2004; Ross et al., 2004; Bradby and Williams, 2006; Mirza et al., 2007).

The relationship of religion to the incidence of HIV/AIDs also falls into this category, where the restriction of sex to monogamous marriage in the Christian tradition, or the practice of circumcision in the Muslim and Jewish traditions, should help to prevent the spread of the condition, and yet these traditions tend to stigmatise those who fall victim to it (Anderson and Doyal, 2003; Gatrad and Sheikh, 2004; Adogame, 2007). On the other hand, there are religious practices that increase the risk of infection, including Catholic teaching on birth control and practices associated with Islamic culture such as polygamy, the sharing of razor blades at the conclusion of *Hajj* and certain conventions of childbirth and breastfeeding.

Religious beliefs themselves can also have implications for the explanation of health conditions, and for their stigmatisation or denial (Rozario, 2005). Pote and Orrell (2002) found, for example, that some ethnic groups viewed schizophrenia as spirit possession or witchcraft. And a series of studies have traced the effects of religion on the social reception and psychiatric treatment of mental illness in a variety of different ethno-religious groups (Hussain and Cochrane, 2003; Dogra et al., 2005; MacKenzie, 2006; Leavey et al., 2007).

Similar themes apply more generally to disability, where religious beliefs – in reincarnation, for example – can lead to disability being seen as a punishment, sin or curse (Confederation of Indian Organizations, 1987; Greater London Association for Disabled People, 1987; Shah, 1995; Atkin et al., 2002). In some cases, cultural beliefs suggest that disabilities can be cured (Channabasavanna et al., 1985; O'Hara, 2003), and the religious issue of the marriage prospects of disabled children can loom large for their families (O'Hara and Martin, 2003; Hussain, 2005). On the other hand, people of faith can be more ready and/or able than those without a religious belief to accept disabled children (Ali et al., 2001; McGrother et al., 2002; O'Hara, 2003; Rozario, 2005). And some of the difficulties may be ascribed to lack of knowledge or understanding, or to language barriers, rather than the effects of religion per se (Begum, 1992; Smith, 1994; Nadirshaw, 1997; Chambra et al., 1998; Shah, 1999; Katbamna et al., 2002; McGrother et al., 2002). The evidence on service provision, and service acceptance, for disabled young people from minority religious backgrounds is similarly mixed, with some studies finding that cultural barriers exist, including concern about lack of sensitivity to religious differences (Shah, 1999; Atkin et al., 2002; Gilliat-Ray, 2007), whereas other studies go against this conclusion (Ahmad et al., 2000).

Perhaps the most difficult issue in this area concerns the relative incidence of learning disabilities, which can reach three times the national average in some South Asian communities, with 19% of families having more than one member with a learning disability (Mir et al., 2001; and see Emerson et al., 1997, for a similar finding). Genetic disorders are also significantly higher in South Asian – particularly Pakistani Muslim – communities than in the general population (Overall et al., 2002; Christianson and Modell, 2004). In Bradford, for instance, 152 different autosomal recessive conditions have been identified, relative to the estimated 15–25 in 'typical' districts (Suleman, 2009). Genetic disorders are sometimes connected to consanguineous marriage, which is estimated to account for 35% to 60% of all marriages among Pakistanis (Shaw, 2001; Hussain and Bittles, 2004). The link between consanguineous marriage and the prevalence of genetic disorders is both complex and contested – the latter particularly by non-medical researchers such as Ahmad (1995), Darr (1997) and Stacey (1997). These concerns also relate to general issues of women's health and family size (Phillipson et al., 2003). Rozario has noted the consequences of religious revivalism, in which contraception, prenatal testing, termination and sterilisation may be seen as un-Islamic (2005: 190, 192). All these factors are linked to material and social deprivation, which are linked, in turn, to inequalities in access to, or use of, maternal health care services and to environmental and genetic risk factors (Baxter, 1998).

Secrecy surrounds the question of genetic disorders, partly because of threats to family marriage prospects, and there are issues about the use of interpreters who are not trusted to maintain confidentiality (Rozario, 2005; and see Gilliat-Ray, 2007). On a positive note, however, Walji (2008) states that the introduction of a screening programme at his local mosque in Birmingham, which includes advising against marriage between carriers, has led to a marked reduction in the incidence of birth defects.

The demonstration of all these varied connections between religion and health or disability supports the case for 'religious literacy' in the provision of services, or perhaps just as importantly 'religious and cultural literacy', given the relevance in many cases of *distinguishing* the impact of religion from the impact of culture and ethnic background. There is, nevertheless, a real requirement in this field for more systematic and comprehensive research in order to provide a secure foundation for efforts to ameliorate the associated inequalities of health or disability.

Towards a balanced perspective on religion and social inequality

The two main conclusions of this chapter pull in different directions. On the one hand, it has been established clearly that 'religion makes a difference' to many key areas of social wealth and personal well-being, in that religious identity affects social attainment independently of other factors. This point applies to economic activity, educational and occupational achievement, residential location, housing, health and disability. Yet it is highly significant that some minority religious groups, especially Jewish and Buddhist groups, are placed above the average on some indicators, and others, especially Hindu groups, are placed at or around the average level. There is at least one finding which reaches the latter conclusion about a Muslim group, regarding the occupational attainment of Indian Muslims noted above (Khattab, 2009). This suggests that minority religious status is not in itself a barrier to social equality in Britain. As far as we are aware, there is no comparable finding in relation to minority racial status. And it is important to note, in comparing the occupational attainment of Jewish and Buddhist groups with that of black Christian groups (both African and Caribbean), that race may indeed be the influential factor, as well as (or even instead of) minority religious status (Khattab, 2009).

This helps to make the general point that it is not usually religious identity *on its own* that makes a difference. A series of findings in the same key areas of social wealth and well-being suggest that a hyphen-group perspective is necessary, because the social position of religious groups is differentiated according to both race and ethnicity. This double-edged conclusion is summed up in the chapter title, 'religion *and* culture make a difference'. An important consequence of this perspective is that there is always likely to be uncertainty about whether a given characteristic of religious groups should be ascribed to the influence of religion in the strict sense or to the influence of its associated ethnic culture. But the empirical connection between religious identity and other aspects of social identity goes well beyond the relationship between religion and culture. The combination of religion and culture with gender is central to the economic position of Pakistani and Bangladeshi Muslim women, for example. And it is very striking how often the pattern of inequality for religious groups matches the inequalities of social class. This occurs to varying extents with educational achievement, residential location, housing conditions and long-term health and disability.

These observations have potentially far-reaching implications for policy in the field of religion and equality. The problem of inequality is largely (but not exclusively) a problem for some specific minority religious groups, especially Sikhs and most (but by no means all) Muslim groups. But it does not follow that the remedy for religious inequality is to rely on measures focused on the religious aspects of identity. For example, Clark and Drinkwater have emphasised the central importance of education: 'the statistical models show that education had a positive, increasing and significant effect on employment for virtually all ethnic groups, with the largest impact for higher (level 4/5) qualifications' (2007: 15) and 'education boosted the employment chances of ethnic minorities by more than for the White group' (2007: 45; and see also Phillips, 2007). Suppose, then, that the educational achievement of disadvantaged Sikh and Muslim groups were to be improved, and that other measures were taken to enhance their class positions. Suppose also that cultural (as opposed to religious) barriers were addressed, and the levels of gender equality improved within some ethno-religious communities. All these measures would impact favourably on religious inequality without any attention having to be paid to the wider social reception of religious identity.

Take as an example the case of material inequality as it affects the poorest ethno-religious groups. Berthoud comments: 'Name any group whose poverty causes national concern – pensioners, disabled people, one-parent families, the unemployed – Pakistanis and Bangladeshis were poorer' (1997: 180). The data summarised above shows that these groups are characterised by larger than average family size; extended family living; a high incidence of children with disabilities; women who do not work outside the home; unemployment or low-paid male employment that is often related to lack of educational qualifications and skills; and the maintenance of enduring links with countries of origin, which have financial implications through, for example, transnational marriage, transcontinental travel and overseas remittances.

The policy initiatives that might help to alleviate the material poverty experienced by a family in situations such as these will obviously depend on the *reasons* for their situation. Thus, if the reason for there being only one wage earner is labour market discrimination, then an appropriate response is through existing equalities legislation. If, however, it is due to the belief that a woman's main role is centred on child rearing and the home, then such legislation will have no effect. Similar points apply to this hypothetical family's need for specialist disability services. If the wife's inability to work outside the home is due to lack of provision of such services, then a logical response is to improve provision, or to remove any element of discrimination surrounding it. If, however, such services are available but are rejected for religious or cultural reasons, as Shah (1995; 1999), Ahmad et al. (2000) and Atkin et al. (2002) suggest, it is more difficult to see how this family can be helped. And since the causes of some aspects of disability affecting some communities lie within the scope of community action as well, it is not clear that measures taken external to the community will have an effect on the inequalities in these cases.

Our appeal, then, is for a broad approach to the question of religious inequality, and for a balanced, evidence-based, assessment of all the factors that contribute to the observed inequalities. Such an approach relies on the following four points. The hyphen-group orientation is the first of these. The second is that there is an important distinction between religious inequality and religious injustice, so that examples of religious inequality cannot be ascribed to the effects of religious injustice without further evidence of these effects. The third point is that a balanced view of the causation of religious inequality will take account of factors that are internal to ethno-religious communities as well as factors that are external to them, derived from their social environments. The final point is perhaps the most far-reaching, and acknowledges the difficult policy choices to be made in this area. In particular, if multiculturalism acts to shield cultural and religious values or practices that reproduce inequalities within communities, the choice may have to be faced between multiculturalism and equality as policy options.

In the course of reaching these conclusions about a balanced perspective, we have begun to trace out some of the consequences of departing from the balance provided by these points. The problems with the recommendations of the Pell Commission arise from their moving too swiftly from inequality to injustice, ignoring the importance of gender and ascribing ethnic inequality solely to external causes. A similar problem applied to the EOC report on minority women's employment, *Moving on Up?* We have touched on two other examples of a similar difficulty. In his analysis of the effects of skills differentials, Khattab (2009) has downplayed the internal factor (the skills differentials themselves) in favour of the external perceptions of these skills by those outside the ethno-religious community. And a similar problem affects some writers on the issue of residential segregation, who seem very reluctant to accept that the observed patterns of residential separation are caused in part by the culturally conditioned choices made by members of ethnic or religious minorities themselves. These writers include both Simpson

(2002; 2004; 2005) and Phillips (D. Phillips, 2006; Phillips et al., 2002; 2005; see Carling, 2008, for further analysis).

In all these cases, we are beginning to see the effects of an approach that is one-sided and therefore 'ideological' rather than analytical, as indicated by the departure from the balanced perspective outlined above. It will be shown in the course of the next chapter that an ideological approach is not confined to one or two solecisms in the text, or to a small number of sources, but appears to be characteristic of a wide range of influential work on religion and equality. In particular, conceptual inflation – such as the treatment of inequality as evidence in itself of injustice – seems to have become an occupational hazard for writers in this field.

3
Social Injustices of Religion or Belief

Religious inequality and religious injustice

The distinction between social inequality and social injustice was introduced in the previous chapter. It was argued that religious inequalities can be addressed by a range of measures involving education, social class equality and/or gender equality that do not refer to religious identity. Religious inequality is not therefore caused solely by injustices suffered by individuals as a consequence of their religious identity. As a key government report made the point: 'not all inequality stems from discrimination, and therefore not all inequality can be addressed by legal remedy' (Phillips, 2007: 37). In this chapter we will, however, focus on the issue of religious injustice, and the related role of the law concerning religion/belief.

Our main concerns are with the minority religions once again, especially Islam, which are thought to bear the brunt of religious injustice. The question of Christian sectarianism in Scotland is also addressed, and its relevance to minority religions in England discussed. The emphasis lies on the injustices faced by religious groups or their members within civil society generally, or at the hands of the state. Our main contention is that the evidence available does not support the widespread beliefs about the pervasiveness of religious injustice. Indeed, the discrepancy between evidence and belief is so marked that it is necessary to invoke a special explanation for it. We identify a prevailing *ideology of religious injustice*, which supports the mistaken beliefs and serves to mask and/or to distort the underlying state of affairs regarding religious injustice.

Britain's legal framework for religion or belief

A new framework of law relating to religion or belief has been established in the UK in recent years through the following enactments:

- The Human Rights Act 1998 (HRA);
- The Terrorism Act 2000;
- The Employment Equality (Religion or Belief) Regulations 2003 (Great Britain) (EER);
- The Equality Act 2006 (Part 2);
- The Racial and Religious Hatred Act 2006 (England and Wales) (RRHA);
- The Equality Act 2010.

In addition to this main domestic legislation, a number of other enactments refer incidentally to religion, and certain offences involving assault, harassment and public disorder can be aggravated by religious hostility. The Equality Act 2010 has created a new Equality Duty for Religion or Belief. The UK is also party to a number of European and international conventions that have implications for religion or belief, including the European Convention on Human Rights (ECHR), and the European Employment Directive 2000. These are covered in greater detail in Macey et al. (2010) (see also Ansari, 2002; Fredman, 2005, and Jahangir, 2008).

The legal framework on religion or belief (including the lack of such belief) gives new rights to *individuals* on the grounds of religion or belief, protecting them in various circumstances against:

- Direct discrimination;
- Indirect discrimination;
- Harassment;
- Victimisation;
- The threat or commission of terrorist violence; or
- Hate crime.

Direct discrimination involves treating members of a group less favourably than others, whereas indirect discrimination involves 'provisions, criteria or practices' that put members of groups defined by religion/belief (or lack thereof) at a comparative disadvantage. A corresponding duty is placed on individuals to avoid discriminatory practices, in all circumstances regarding direct discrimination, and in cases of indirect discrimination where the discrimination is not considered to be 'a proportionate means of achieving a legitimate aim' (EER 2003, Part 1,3,1b; Department for Communities and Local Government [DCLG], 2007b). Throughout this book, the term 'religious discrimination' is used in the legal sense(s) defined above, with the distinctions 'direct' or 'indirect' as appropriate. For clarity, the term 'discrimination' is confined to inequalities that are regarded as unjust.

The RRHA protects individuals (and groups) against the expression of religious hatred in a variety of circumstances. But it also contains a robust defence of freedom of expression on matters of religion/belief, which was introduced during the passage of the Bill through the House of Lords:

> nothing in this [amendment to the Public Order Act 1986] shall be read or given effect in a way which prohibits or restricts discussion, criticism or expressions of antipathy, dislike, ridicule, insult or abuse of particular religions or the beliefs or practices of its adherents, or of any other belief system or the beliefs or practices of their adherents, or proselytising or urging adherents of a different religion or belief system to cease practising their religion or belief system. (RRHA 2006, Schedule, S.1, 29J)

The HRA further guarantees an individual's freedom of conscience, including the right to hold, 'manifest', 'practise or demonstrate' religious beliefs in public or in private, and to reject or to change religious allegiances (Department of Constitutional Affairs, 2006: 22).

At the same time, it has been argued that the new framework 'recognises that religious groups and faiths have rights to order their lives and communities according to their beliefs and doctrines' (Southwark, 2004: 3), so that in this sense it may confer some group rights. In addition, there are a number of explicit exemptions that permit religious organisations or faith-based organisations (FBOs) to act in a manner that would otherwise amount to discrimination on the grounds of religion/belief, or on one or other of the protected grounds. The Equality and Human Rights Commission (EHRC) describes these exemptions as follows:

> Certain organisations which exist to practise, advance or teach a religion or belief may, under certain circumstances, restrict membership to people of that religion or belief. They can similarly restrict participation in their activities; the way they provide goods, facilities and services as part of their activities; and the use of their premises. (www.equalityhumanrights.com)

FBOs can also restrict membership and services on the grounds of sexual orientation in certain circumstances. This side of the justice issue is considered further below, in Chapters 5 and 6.

There appear to be four main reasons why the legal framework has been extended in recent years to embrace religion.

First, some particular enactments (including the HRA and EER) were necessary in order to fulfil international legal obligations.

Second, there were a range of political considerations that pressed the New Labour government in the direction of primary legislation, including direct lobbying from religious (especially Muslim) organisations, and the felt need, perhaps, to balance the political agenda after 9/11 between security and social inclusion.

Third, courts and tribunals had ruled that Muslims, Jehovah's Witnesses and Rastafarians were not covered by the Race Relations Act 1976, or subsequent amendments (Jahangir, 2008). This created a legal anomaly, and a position of formal religious disadvantage for these groups (in the sense defined in Chapter 2), compared with other groups, such as Jews and Sikhs, who were covered by existing legislation because of the strength of their respective claims to be regarded as (unitary) ethnic groups. Formal recognition in law was seen as a remedy for this anomaly, although it is worth pointing out that ways had been found to address religious interests informally, in the absence of explicit legal recognition (see, for example, CRE, 2005b). So it is not absolutely clear that new legislation was necessary to provide a practical remedy for the anomaly.

Fourth, there was a widespread belief that members of religious minorities, and especially Muslims, were subject to specific injustices of the kind that the laws were intended to address. We will see below, however, that, insofar as the new laws were enacted for this reason, the enactments took place before the facts, that is, in the absence of persuasive evidence that social wrongs existed on the scale that might justify legislative intervention to correct them.

The new legislation has nevertheless drawn religious individuals/believers and their organisations into new *relationships* with each other, and with the state and with civil society. It has created, in effect, a new basis of settlement for 'the question of religion' within the British polity. The character of this settlement was never articulated explicitly, however, and it exists in some tension with other aspects of the British constitution. One of the purposes of this book is to identify the principles behind this settlement, and to consider some of its ramifications, particularly in relation to ethno-religious equality or inequality.

Equality principles for religion or belief

The current legal framework rests implicitly on three distinct equality principles:

1. equality of individual treatment on the grounds of religion or belief;
2. formal equality of recognition of all religions or belief systems;
3. equal consideration for identities of religion or belief alongside other aspects of social identity.

The first principle of *equal individual treatment* is the most familiar one. It extends to religion or belief the legal protection that individuals have enjoyed for some time on grounds of race, ethnicity and gender, and more recently age, disability and sexual orientation. The Equality Act 2010 potentially extends protection even further, to social caste,[1] which will be activated if research demonstrates that this is appropriate (www.equalities.gov.uk). These protections cover such forms of unequal or harmful treatment as discrimination or hate crime, as listed above.

The second principle of *equal religious advantage* treats any particular religion or 'similar philosophical belief' (EER 2003, Part 1,2,1) as one among many religions or belief systems, with none given any distinctive status. The CIPD notes, for example, that the 'European Court of Human Rights protects the Church of Scientology, the Moon sect, Druids, Vegans, the Krishna Consciousness movement, Atheists and the Divine Light of Centrum' (2003: 6).

The third principle of *strand equality* gives equal consideration to the claims of religion or belief alongside the claims of other strands of social identity such as race, ethnicity, gender, age, disability and sexual orientation. Strand equality for religion or belief is a consequence of including religion or belief within a normative framework that already applies to these other aspects of social identity. Just as equal religious advantage gives no special status to any particular religion, so strand equality gives no special status to religion in general, compared with gender, age, sexual orientation and so forth.

It is not obvious that exponents of certain religious or secular worldviews will be entirely comfortable within this new dispensation, because they may wish to prioritise religious identities over all others, or to advance the cause of a particular viewpoint – religious or secular – as providing privileged access to the truth. The two equality principles stand back from such judgements in the name of even-handedness between all religious institutions and secular worldviews.

The principle of equal advantage is evidently incompatible with the position of the Anglican Church as established within England and with the UK Monarch's position as 'Defender of the (Anglican) Faith'. Interestingly, the current heir to the UK throne has proposed that he would become in due course 'Defender of Faith' rather than 'Defender of the Faith', to reflect the UK's multicultural society (*Daily Telegraph*, 2008). But this change, although moving in the right direction (from the standpoint of equality), would still violate the non-advantage principle. To comply fully with the current drift of policy, the heir presumptive would have to become 'Defender of Faith or Belief'. The Monarch's equal protection would thus have to extend to dedicated Atheists among his or her subjects, as much as to devout Muslims or observant Christians. This would amount to a profound constitutional change, of historic proportions. So the stakes at issue in this debate are quite high.

Equal advantage is consistent with secularism, which gives no recognition to any religion or belief system within the public domain (Allison, 2006). This is because no recognition for anyone gives the same level of recognition to everyone. Equal advantage nevertheless goes beyond secularism, since it can accept public recognition of any religion or belief system, so long as every other religion or belief system receives the same level of recognition. To bring out the contrast involved, consider two cases heard recently in Britain: 'in Eweida v British Airways 2008, a British Airway's employee lost her right to wear a cross with her uniform, whereas Singh v Aberdare School 2008 upheld a Sikh girl's right to wear a *kara* bracelet to school' (Woodhead, 2009: 21). The two decisions are inconsistent with the equal advantage principle, since they permit a freedom to a Sikh that they deny to a Christian. But equal advantage could be restored in two different ways: either by prohibiting both the *kara* and the cross or by permitting both the *kara* and the cross. Both outcomes treat Christianity and Sikhism the same, but only the first resolution is consistent with (thoroughgoing) secularism, which would not permit any display of religious symbols. This demonstrates the difference between secularism and the equal advantage principle. It follows that the equal advantage principle still allows much room for discussion about the (equal) level of recognition that every religion or belief system should be granted within the public domain.

Another area of discussion is whether equal recognition requires equal recognition of religions considered as collective entities, or recognition proportional to the numbers of members of each religion. We have encountered one example already. Does equal recognition for Islam require that there is a Muslim prison chaplain alongside every Christian one? Or does it mean that 3% of prison chaplains should be Muslim, reflecting the proportions in the population as a whole?

Another difficulty arises from the provisions of the 2010 Equality Act that impose a duty to promote equality of religion/belief on such public bodies as the police, prison, probation and fire services. This involves setting targets for recruitment, retention and progression (Home Office, 1999). And private employers are allowed under law to take positive action in favour of minorities in employment decisions, at least in 'tie-break' situations.

Khan (2006) argues that 'preferential treatment' is fair in relation to disadvantaged groups and O'Neill and Holdaway (2007) justify it for the purpose of changing (racist) police culture. The need to recruit officers from minority ethno-religious backgrounds is also felt acutely by the police. On the other hand, positive discrimination is still illegal, so that a considerable tension is developing in law and practice in this field. This tension might be resolved by arguing that (legal) positive action does not constitute (illegal) positive discrimination, but this position is hard to maintain in the face of evidence about the operation of institutional targets, provided, for example, by formal investigation into the police service in England and Wales carried out by the CRE (2005a). This found that there was direct discrimination against white applicants. It is noteworthy that the chair of the Police Federation of England and Wales has argued against positive discrimination on any grounds, stating that the way to increase the trust and confidence of all communities is by sustained non-discriminatory action (Berry, 2004). We will not pursue all the philosophical and practical issues involved in the question of positive action, in part because the law on the religious equality duty is intended to come into effect only in April 2011. But there is no doubt that the trend of current law-making will bring this aspect of the justice issue into increasing prominence (see Baker et al., 2004, Fredman, 2005, and Choudhury, 2007, for further discussion of the equalities issues involved).

The principle of strand equality also raises some difficult issues, especially those surrounding the limits of toleration (McKinnon, 2006). These issues will be discussed further in Chapter 6. We return in this chapter to the most familiar aspect of the justice question, concerned with the equal treatment of individuals in civil society, and the current prevalence of religious injustice.

The evidence for religious injustice: direct and indirect techniques

It has been claimed that 'clear proof of any form of discrimination is often hard to obtain since admissions by the perpetrators are rare' (Conway, 1997: 58), and it is certainly true, as noted previously, that 'proof of religious discrimination is difficult to establish in the absence of hard statistics' (Brown, 2000b: 1037). But these observations should not be taken as a counsel of despair, since evidence amounting to 'clear proof' and/or 'hard statistics' can come from two sources especially.

Case law provides the first such source. Since the legal framework surrounding religion/belief is so recent in origin, there are at most some early indications available from this source, especially via the analysis conducted by the Advisory, Conciliation and Arbitration Service (ACAS) into claims brought under the legislation on religion or belief, which include cases of harassment, bullying and violence (Savage, 2007). Here it is interesting to note that two-thirds of these claims cited race as a secondary jurisdiction to religion or belief. Analyses of case law cannot, however, provide conclusive evidence for the overall levels of discrimination, since it is not clear whether the cases that come before the courts form a representative sample of incidents.

The most conclusive evidence regarding these overall levels of religious discrimination arises from discrimination-testing, using actor techniques, for example. The use of such techniques provided compelling evidence for the incidence of racial discrimination in Britain in the 1970s (see, for example, Smith, 1977). Perpetrators may be reluctant to admit what they are doing, as Conway suggests, but they can sometimes be caught in the act by the use of such techniques. The *Pell Report*, mentioned at the end of the previous chapter, noted that 'the first requirement is to measure the level of [ethnic minority] discrimination in the labour market' (Pell, 2007: 22). This comment implies, of course, that the level of discrimination was still in need of measurement in 2007. The report advocated the use of the direct techniques developed by the International Labour Organisation (ILO), including '"mystery shopper" CVs and actor interviews' (Pell, 2007: 22). Although this recommendation applies to ethnic discrimination, it could easily be adapted to the case of religious discrimination, and it could also be used to *distinguish* religious discrimination from ethnic and racial discrimination, by the introduction of, say, a 'white Muslim' persona for the actor tests.

A survey of recent literature (Macey et al., 2010) nevertheless yields only one example of the use of such techniques to test for religious discrimination, involving an informal telephone survey on behalf of BBC Radio Five Live with about fifty employers (European Monitoring Centre on Racism and Xenophobia [EUMC], 2006a). Any conclusions drawn about the incidence of religious injustice therefore depend on indirect techniques.

Indirect evidence of religious discrimination arises not from the testing of discriminatory actions but from opinions about whether discrimination has taken place. The opinion that is 'closest to the action' is the first-hand view of the person who is vulnerable to discrimination of the relevant kind. The corresponding research instrument is a questionnaire that invites respondents to report their own personal experiences, by specifying how often, or in which contexts, they believe themselves to have been discriminated against on grounds of religion or belief.

Although it may be assumed that such methods provide an accurate account of the respondent's own understanding of his or her personal situation, such self-reports may not be the most accurate way of establishing either the existence or the extent of injustice. On the one hand, self-reports may *under*estimate the extent of discrimination, because respondents may not be aware of the actions that affect them, or because the social climate discourages disclosure (Ameli et al., 2004). On the other hand, self-reports may *over*estimate the extent of discrimination, because respondents mistake their own experiences as examples of discrimination, or the grounds on which it occurs – believing, for example, that the unfair treatment arises from religious discrimination, rather than from ethnic or racial discrimination.

There is also the problem of whether respondents share the investigators' (or the legal) understanding of terms such as 'unfair treatment' or 'discrimination', since 'in [some] contexts, religious individuals can come close to claiming that others are discriminating against them because they do not happen to share the same values' (Weller et al., 2001: 116; see also Jayaweera and Choudhury, 2008, on this topic and on the relationship between religious and ethnic or racial discrimination).

Although studies based on respondents' self-reports may not be as conclusive as direct methods, they offer a more reliable guide than studies that ask respondents for their *third-party opinions* about the incidence of injustice in society at large, independently of whether, or how or where, they may have encountered discrimination themselves. The operative distinction is between research that focuses on the respondent's personal *experience* of discrimination as an individual and that which focuses on the respondent's *perception* of the discrimination (or other harms) suffered by members of a given social category in society more generally. To underline the nature of the distinction, research into the experience of discrimination will address the question 'how much religious discrimination is there in society?' whereas research into the perception of discrimination will address the question 'how much religious discrimination is there *believed to be* in society?'

This distinction would not be very significant, perhaps, if the research generated answers to these two questions that were broadly comparable. It turns out, however, that this is not the case. There is a considerable discrepancy between what is believed to be true and what is true regarding religious discrimination, granting all the caveats entered earlier about the uncertainties of current knowledge in this area. This is another peril of subjectivity, when the *belief* in discrimination is taken to show the *existence* of discrimination, in the absence of more objective tests. We document this point first in relation to Christian sectarianism in Scotland, and then in relation to the minority religions in England and Wales.

Christian sectarianism and religious discrimination in Scotland

Bruce et al. (2005) conducted the key study on this topic. They began with a critique of a small-scale interview study undertaken by Walls and Williams (2003). This claimed to 'establish the *fact* of discrimination' against Catholics in Scotland (Bruce et al., 2005: 155, citing Walls and Williams, 2003, with emphasis in the original). Bruce et al. show, however, that Walls and Williams' evidence demonstrates at most the existence of the *belief* that anti-Catholic discrimination occurs in Scotland, not the existence of such discrimination itself. This finding about belief is mirrored in other sources, with the result that 'many Scots believe religious discrimination [directed against Catholics] to be common' (Bruce et al., 2005: 165; see also Adams and Burke, 2006, and Bradley, 2006).

Yet Bruce et al. find that there is 'a gulf between perception and experience' in this area (2005: 162). In the 2001 Social Attitudes Survey for Scotland, for example, one half of respondents raised as Catholics thought that 'religion still matters' in limiting opportunities for Catholics, and a third of other respondents shared this view. But the proportion of Catholic respondents who had experienced discrimination themselves was much smaller, so that 'two-thirds of those who thought discrimination was a problem did not feel that they had suffered it themselves' (Bruce et al., 2005: 161). An even more striking illustration of the gulf was that '98.3 per cent of Catholics in [one] Glasgow survey declined the chance to claim to have been victims of discrimination' (Bruce et al., 2005: 162). What is generally believed to be the case – that is, the *perception* of discrimination – thus far exceeds the (self-reported) *experience* of discrimination in Scotland.

The study cites several possible reasons why the problem of sectarianism looms larger in the public imagination than it does in everyday life. These include a number of contexts in which Catholic and Protestant institutions or representatives are 'paired', which gives the impression of equal numerical weight, when in fact just 16% of the population was recorded as Catholic in the 2001 Census. This leads to a general overestimation of the number of Catholics to be found in each social context, so that their relative absence in a given context seems disproportionately severe, and unnecessarily incriminating for the social system. Relative Catholic prominence in the media, and the impact of high-profile symbolic events – above all the Celtic-Rangers football rivalry in Glasgow – may also act to magnify the salience of the underlying issues of religious difference (Bruce et al., 2005). There are some interesting parallels here with the case of Islam in England and Wales, which will be touched upon below.

The study by Bruce et al. also presents evidence about religious inequality in Scotland, which has historically placed Catholics in lower socio-economic positions than Protestants, especially in relation to members of the Church of Scotland. These differences are most evident, however, in older age cohorts and diminish rapidly among the younger age groups, so that 'religious differences in social class are largely restricted to older Scots' (Bruce et al., 2005: 158). A very similar finding applies to basic educational achievement, where there has been a striking narrowing of the gap between Catholics and Protestants. (See the Statistical Appendix, Figure 6.) Paterson (2000) has linked improved educational attainment with the changing socio-economic position of younger Catholics, so that education has had a marked impact in reducing religious inequality in Scotland. This is in the absence of any legislation targeted specifically at religious discrimination. These findings are in line with the argument developed at the end of the previous chapter about the potential importance of improved educational achievement in equalising the social position for the minority religions. (And see also Paterson and Iannelli, 2006.)

Since there is so little inequality in socio-economic terms between Catholics and others (in all but the oldest age cohorts), Bruce and his colleagues conclude that 'such patterns as we find are entirely consistent with an explanation in which discrimination plays no part'

(Bruce et al., 2005: 166). According to this evidence, then, contemporary Scotland presents a case in which there is (a) a widespread perception of extensive (intra-Christian) discrimination, but (b) little (self-reported) experience of it and (c) low levels of religious (intra-Christian) inequality in social or economic terms.

Religious discrimination in England and Wales

The main concern in England and Wales lies with discrimination directed against members of the minority (non-Christian) faiths, especially Muslims (Weller, 2006). It is already evident from the findings given in the previous chapter that the situation of minority religious groups in England and Wales is different from that of Catholics in Scotland, since there are significant socio-economic inequalities in the former case, but not in the latter. It is more of a live issue within this context to what extent these inequalities are caused by religious injustice.

One of the most influential recent studies of the question was entitled *Religious Discrimination in England and Wales* (Weller et al., 2001), which will be called the *Weller Report* after the chair of its research team. This report was one of the two main official studies, along with Hepple and Choudhury (2001), that paved the way for the new legal framework on religion/belief. The brief given to Weller and his colleagues by the Home Office was 'to assess the evidence of religious discrimination in England and Wales, both actual and perceived' (Weller et al., 2001: vi).

The principal research instrument chosen for the study was a survey question addressed to representatives of a wide range of religious organisations, as follows: 'do your members experience unfair treatment because of their religion in any of the following areas?' covering education, employment, housing, health, law and criminal justice, access to funding and the media (Weller et al., 2001: 136). As the researchers comment, 'the representative from each organisation who completed the questionnaire was set the difficult task of trying to reflect the collective experience of his or her membership' (Weller et al., 2001: 5). This survey was backed by interviews with a very small sample of individuals (N = 29) 'who claim to have experienced discrimination on the basis of religion' (Weller et al., 2001: 161).

It follows that the *Weller Report* belongs almost entirely on the 'perception' rather than the 'experience' side of the research agenda, despite the fact that the Home Office specifically asked the Weller team to look at both aspects of the justice question and investigate 'both actual and perceived' discrimination. The only element of the research design which comes close to first-person experiences of discrimination – the 'biographical' interview process – involves a self-selected (non-random) sample, which cannot provide any independent evidence of the general extent of discrimination.

The *Weller Report* is nevertheless cited prominently as contributing significant evidence for the incidence of religious discrimination as it is actually experienced in England and Wales (see, for example, Purdam et al., 2007). Denvir et al. described the *Weller Report* in an important ACAS review paper as 'the main study documenting religion or belief discrimination in the workplace, and wider society' and 'a comprehensive and detailed empirical study of the *experience* of discrimination on grounds of religion or belief' (2007: 26–7, emphasis added). The latter verdict would be more apt if the word 'experience' were replaced by the word 'perception'. And a recent report of a series of expert seminars held by the EHRC reiterated the conviction that the *Weller Report* 'found that religious discrimination existed, and was manifest in different forms, including...direct discrimination...and...indirect discrimination' (Woodhead, 2009: 14–15). The tendency to conflate perception with experience, and to view evidence of the former as evidence of the latter, is the third example of conceptual inflation encountered in this book. This key feature of contemporary debates on minority religion seems to have escaped most commentators, with a few notable exceptions, such as Malik (2005a,b) and Mirza et al. (2007).

The main finding of the *Weller Report* is that religious discrimination is widely perceived by (representatives of) minority religious organisations to be a pervasive problem affecting their members. A majority of Muslim organisations reported very frequent unfair treatment across every institutional domain, with Hindu and Sikh organisations reporting relatively high levels of unfair treatment (Weller et al., 2001). High levels of perceived unfairness were also found by the 2005 Citizenship Survey, which applies like the *Weller Report* to England and Wales. Almost two-thirds of respondents (64%) – without prompting – named Muslims as a group against which prejudice had recently increased (Kitchen et al., 2006). These sources show that there is a widespread belief in the existence of pervasive religious discrimination. But despite the claims made by Purdam et al. (2007), Denvir et al. (2007) and Woodhead (2009), the evidence contained in the *Weller Report* does not show that religious discrimination itself is a pervasive reality of English or Welsh society.

The 2005 Citizenship Survey also asked, however, about respondents' first-hand experience of religious discrimination, which allows perceptions and experience to be compared directly for the same large (and carefully constructed) random sample (N>9,600). The main findings are that just 2% of respondents reported that they had been discriminated against because of their religion by any organisation. Among (self-identified) members of religious groups, 2% of Christian respondents and 3% of those of No Religion reported experiences of discrimination, rising to 7% for Hindu respondents, 12% for Sikhs and 13% for Muslims (Kitchen et al., 2006).

A separate set of questions regarding the experience of discrimination in employment found that just 1% of the white respondents with adverse employment experiences specified religion as a reason for refusal of a job, and 2% specified religion as a reason for unfair treatment regarding promotion. The corresponding figures for black respondents were 2% and 4%, and for Asian respondents 10% and 16% respectively (Kitchen et al., 2006: 30). Religion is consistently the weakest of the specific social factors identified by this research as the reason for adverse employment experiences, with lesser adverse impact than race/ethnicity, age or gender (see Macey et al., 2010, for further detail on this and other statistical findings covered in this section).

Although Muslim respondents were more likely than others to cite religion as a reason for adverse treatment, the proportion of Muslim respondents who reported such treatment is very small. It affected just over 2.5% – that is just over one in forty – of the Muslim respondents in the relevant samples. This evidence is in marked contrast to the confidence expressed by the religious organisations approached by Weller that religious discrimination is a widespread and serious phenomenon in contemporary England and Wales.

The need to distinguish perception from experience applies equally to the question of housing. There is a striking contrast between the perceptions of pervasive unfair treatment in the housing market presented by religious organisations to the *Weller Report* team (with two-thirds of the Muslim organisations reporting frequent or occasional unfair treatment) and the reports of unfair treatment experienced by religious respondents themselves. According to respondents to the 2005 Citizenship Survey, there is almost no discrimination against Christians, Hindus, Sikhs or Muslims in either public sector or private sector housing. The highest figure was that 2% of Muslim respondents claimed to have been discriminated against in public sector housing.

A similar picture applies to the public services. When minority religious respondents were invited to report on their own experiences of the public services, at least 94% of respondents in every religious group expressed their satisfaction with each of the public services, ranging across health, education and criminal justice. Muslims expressed the highest level of dissatisfaction (6%) in relation to discrimination at the hands of the police services.

This last finding is particularly surprising, given how the Muslim Council of Britain (MCB) responded to statistics released by the Home Office in 2004 which showed that there had been a 300% increase in the number of Asians stopped and searched under the anti-terror laws: 'The whole Muslim community is being targeted by the police' (Sofi, cited in Malik, 2005b: 1). And the MCB's general secretary insisted that '95–98% of those stopped and searched under the anti-terror laws are Muslim' (Sacranie, cited in Malik, 2005b: 1). In fact, as Malik pointed out to the MCB, out of a total of 21,577 people stopped and searched under the terror laws, 14,429 were white and just 3,000 were Asian, of whom probably half were Muslim, that is 'around 1,500 Muslims out of a population of more than 1.6 million' (Malik, 2005b: 1). But the real issue of concern is that no matter how many times Malik showed the true statistics, the MCB refused to budge, continuing to relay the message of widespread anti-Islamic injustice.

This is not to deny the existence of racism in the police in general (MacPherson, 1999; Bland et al., 2000; Miller et al., 2000; BBC, 2003; Whitfield, 2004), nor particularly with respect to their use of stop and search. However, Malik (2005b) points out that these are predominantly directed at black – not Asian – people, with the former being five times more likely to be stopped and searched than the latter (Home Office, 2004; Metropolitan Police Authority Scrutiny Panel, 2004).

In terms of other studies, Marsh (2002) found a very low total of less than 2% self-reported religious discrimination in a Europe-wide sample. There are three studies that report higher levels of anti-Muslim discrimination in Britain, whose findings must, however, be questioned on a variety of methodological grounds. Although one investigation conducted by the Islamic Human Rights Commission (IHRC) found that up to 80% of the Muslim respondents reported experiences of discrimination, the sample selection appears to have been biased in favour of those who believed they had experienced discrimination, because of the channels through which the sample was recruited (Ameli et al., 2007). In the second case, the results are certainly obtained from non-random 'snowball sampling' and the authors themselves volunteer that 'it is not possible to generalise the results of this research' (Jayaweera and Choudhury, 2008: 15). The relevant sample size is also small (N = 155). A third case involves an official report prepared for the Cabinet Office by Abrams and Houston (2007). The size of the Muslim sub-sample was also small in this case (N = 128). But the main difficulty with the study is that Abrams and Houston asked respondents about their recent personal experiences of *either* prejudice *or* unfair treatment. So the study is not focused on the question at issue in this section. In contrast to all these studies, the 2005 Citizenship Survey used a random sample of much larger size and asked specifically about discrimination in ways that directed respondents towards particular social contexts, such as employment, health care or criminal justice.

The principal sources thus show that the situation with minority religions in England and Wales resembles that in relation to Christian sectarianism in Scotland – there is a 'gulf between perception and experience' (Bruce et al., 2005: 162). Unfair treatment is widely believed to be pervasive, but the evidence for these widespread beliefs must be treated with extreme caution as a statement of the levels of discrimination *actually experienced* by members of minority religions. The best evidence available in relation to the latter question shows that the levels of (self-reported) religious injustice are very low, in a range of areas including employment, housing and the public services. The highest reported rate is that 13% of Muslims believe themselves to have suffered discrimination in at least one institutional sector. But this implies, of course, that 87% of Muslims (in the relevant sample) believe that they have not suffered discrimination in any institutional sector.

Religious prejudice

Strictly speaking, prejudice of religion or belief involves an opinion about a religious tradition or a secular belief system that is pre-conceived or biased and is therefore based on lack of knowledge, or an unreasonable or unfair assessment of its beliefs and/or practices. Demonstrating the existence of prejudice thus requires evidence not only about the negative opinion held by the respondent about a religion or belief system, but about the grounds on which the opinion is held.

The Global Attitudes Project on religion conducted by the Pew Research Center in Washington DC is able to finesse this issue, because its survey questions refer merely to 'favourable' and 'unfavourable' opinions, and the term 'prejudice' is not used. The headline findings are that in the four surveys conducted from 2004 to 2008, between 14% and 23% of British respondents expressed unfavourable opinions of Muslims – compared with large majorities (of between 63% and 71%) who expressed favourable opinions (Pew, 2008). The proportions of unfavourable opinions expressed about Christians ranged between 5% and 7% over the four surveys, and those about Jews ranged between 6% and 9%. The differences in the results of the surveys are broadly within the error margin of 4% quoted for the British sample, which included about 750 respondents in 2008 (Pew, 2008). The Pew research does not, therefore, suggest that attitudes have changed markedly over this period.

These figures for attitudes towards religious groups in Britain may be compared with those for countries such as France, where unfavourable opinions of Muslims, Christians and Jews were held by 38%, 17% and 20% of the sample respectively in the 2008 survey. The equivalent figures for the US were 23%, 3% and 7%; for China they were 55%, 55% and 55%; for Turkey 9%, 74% and 76%; for Pakistan 1%, 60% and 76%, and for India 56%, 37% and 32% respectively (Pew, 2008).

It was noted above that Abrams and Houston did not differentiate prejudice from unfair treatment in their survey question. In the interpretation of their findings, they also speak about prejudice as if it is demonstrated by any expression of negative feelings, so that they have not recognised the distinctive character of prejudice (see, for example, their 'Summary and Conclusions' at Abrams and Houston, 2007: 45–7). Their research question asked: 'In general how negative or positive do you feel about the following groups in Britain?' The answers to this question, which range from 'very positive' to 'very negative', therefore involve favourable or unfavourable attitudes, as in the Pew surveys. But the answers are considered under the heading 'Overt Prejudice' and are used elsewhere in the report to provide 'a very basic measure of direct prejudice' (Abrams and Houston, 2007: 86, 33). This is a fourth example of conceptual inflation, because it extends the concept of prejudice to include every variety of unfavourable attitude.

Abrams and Houston also invited their respondents to give an opinion about Muslims, but not the adherents of any other religion or belief system. Their findings regarding Islam are nevertheless consistent with the Pew research: 19% of their sample expressed negative feelings about Muslims, in comparison with 22% who expressed such feelings about gays/lesbians, as against 10% for black people and 8% for people under 30 (Abrams and Houston, 2007). Overall then, large majorities of the British population appear to hold favourable opinions of adherents of all the Abrahamic faith groups, with only very small minorities holding unfavourable opinions of either Christians or Jews. It is a concern that a sizeable minority in Britain (of around 20%) hold an unfavourable opinion of Muslims, although this proportion is considerably lower than in many other countries, including France, China and India. This level of anti-Muslim opinion in Britain is also much lower than the proportions found to hold unfavourable opinions of Christians and Jews in China or India, or of the same groups in countries with predominantly Muslim populations such as Turkey or Pakistan.

In a synoptic article entitled 'Islamophobia in Contemporary Britain', Field (2007) analyses the findings of 104 opinion polls conducted with non-Muslims between 1988 and 2006 (90 of them since 2001) and 29 polls of Muslims (26 since 2001). Field is careful to stress the need for caution in interpreting these polls for a number of reasons, particularly the fact that most of them were conducted at 'crisis points' in which Muslims were involved (such as the terrorist attacks on the US, Britain and Spain, the 'Rushdie Affair', the Gulf and Iraq Wars and the 'Danish Cartoons' controversy). Field's 'poll of poll' findings are broadly in line with the Pew surveys, in that large majorities (usually of 60% or more) continue to express favourable attitudes towards Islam, even in circumstance dominated by crisis incidents, and there is little evidence of deepening hostility over the decade. It is not, therefore, entirely clear why he concludes that there is increasing Islamophobia in Britain, especially since 2001, which takes the form of:

> a stereotypical portrait of Muslims in the eyes of the majority British population…an increasing perception that Muslims in Britain are slow to integrate into mainstream society, feel only a qualified sense of patriotism and are prone to espouse anti-Western values that lead many to condone so-called Islamic terrorism. (Field, 2007: 466)

But even if this were a defensible description of the poll findings for 'the majority British population', it is interesting to note that such a perception of Muslim attitudes is to some extent confirmed by the polls carried out among Muslims themselves. Thus:

> At least one in twenty, disproportionately young Muslims, are so disaffected as to be willing to contemplate complete rejection of mainstream society and the use of violence against it. A further 15% are partially alienated to the extent of finding Western values decadent, experiencing no great sense of loyalty to Britain, feeling that Muslims have allowed themselves to become too integrated into British culture and sympathizing with the motives of those who take up arms for Islam. A further third co-exist with British society but consider themselves more Muslim than British. (Field, 2007: 469)

These findings raise some important questions about the use of language. Is it 'prejudicial' or 'stereotypical' to take a view (of Muslim opinion) that conforms with a good deal of the evidence? And does equality of religion or belief imply an even-handedness about language, so that negative judgements on one side should not be described as 'Islamophobic' when judgements on the other side are described in the more sympathetic terms of 'disaffection' or 'alienation'?

We return to the question of 'Islamophobia' below. The main point here is that negative attitudes, however strongly felt or expressed, do not necessarily translate into hostile actions. As a result, there are vital lines to be drawn within a free society regarding which attitudes and behaviours are to be criminalised, as opposed to being (merely) disapproved. The recent repeal of the Blasphemy Act, which gave unequal protection to Christianity, delivered equal advantage of religion or belief in a manner that also extended the domain of free speech. As noted above, this freedom has been made explicit because the law exempts from regulation 'expressions of antipathy, dislike, ridicule, insult or abuse of particular religions or the beliefs or practices of its adherents, or of any other belief system or the beliefs or practices of their adherents' (RRHA 2006, Schedule, S.1, 29J).

There are nevertheless detectable movements in the opposite direction, which would circumscribe anti-religious expression even more tightly than under the Blasphemy Act. Brown has, for example, claimed that 'a reverence for the transcendental sacred is privileged above other forms of reverence', and proposed that the law should be changed accordingly to prohibit 'the harm done directly to a person by deliberately wounding her sense of the sacred' (2003: 189). This would in effect extend the previous law on blasphemy to cover most religious faiths, though not secular worldviews. Even more broadly, experts convened by the EHRC have come up with a new concept of *cultural and attitudinal discrimination*, which:

> has to do … with religion being misunderstood, denigrated, ignored, trivialised, distorted or ridiculed, including by the media, in education, and in public discourse. It can also include the expression of personal prejudice and hostility against religion and religious individuals. (Woodhead, 2009: 15)

Recall, however, that religious discrimination is a criminal offence. Given that a person can manifest 'attitudinal discrimination' simply by ignoring a particular religion, are these experts seriously considering the possibility that displaying indifference to religion should constitute a criminal offence? Thought crime is evidently alive and well at the EHRC! And the concept of 'cultural and attitudinal discrimination' provides our fifth example of conceptual inflation, because it extends the concept of discrimination beyond its proper field of application. Properly conceived, discrimination involves unfair, unequal treatment, not simply the holding of different views, or the manifestation of the 'wrong' attitude.

Religious hate crime

In ordinary parlance, a religious hate crime is a crime that is motivated (or exacerbated) by the perpetrator's hatred of others' religion(s) and/or belief(s). In the British legal definition, however, a religious hate crime is:

> any criminal offence which is perceived, by the victim or any other person, to be motivated by a hostility or prejudice based on a person's religion or perceived religion.
> (www.crimereduction.homeoffice.gov.uk/hatecrime)

Notice how the requirement of motivation has been replaced by a requirement about the *perception* of motivation, and how, moreover, this perception can be entertained by any person whomsoever in order for the crime to count as a hate crime. 'Hate incidents' are treated in a parallel fashion. This supplies a sixth example of conceptual inflation, and the most egregious to date.

It is difficult to believe that these definitions can be intended seriously in legal terms, however well meaning they may be politically. The test here involves absolute subjectivity, because the relevant opinion about motivation could be entertained by an individual who has no connection whatever with the alleged crime or incident, as a victim or as a witness, and no information regarding it. And there is no qualification to the effect that the person has to be 'reasonable' in his or her judgement, which is the commonly applied legal safeguard. It follows that any crime or incident whatsoever could become a religious hate crime or incident (or indeed a race hate, sexual orientation hate, or disability hate crime or incident) just because one person perceives it to be so, regardless of the evidence – or lack of evidence – for this perception. Among other consequences of this approach, the latitude of classification makes it very difficult to interpret the official statistics, and therefore to determine the true dimensions of religiously motivated crime, because it is not at all clear that the relevant officials in the police service or the Home Office will have used the same test as to what counts as a hate crime.

This subjectivist approach stands in marked contrast to the careful work undertaken by the Community Security Trust (CST), which provides a detailed annual report of antisemitic hate crimes and incidents in Britain. CST's methods of data collection and analysis take account of the motivation, content and target of any incident, and the context in which it occurs. The analysis also distinguishes between antisemitic and anti-Israeli activity. In 2009, almost 500 potential incidents were rejected in this way as being anti-Israeli but not antisemitic, leaving 924 recorded antisemitic incidents. Of these, 3 involved extreme violence, 121 assault and 89 damage to, or desecration of, property. The majority of incidents – 605 – concerned abusive behaviour, whilst 62 were concerned with antisemitic publications and 44 involved threats (CST, 2010).

It is unfortunate that the available research does not cover the non-Jewish minority religions with the same care and attention to detail. The IHRC, for example, bases many of its claims about anti-Muslim aggression on data culled from an online questionnaire which includes incidents that people have *heard about*, rather than experienced. And in arriving at its assessment of the extent of Islamophobia, it includes *'dirty looks'* as *'anti-Muslim harassment'* (IHRC, 2008), another example of conceptual inflation that will create exaggerated statistics. Ameli et al. (2004) nevertheless report a number of incidents in which Muslim women were punched, shouted at, spat on or had their *hijabs* pulled off. An important consultation with the Muslim Women's Network (MWN) found safety to be the issue of greatest concern, with the majority of participants recounting personal experiences ranging from harassment and verbal abuse to serious threats and assaults (Raz, 2006). Franks' (2000) research is relevant here, because it looked particularly at white women who wear the *hijab,* so that, in theory, instances of harassment and violence relate to *religion,* rather than ethnicity. This research raises the question of how racism and religious hostility intersect and the differential impact of ethnic or religious hostility on women relative to men. We should emphasise that we are in no way opposed to the idea that racially (or religiously) motivated hate crimes merit differential treatment (Iganski, 2002; 2008). We *are* opposed to the idea that the character of such crimes can be determined on an entirely subjective basis.

A finding that is common within this literature is that hate activity is sparked by 'trigger events' of various kinds, which may be related to national or international incidents or conflicts. For example, the total of antisemitic events recorded by the CST in 2009 was almost 70% higher than in the previous year (924 compared with 546). This 'occurred largely because of the extreme reactions to the trigger event of the Gaza conflict', which produced almost 300 incidents in January 2009 alone (CST, 2010: 23). A previous 'spike' had occurred in 2006, related to Israel's war against Hezbollah in Lebanon. There is a tendency nevertheless for the level of incidents to fall away fairly swiftly after the effect of the trigger event has passed, although it took four months (until May 2009) for the monthly total of antisemitic incidents to return to the previous year's levels (see also EUMC, 2004a,b, on antisemitism in Europe).

EUMC recorded a very similar pattern in anti-Islamic incidents following 9/11 (Allen and Nielsen, 2002), which increased dramatically in its immediate aftermath, but decreased equally quickly and a few weeks later fell below those for the previous year (EUMC, 2006a). Malik (2005b: 2) notes that the EU discovered around a dozen serious physical attacks on British Muslims in the four months following 9/11, but reports Christopher Allen as stating that 'There were very few serious attacks... [rather, Islamophobia] manifested itself in quite basic and low level ways.' It is notable, however, that following 9/11, a number of *Sikh* people and properties were attacked, presumably in the belief that they were Muslim. One Sikh interviewee in Farnell et al.'s research commented (laughingly and indicating his beard): 'The problem is we look more like the Taliban than the Muslim does' (2003: 38).

Although the provision of information about religious hate activity is by no means comprehensive or satisfactory, it seems fair to conclude that it does take place in the UK on a scale giving rise to concern, with a degree of seriousness ranging from incidents of personal abuse to violent assault. Women in recognisably Muslim styles of dress seem to be at particular risk of hate crime, but it has been argued by Mirza et al. (2007) that – contrary to popular belief – Jews as a group are more likely to be the targets of hate crime than Muslims. They estimate that one in 1,700 Muslims is likely to fall victim to 'faith hate' attacks every year, whereas Jews are more than four times as likely to be attacked in this way, with a ratio of 1 in 400. This finding may support Wistrich's suggestion that antisemitism is 'the longest hatred' (1992) (see also Taguieff and Camiller, 2004, Chesler, 2005, and Bunzi, 2007, on the rise of antisemitism).

'Islamophobia' and the role of the media

Islamophobia: A Challenge for Us All is the title of an influential report commissioned by the Runnymede Trust in the 1990s, which has probably done more to establish the currency of the term 'Islamophobia' in public life in Britain than any other single source.

The report defines 'Islamophobia' as 'unfounded hostility towards Islam' (Conway, 1997: 4, hereafter referred to as the *Conway Report*). It went on immediately to extend this definition to 'refer...also to the practical consequences of such hostility in unfair discrimination against Muslim individuals and communities, and to the exclusion of Muslims from mainstream political and social affairs'. Notice that the definition starts from a psychological state – unfounded hostility – and extends it to apply to a potentially wide range of social and political phenomena. This provides yet another example of conceptual inflation. It was perhaps unwise to link the psychological aspect of the definition so closely with the social and political aspects, since discrimination and exclusion can come about for a variety of reasons, not all of which involve psychological hostility. As the authors of the report also recognise, the wording of the definition implies that it is not sufficient for a finding of Islamophobia to show that there is hostility towards Islam. The hostility must in addition be 'unfounded' – that is, it must go beyond a reasoned opposition to Islam (or a reasonable emotional response to Islam) in some context of application. As its name implies, Islamophobia thus requires not just an unfavourable attitude towards the religion, but an element of phobia – irrational dread.

This distinction may be easy enough to state in principle, but it is more difficult (and controversial) to apply in practice, since it implies, strictly speaking, that every accusation of Islamophobia must be accompanied by a diagnosis of the accused person's mental state. The problem is similar to that posed by the need to distinguish a prejudice from an unfavourable attitude. As the *Conway Report* asks: 'how...can one tell the difference between legitimate criticism and disagreement on the one hand, and Islamophobia on the other?' The authors of the report attempt to answer their own question by developing a contrast between 'open' (unprejudiced) and 'closed' (prejudiced) views of Islam (Conway, 1997: 4–5). They find some difficulty in pinning the contrast down, however, and in any case it would be very difficult to operationalise. To give just one example, 'Islam seen as a political ideology, used for political or military advantage' is cited as an instance of a closed view of Islam, and thus as evidence of Islamophobia (Conway, 1997: 2). But the cited view (whether defensible or not) is a conclusion of social science and historical analysis, and not a description of a psychological state. So the precise definition of Islamophobia remains elusive, even though it is said to have 'four separate aspects: (a) social exclusion (b) violence (c) prejudice and (d) discrimination [which are] inter-connected and mutually reinforcing' (Conway, 1997: 12).

At the same time, the report claims that 'Islamophobia' 'describes a real and growing phenomenon – an ugly word for an ugly reality' (Conway, 1997: iii). The report continues:

> The word is not ideal, but ... is a useful shorthand way of referring to dread or hatred of Islam – and, therefore, to fear or dislike of all or most Muslims. Such dread and dislike have existed in Western countries and cultures for several centuries. In the last twenty years, the dislike has become more explicit, more extreme and more dangerous. It is an ingredient of all sections of our media, and is prevalent in all sections of our society. (Conway, 1997: 1)

These are very sweeping claims, which maintain that Islamophobia is virtually endemic within Britain and 'Western countries and cultures' more generally. Is there evidence for these claims? And was the evidence available to the authors of the report at the time that the claims were made? The answer to both questions is in the negative, at least as far as Britain is concerned.

First, as the evidence considered in the previous sections shows, anti-Muslim feeling is by no means 'prevalent in all sections of society'. It appears to be confined to about a fifth of the population in Britain. Incidents of violence and discrimination do occur on a scale that merits concern, but not to the extent suggested by the heightened language used in the *Conway Report,* which represents anti-Muslim hostility as 'more explicit, more extreme and more dangerous' than ever before. What the evidence does show is the widespread *belief* in the prevalence of Islamophobia, which the contents of the *Conway Report* reflect, and which the reception given to the report no doubt reinforced.

Second, the *Conway Report* provides little systematic evidence for the claims it makes about the prevalence of Islamophobia at the time the report was written. Descriptions are given, for example, of eleven specific hate incidents, but only four of these appear to involve religious hostility or discrimination, as opposed to racism. And no context is provided for a number of the incidents. Among incidents that are said to be 'relatively trivial in themselves but which have a cumulative effect on the victims', the two examples described in the report involve 'rotten fish is left on doorstep' and 'corrosive liquid is poured over a car'. Although the authors say that they know of 'many other' incidents, they provide no further information. In terms of their general evidence of hate crime, the authors acknowledge that the analysis of the data available to them led to conclusions about a specifically religious component that were 'speculative' (Conway, 1997: 41).

The *Conway Report* is on slightly stronger ground in its claim that Islamophobia 'is an ingredient of all sections of our media', although this claim, too, is unqualified – is it really intended to apply to *every* section of *all* media? Nevertheless, the report does reproduce a number of examples of individuals identified in context as Muslim and represented in the print media in an unsympathetic or unflattering light. As such, the examples constitute evidence of opposition, or even hostility, to Islam within the mainstream media. Subsequent publications have also claimed that Islamophobia is institutionalised, particularly in television (Ansari, 2002; The Media Diversity Institute, 2002; Poole, 2002; Allen, 2004; 2007; Ameli et al., 2007; In-Service Training and Educational Development, 2007; Richardson, 2007). Otherwise, there are a few studies of the reception of news coverage, especially of dramatic events such as 9/11, in (typically) small samples, and with a quality of evidence best described as 'anecdotal' (Ahmad, 2006; Banaji and Al-Ghabban, 2006; Harb and Bessaiso, 2006). There are some recent studies of (Christian) sectarianism in the media in Scotland, including coverage of the Celtic-Rangers rivalry (Adams and Burke, 2006; Bradley, 2006). There is discussion of 'Anglophobia' in some sources on Scotland, but this does not appear to have any religious dimensions (Bruce and Glendinning, 2003; McAspurren, 2005).

Care must be exercised, nevertheless, in proceeding from examples of hostile representation of Islam, or Muslims, to findings of Islamophobia, for several reasons.

First, the definition of Islamophobia requires it to be shown that the description or the portrayal is an unreasonable one, given the specific individuals or events portrayed.

Second, the genre of representation is a factor that must be taken into account in the analysis of meaning, in that cartoons, for example, involve caricature – that is, deliberate exaggeration or distortion. Context is relevant to the interpretation of media representation, just as it is to the classification of hate crime.

Third, Islamophobia involves a specific targeting of Islam, and a religious disadvantage that treats it adversely compared with other religions or belief systems. In terms of media representation, it would be relevant to ask, for example, whether the portrayal of imams is more hostile than the portrayal of priests. This highlights the need to distinguish between general criticism of the way the media operates in Britain (which may be exemplified in some cases by its treatment of

Islam or Muslims) and an accusation of specific animosity. A further reason for making this distinction is that the remedy differs between the two cases: either raise the general standards of media coverage on the one hand or deal with anti-Muslim bias on the other.

Fourth, the guidance now offered by the law on religious hatred was noted above. Is Islamophobia involved only when hostile expression crosses the line into incitements of hatred, or is it defined more broadly, to include, say, every instance of dislike, ridicule or insult (or even indifference to Islam, as the concept of 'attitudinal discrimination' seems to imply)? Here it is worth noting that the CST declined to classify the following email received by a pro-Israeli group as antisemitic, because it was thought to be political rather than religious in intent: 'Murderers, thieves, swindlers! You are the bane of this earth, a blot on our landscape. Go to Hell' (CST, 2010: 26). Is there an analogous line to be drawn between religiously motivated and politically motivated expressions of opposition towards Islam?

It is not argued here that it is an easy matter to draw any of these lines, or to make judgements about every individual case. The point, rather, is that the *Conway Report* did not dwell on the need to draw these lines, or the difficulties of judging cases, although it did at least attempt to explore the distinction between prejudicial and reasoned views of Islam. The subsequent literature on Islamophobia has been, if anything, even less concerned to approach its topic with the required precision. This is evident in work that now applies the concept to the European context beyond the UK (EUMC, 2006a,b). And the *Conway Report* was followed up by a second report from the Commission on British Muslims and Islamophobia (Muir et al., 2004), which provided very little systematic evidence for the harms suffered by Muslims, and yet continued to make a wide range of policy recommendations designed to combat Islamophobia. And it is interesting to note that Christopher Allen, whose work with both EUMC and the Forum against Islamophobia and Racism (FAIR) has done much to popularise the idea of Islamophobia over the past decade, had by 2004 reached a similar conclusion about this lack of empirical substantiation: 'the reality remains that very little research [on religion] has actually been undertaken that offers any concretised or grounded evidence' (2004: 11).

An exception to this generalisation in the field of media representation is an article published by Richardson (2001), which analysed the coverage of Muslims in broadsheet newspapers in Britain over the period October 1997–January 1998. The coverage was nearly all of non-British Muslims – nearly 90% of the reports – reflecting the international situation of the time. This counts as a 'pioneer study' in the field because of its relatively systematic approach towards the sampling of news coverage. And it also established two themes that have featured in subsequent research: a tendency to associate Islam and Muslims only with negative news contexts, and to exclude Muslim voices from the coverage.

It is surprising that Richardson's approach was not followed up for the media post 9/11 until the appearance of a study in 2008 from the Cardiff School of Journalism, Media and Cultural Studies of the coverage of Islam (and of Muslims) in the national UK press from 2000 to 2008 (Moore et al., 2008). The context of this coverage had been transformed by 9/11, the 7/7 bombings in London and UK participation in the conflicts in Afghanistan and Iraq. Unsurprisingly, the coverage was now domesticated, compared with the reports analysed by Richardson, by making extensive reference to Muslims within the UK. Findings from this show that the volume of news stories referring to Islam in Britain (or British Muslims) increased quite sharply in 2001–2 and 2005–6, immediately following 9/11 and 7/7. These local peaks in coverage, however, combined with a steadily rising trend, which saw coverage increase almost tenfold over the review period, from 350 stories a year in 2000 to an estimate of nearly 3,500 in 2008.

A sample of almost 1,000 of these stories was chosen for further analysis (about 5% of all the news stories). Three 'news hooks' dominated the coverage in the sample: terrorism (or the war on terror), religious and cultural issues, and Muslim extremism, amounting to 36%, 22% and 11% of coverage respectively. The relative proportions of these stories, which together account for over two-thirds of coverage on British Muslims, were similar for the broadsheet and the tabloid press.

The most frequent discourses within this coverage linked Muslims to the threat of terrorism; viewed Islam as dangerous, backward or irrational; covered Islam in relation to multiculturalism, or spoke of Islam in terms of 'a clash of civilisations' or a threat to the British way of life. The authors comment: 'four of the five most common discourses about Muslims in Britain in the British press associate Islam/Muslims with threats, problems or in opposition to British values' (Moore et al., 2008: 15).

An analysis of word associations found further that a majority of the most commonly used nouns ('terrorist', 'extremist', 'cleric', 'Islamist', 'suicide bomber', 'convert', and 'militant') and adjectives ('radical', 'fanatical', 'fundamentalist', 'extremist', 'militant', 'moderate', and 'evil') held negative connotations. The authors point out that:

> This is not to say that these nouns were used inaccurately or indiscriminately: as our other findings suggest, if British Muslims are most likely to feature in news about terrorism, extremism or religious and cultural differences, then it is not surprising if the nouns used reflect these topics. What these findings do indic- ate, however, is the extent to which the dominant 'news hooks' have implications on [sic] the way British Muslims are generally described. (Moore et al., 2008: 17)

If the negative portrayal of Islam thus followed on from the newspapers' choice of newsworthy topics, it was also compounded in some cases by ordinary kinds of journalistic faults, such as 'decontextualisation, exag- geration and misinformation' (Moore et al., 2008: 32). These problems are traced out in several stories that dominated headlines at various times in 2007–8, including the genetic dangers posed by first-cousin marriage, the analogy between Islamophobia and the situation in 1930s Germany, the Archbishop of Canterbury's 2008 statement on *shar'ia* law, the existence of social separation in Britain along religious lines, and future demographic trends (Moore et al., 2008).

The content of the newspaper articles creates a strong impression of the way in which Muslims are talked about rather than spoken with. Statements by public figures and politicians, criminal justice profes- sionals or (non-Muslim) campaign groups account for over a half of all quotations about British Muslims, whereas the MCB accounts for 8%, radical Islamic groups 4% and Muslim religious leaders 3%. Although 'the Muslim community' is frequently the topic of debate, community sources were used in just 1% of quotations (fifteen in all), only slightly ahead of the nine quotations from the BNP. And the BNP may not provide the most insightful appreciation of community issues (Moore et al., 2008).

It is possible that the focus on national media in these studies gives a misleading view of press coverage in its totality, because local newspapers in areas with higher Muslim populations may cover a broader range of issues, with a more balanced representation of Muslim voices. This is our informal impression, for example, of the coverage in the Bradford *Telegraph and Argus*. And there is very little systematic research into television coverage, which arguably has the greater social impact, or the Internet, whose significance as a source of information (and disinformation) grows daily.

Overall, these studies add to the general sense that the public and official discourses surrounding Islam take place in their own realm, which is established at some distance from the experience of ordinary people. In the same way that government policy-makers seek out (and in the process help to create) 'community leaders' to articulate a community view, so do newspapers – when they attend to Muslim voices at all – seek out community spokesmen to provide a Muslim reaction to the news of the day. It appears that the MCB fulfils this role for the national print media more than any other Muslim organisation, and it has been described as 'the best-known and most representative Muslim umbrella organisation' (Muir et al., 2004: 1) and 'the single most representative and successful national Muslim organisation' (Modood, 2007: 83). Yet the MCB has a very particular political agenda of its own, with settled and uncompromising views on a wide range of issues (Bright, 2006; Malik, 2009). Its attitude towards the evidence of injustice was noted above. And it is difficult to regard it as speaking with authority for Muslims in general, given the very small fraction who name it in surveys as representative of their interests or views. (The fraction is 4% according to Channel 4 Dispatches, 2006, and 6% according to Mirza et al., 2007.) The position of the MCB is sustained to a significant extent from the top down, via its role in relation to government and the media, rather than from the bottom-up, as an expression of popular Muslim opinion.

The assessment of the media coverage of Muslims is made more problematic by the difficulties in establishing an appropriate frame of comparative reference. The volume of news coverage of Muslims has understandably increased in response to the events of the past decade. And it is also unsurprising that this news coverage has been negative, not only in the sense that most news coverage is negative, but because of the roles – often motivated ostensibly by religion – that Muslim men have played in these events. It is not easy to judge against this background whether, or how far, the coverage strays beyond 'fair comment' into the territory of Islamophobia. Without this background of events, how much coverage of religious or other issues relating to Muslims might one expect to see in the mainstream media – more than 3% or less than 3% (given that Muslims form 3% of the UK population)? How similar, or different, would one expect the coverage to be of Islam compared with Hinduism, say, Sikhism, Judaism, Christianity or Atheism, particularly if individuals claiming to be acting for these groups were involved in similar acts of violence? And does the media profile of Islam itself create misleading perceptions of issues surrounding inequality and injustice, as seems to have happened in relation to Catholicism in Scotland?

A corresponding uncertainty surrounds the wider social effects of this increasing media coverage. It might be thought that the continual portrayal of Muslims in negative news contexts is likely to reinforce stereotypes that impact negatively on the experience of individual Muslims and their communities, and thus feed back onto processes of discrimination, harassment or violence considered earlier in the chapter. All that can be said, however, is that the evidence considered in this chapter does not bear out this gloomy prognosis. Even though levels of (self-reported) injustice are higher for Muslims than for other religious minorities, they remain at a low level. A two-thirds majority of non-Muslim respondents hold favourable views of Islam. Perhaps most significantly, there appears to be no long-run tendency for Muslims to be seen less favourably over time, and the level of anti-Muslim violence has not increased as a trend, although it does respond in peaks to particular events, and then falls back again. In these respects, as in others, the view from the ground looks much more promising than the impression received from mainstream public discourse, whether from government, the press or most academic research.

Conceptual inflation: an ideology of religious injustice

The evidence considered in this book so far reveals a striking *disjunction* between the place of organised religion in the spheres of politics, culture and the law and its place in people's lives. The interesting question then becomes how this disjunction is sustained and reproduced. The analysis presented in this book suggests that part of the answer consists in the existence of a powerful ideology of religious injustice. The hallmark of this ideology is what we have called *conceptual inflation*. This involves a tendency to stretch the definitions of value-laden concepts beyond their proper range of reference. As a result of this process, the claims of inequality, oppression or injustice suffered by some religious groups are magnified or exaggerated beyond what the evidence will bear.

Examples from the previous chapter include the direct inference of injustice from inequality and the assumption that inequality is caused solely by factors external to groups. But the same pattern has emerged time and again in relation to the topics of this chapter. Examples include the definition of religious hate crimes/incidents in purely subjective terms, the treatment of anti-religious attitudes (or even 'indifference or ignorance about religion') as 'cultural and attitudinal discrimination' (Woodhead, 2009: 15), the assumption that an unfavourable view of religion constitutes evidence of 'overt prejudice' (Abrams and Houston, 2007: 86) and the failure to distinguish the perception from the experience of discrimination.

In addition to these problems, there are cases where sweeping conclusions about the prevalence of injustice are based on insufficient evidence, derived, for example, from samples that are either very small or gathered on a non-random basis. There is the example of the MCB's exaggeration of stop-and-search statistics, which was not withdrawn even in the face of compelling criticism. Another symptomatic case is the IHRC's (2008) contention that 'dirty looks' constitute 'anti-Muslim harassment'.

Although we have not given a full analysis of 'Islamophobia' in this chapter, the use of the expression offers examples of conceptual inflation in at least two senses: first, because the very term 'Islamophobia' makes opposition to a religion resemble a deep psychological malady (a type of psychosis); and second, in cases or contexts in which any criticism of the religion or its adherents is regarded as 'Islamophobic', which tends to close off the space for reasoned argument or debate. The conventional assimilation of anti-Islamic sentiment to racism works in a similar fashion. And the *Conway Report* (1997), which did so much to popularise the concept of Islamophobia, made sweeping claims that were based on very little concrete evidence.

The power of this tendency towards conceptual inflation is indicated by the fact that it occurs not just in marginal or incidental texts, but in a series of major publications that have helped to define the terms of the debate about religion and equality in the UK. These include the *Conway Report* as mentioned above and its successor report (Muir et al., 2004), the *Weller Report* for the Home Office (Weller et al., 2001), the study by Abrams and Houston submitted to the Cabinet Office (2007), the *Pell Report* (2007) prepared by the Business Commission on Race Equality in the Workplace, the EOC study *Moving on Up?* (2007) and the first publication in the field of religion or belief by the Equality and Human Rights Commission (Woodhead, 2009). The same problems are reproduced in influential survey articles, including Purdam et al. (2007) and Denvir et al. (2007).

We should emphasise that what makes these examples problematic – and what therefore makes the ideology of religious injustice ideological – is a lack of balance in the treatment of issues. For example, we are not denying that religious discrimination is a factor in religious inequality; we are, however, insisting that it is not the only factor. Likewise, we are not suggesting that religious hate crimes do not occur, but we are saying that it takes more than the opinion of one person to make a religious hate crime; it also requires evidence of content, context and motivation (as taken for granted, for instance, in the exemplary surveys of anti-semitic activity produced by the CST).

Our concerns about the power of this ideology are partly scientific and partly political and personal. We regard it as important that policy on religion and equality should be based as far as possible on the factual situation of the ethno-religious groups concerned, regardless of whether their situations are evaluated as 'good' or 'bad' from various points of view. The influence of the ideology makes it very difficult to achieve this kind of balanced perspective, since it serves to misdirect attention in the field. It acts to magnify some issues or problems and to conceal or to marginalise others. And the ideology spreads by repetition. Once the belief in widespread injustice had taken hold, it was simply reproduced, so that 'what everyone knows' became treated as a fact. And, as we have just seen, a series of official reports, not to mention legal enactments, have been readily available to reinforce these popular beliefs. As social scientists, we are interested in 'seeing through' this ideology, and restoring a balanced perspective on the situation of religious groups that conforms to the evidence (so far as that can be determined). In this respect, we might do worse than follow Tom Bottomore's lead:

> if the sociologist has a highly important intellectual role as a critic of society…he [sic] is not simply a critic, but a sociological critic; and the quality of his criticism will depend upon the quality of his understanding of the institutions and movements in present day and past societies ... he has a duty to resist being swept off his feet by every passing wind of ideology. (1970: xii–xiii)

A balanced perspective on the question of religious injustice suggests that, while religious injustice does exist, its scale of occurrence in Britain is considerably less severe than is commonly believed. It follows that the elimination of religious injustice, thoroughly desirable though this is, will have less effect on the reduction of religious inequality than is commonly anticipated. This reinforces the conclusion reached at the end of the previous chapter, that if the main target is the reduction of inequality, measures may be more effective that make no reference directly to religious identity.

Our concerns about the ideological treatment of religious injustice are not exhausted by our role as social scientists, however. As citizens, and not least as citizens of Bradford, we have another, and perhaps deeper, concern. The ideology of injustice has an effect on relations between groups because of the way it portrays religious minorities, and especially Muslims, as perpetual victims of their society. As a conclusion, we cannot improve on the words of Malik, and of Mirza and her collaborators, who deserve credit for their early diagnosis of the ideology and its effects:

> Pretending that Muslims have never had it so bad might bolster community leaders and gain votes for politicians, but it does the rest of us, whether Muslim or non-Muslim, no favours at all. The more that the threat of Islamophobia is exaggerated, the more that ordinary Muslims come to accept that theirs is a community under constant attack. It helps create a siege mentality, stoking up anger and resentment, and making Muslim communities more inward looking and more open to religious extremism. Muslim leaders constantly warn that Islamophobia is alienating Muslims and pushing many into the hands of extremists. However, it's not Islamophobia, but the perception that it blights lives, that is often the bigger problem. (Malik, 2005b: 3)

> The authorities and some Muslim groups have exaggerated the problem of Islamophobia, which has fuelled a sense of victimhood amongst some Muslims. (Mirza et al., 2007: 6)

> This victim mentality is given social credence by institutions, politicians, the media and lobby groups. It is unsurprising that young people believe they are being discriminated against when everyone tells them so. (Mirza et al., 2007: 72)

4
The Trouble with Multiculturalism

Multiculturalism and diversity

We focus specifically on multiculturalism in this book because for some years now, it has been the dominant approach to cultural and religious diversity around the world (Kymlicka, 1998; 2001a,b; 2007). It is thus important to clarify *what* the term means, *why* it was introduced into Western societies and *how* it operates in policy and practice. Since our concern is with equality and human rights, our focus is mainly at the policy and practice levels and the question of whether multiculturalism has promoted or obstructed these in relation to minority ethnic groups (for a theoretical critique, see Macey, 2009).

What is multiculturalism?

It is important to distinguish at the outset between (a) multiculturalism as a description of society, (b) multiculturalism as a policy and (c) multiculturalism as an ideology and practice.

Multiculturalism in the first sense is a fact of life for nearly all developed societies in Europe and elsewhere. International migration over the past half-century may not have been as extensive in numerical terms as earlier population movements (Casanova, 2007), but it has considerably extended the range of racial, ethnic and religious identities represented significantly in the populations of receiving countries. As one of these countries Britain is, and will remain, a multicultural society, as documented in Chapter 1.

Multiculturalism as a policy applies worldwide to a variety of historically influenced social situations. These include the position of national minorities (groups that have some claims to establish national or regional autonomy) and of indigenous peoples, as well as minority ethnic or religious groups formed as a consequence of immigration (Kymlicka, 2007). We are concerned in this book only with the latter application of multiculturalism.

Multiculturalism as a policy response to the consequences of immigration takes its place among other approaches to the same set of social issues, including assimilation, integration, antiracism, secularism, pluralism, community cohesion and the position we have identified in the previous chapter – equality of religion or belief. Some of the strengths and weaknesses of multiculturalism as a policy will be considered below.

Multiculturalism as an ideology involves a broader set of attitudes towards minority relationships. These attitudes can be held uncritically, and generate reflex responses to issues of the day. This ideology may be reflected more or less explicitly in policy initiatives, or it may operate less directly, by creating a climate for considering issues of diversity and equality whose effects can be detected nevertheless in practical outcomes. We will describe the elements of this ideology in greater detail below; first, we explore the meaning(s) of the basic term 'multiculturalism'.

The difficulty of reaching a consensus about the policies covered by multiculturalism is illustrated by the following list of quotations:

(a) 'in broad terms, multiculturalism advocates dealing with diversity not by assimilating, or expelling, cultural minorities, but by accommodating them' (Kukathas, 2001);

(b) 'Multiculturalism ... is underpinned by notions of respecting diversity and valuing cultural difference' (Meeto and Mirza, 2007);

(c) 'Multiculturalism is a policy agenda designed to redress the unequal treatment of cultural groups and the "culture-racism" to which members of minority cultural groups are often exposed' (A. Phillips, 2007);

(d) 'Multiculturalism as a political, social and cultural movement has aimed to respect a multiplicity of diverging perspectives outside of dominant traditions' (Willett, 1998);

(e) 'Multiculturalism is a political and normative perspective on cultural diversity, where this is positively valued and worth securing and promoting' (Parekh, 2000b);

(f) 'Multiculturalism involves a range of rights, different foci, including political representation, affirmative action, exemptions from laws, recognition of traditional legal codes, etc' (Kalev, 2004);

(g) 'Multiculturalism – the belief that all cultures are equal in value ... [we must regard] every individual, and every culture in which individuals participate, as being equally valuable' (Minogue, 2005);

(h) 'Britain should develop both as a community of citizens (the liberal view) and as a community of communities (the pluralist view)' (Parekh, 2000b);

(i) 'the political idea of multiculturalism – the recognition of group differences within the political sphere of laws, policies, democratic discourses and the terms of a shared citizenship' (Modood, 2007);

(j) 'A shift to true multiculturalism...would involve the abandonment of cultural hegemony by the native Britons' (Melotti, 1997).

This abundance of definitions bears out Kukathas' comment that 'What exactly multiculturalism amounts to...is not so clear, since policies bearing that name vary, and principled defences of multiculturalism do not always defend the same thing' (2001: 85). Anthias adds that 'there are as many varieties [of multiculturalism] as Heinz or blossoms' (2002: 279), and Cantle even suggests that 'multiculturalism no longer has any real meaning' (2008: 68). The key to further understanding is to regard multiculturalism not as a single policy option, but as a portmanteau term for a large spectrum of positions, with varying implications for policy. Anthias distinguishes in this sense between 'liberal...and critical or reflexive multiculturalism...hard and soft versions' (2002: 279); Cantle refers to 'a spectrum from "assimilation" to "co-existence"' (2008: 90), and Patel and Siddiqui (2010) contrast 'early' and 'mature' multiculturalism.

It is certainly clear from the quotations above that the different versions of multiculturalism vary considerably in their potential implications for human rights, and how deeply they cut into the social and political fabric. At one end of the spectrum, multiculturalism expresses the liberal values of accepting different ways of being (May, 1999), treating minorities with respect (Meeto and Mirza), reducing disadvantage (Phillips) or preserving diversity by resisting calls for the repatriation of immigrants (Kukathas). Towards the other end of the spectrum, liberal or democratic values may be challenged by the demands that all cultures be regarded as equal (Minogue), that group differences should be recognised within the *public* arena (Modood), that diversity should be 'promoted' as well as respected (Parekh), that traditional legal codes should be recognised (Kalev) or that Britain should cease to define its own culture (Melotti).

Modood has addressed this variability by pointing out that 'multiculturalism is conceived differently in different countries and is given varied institutional expression depending upon the local and national political culture' (1997: 4). As we will see in the next two sections, this claim is certainly true descriptively, because societies have varied in their approaches to diversity (Esman, 2004), and these have also varied over time. The claim is potentially misleading, however, if it is taken to imply that there is an essential core to multicultural policy that is preserved across every political context and is merely adapted to take account of local circumstances. Perhaps the most that can be said is that multiculturalism is a name given to a wide range of policies that attach weight of some kind to minority ethnic cultures and religions. As such, multiculturalism definitely excludes assimilation and probably excludes secularism, but otherwise leaves the policy field wide open. It is arguable, however, that there are a number of key elements that underpin the multicultural enterprise in many of its variants, and we briefly discuss some problems of these at the end of this chapter.

This vagueness of definition may help nevertheless to explain the worldwide success of the concept, since multiculturalism is a position that almost everyone can endorse in one form or another. But the resulting ambiguities create real difficulties for the topics considered in this book. For example, multiculturalism equivocates between separatism and accommodation/integration as objectives of policy; it provides little guidance about the principles that should regulate the relationships between groups, and whilst it says that some weight should attach to minority ethnic cultures and religions, it does not specify how much. In particular, it is silent as a whole over the circumstances under which this weight might be decisive, and thus potentially override considerations of equality or human rights. These points establish a first set of difficulties with multiculturalism as an approach to diversity at the level of policy. In the following sections, we sketch the historical evolution of British approaches to multicultural and multi-faith societies, before returning to the difficulties of multiculturalism as ideology and as practice.

The evolution of policy I: from assimilation to multiculturalism to anti-racism (and back to multiculturalism again)

Multiculturalism has arisen as a response to the changing demography of developed societies, as a perceived alternative to previous policy approaches and as a response to the accumulating evidence of racial and ethnic inequalities discussed in Chapter 2. Roughly speaking, the pendulum has swung back and forth between greater and lesser weights of influence afforded to minority cultures. Policies have therefore moved – or sometimes veered or swerved – in more or less multicultural directions, depending on a range of different circumstances and events.

In Western Europe, for example, Britain and France are generally held to be at opposite ends of the multicultural spectrum, with the former being fairly relaxed about cultural and religious diversity and the latter insisting on assimilation into the secular state (Bertossi, 2007; Hamdan, 2007). More recently, however, it has been argued that France is not only *de facto* multicultural (Schain, 1999), but that it has moved towards recognition and acceptance of cultural and religious differences (Aitsiselmi, 2006; Echchaibi, 2007). However, this might be questioned in light of the recent ban on religious symbols in schools (including the *hijab*) and the ban on the *burqa*[2] in public places.

Multicultural societies developed initially in much of Western Europe as a consequence of labour shortages following WWII, which forced states to recruit overseas workers – initially European, and subsequently non-European. Migrant workers were treated as units of labour, and were expected to return to their homelands when they were no longer needed. Many workers shared this expectation, particularly, in Britain, those from the Indian subcontinent (Anwar, 1979; Ballard, 1994). Those from the Caribbean, on the other hand, tended to regard England as the 'motherland' (Green, 1990) and often planned to settle here permanently. And while the rights accorded to migrant workers differed between states – from Germany's restrictions on 'guestworkers' to full citizenship rights in Britain (Cohen, 1988) – the assumption of temporary residency affected both state policies and minority group attitudes.

Because people from the Caribbean thought of themselves as permanent citizens, their orientation was towards achieving racial equality and they were instrumental in the development of an anti-racist movement (Gaber, 1994). Pakistani Muslims, on the other hand, planned to return home and were concerned to avoid the potential impact on the norms, values and traditions of the homeland of what was often regarded as an immoral British society (see Ballard, 1994, Shaw, 1994, Lewis, 2002, Macey, 2006, and Yip, 2004, for examples of historical and contemporary evaluations of British morality). This resulted in a 'separatist' orientation and was encouraged by chain migration, which enabled the establishment of ethnic enclaves comprised of close-knit, often related, people (Ballard, 1994). The different orientations of groups of post-war settlers have had a significant influence on their subsequent trajectories – which, in turn, have impacted on the evolution of multicultural policy.

At the state level, Britain initially dealt with overseas workers by doing nothing, that is, making no provision for the needs of the people it had recruited to work and live here. It then adopted a *laissez-faire*, and implicitly assimilationist, approach (Macey, 2009), though later (along with the Netherlands) made the most ambitious commitment to multiculturalism of all the Western European importers of labour (Joppke, 2004; Sniderman and Hagendoorn, 2007). France assumed that workers would totally assimilate into French culture (Melotti, 1997), and Switzerland used permits of abode to police foreign workers (Cohen, 1988).

It was not until the mid-1960s that the British government stopped assuming that assimilation was the best way of dealing with social diversity and started talking about integration, famously defined by Roy Jenkins as 'equal opportunity, coupled with cultural diversity, in an atmosphere of mutual tolerance' (1970 [1966]: 267). This change was brought about when families from the Indian subcontinent began to arrive and it was realised that the 'temporary' workers were 'here to stay' (Gilroy, 1987).

Education provides a good illustration of the evolution of policy, as government objectives moved between 'assimilation', 'integration' and 'pluralism' (Mullard, 1982; 1985). The first intervention was the establishment of language centres to cope with the large numbers of children in some areas who could not speak English. This was followed by the 'bussing' of children to schools outside their neighbourhoods, with the aim of achieving balanced intakes. Both of these policies were condemned as racist (Troyna and Williams, 1986), and both were based on an *assimilationist* ideology, that is, the notion that the best way of achieving ethnic harmony was by minimising differences of language and culture.

By the 1970s, and through the 1980s, the government adopted a policy of *cultural pluralism* which implied the acceptance of distinct cultural/ethnic groups in Britain. This was the beginning of contemporary 'multiculturalism', with the government stating that schools must take account of Britain's multiracial nature. Rattansi (1992) criticised this approach as being based on creating tolerance for minority people and their cultures (rather than tackling racism). And certainly the focus was on prejudice, not racism, in the belief that this could be addressed by teaching white children about minority cultures. We would note in passing that this is not significantly different to the 'contact hypothesis' (Brown, 1995; Hewstone et al., 2006) that underpins today's focus on 'cohesion'.

The next phase in the education arena involved the limited application of *anti-racism*, which had developed as a social movement partly out of anger at the failure of multiculturalism to eliminate racism in schools and society. Anti-racism focused on social structures and institutions in the belief that it was at this level that ideologies and practices needed to be challenged. It also insisted that links must be made with such other forms of oppression as those based on class and gender. However, in 1989 the report of an inquiry into the murder of an Asian boy by a white one castigated the anti-racist policies of the school and local education authority as contributing to the murder, labelling them 'doctrinaire, divisive, ineffectual and counterproductive' (McDonald et al., 1989).

But it was not only such shocking events as a murder on school premises that impacted on anti-racism, for during the 1980s and 1990s a number of articles criticised it on conceptual, theoretical and policy/practice levels. Criticisms included the essentialising of black people through not deconstructing ethnic identities; failing to locate anti-racism within an economic context, or properly considering the intersections and interactions of class and gender; ignoring Asian and religious identities, and excluding the growing number of 'mixed parentage'/dual heritage people (Modood, 1988; Miles, 1989; Mason, 1990; Gilroy, 1992; Hyder, 1993; Lindsey, 1994; Macey, 1995a,b).

With the benefit of hindsight, some of these criticisms may have paved the way for the major division between ethnic, racial and religious groups that arguably destabilised the struggle for racial justice, led to religious minorities (notably Muslims) developing a form of identity politics which prioritised religion and to the growing focus on multicultural, rather than anti-racist strategies (Macey, 1995b; Malik, 2009).

These changes were supported by two official inquiries which put pressure on the government to adopt a pluralist, or multicultural, approach to education and through this to society as a whole. One of these – the *Swann Report* – was into the underachievement of black children in schools (DES, 1985); the other – the *Scarman Report* – was into the reasons for the urban disorders/riots in the 1980s (Scarman, 1982).

By the early 1990s, then, the pendulum had swung (back) from anti-racism to multiculturalism, albeit a multiculturalism claimed by its adherents to incorporate the best of anti-racism and, through its emphasis on access to power, to constitute a move towards real cultural pluralism (Modood and Werbner, 1997).

The evolution of policy II: from multiculturalism to cohesion

By the late 1990s, concerns were being expressed in many Western European societies that multiculturalism had reached an 'impasse' and that a new, multicultural model of integration was needed (Melotti, 1997;

Joppke, 2004). These concerns were given a new urgency by the terrorist attacks on the US in 2001 (9/11), in Spain in 2004 and in England in 2005 (7/7) (see Sniderman and Hagendoorn, 2007, on the Netherlands and Abbas, 2005, 2007, on Britain). Law (2010) has recently contended that integration is a political priority in virtually every Western European state.

In Britain, however, it was more local events prior to the London bombings that prompted a modification of multiculturalism via the development of the concept of 'community cohesion' (later to be called 'social cohesion', then simply 'cohesion'). These events comprised a series of violent public disturbances and riots in a number of Northern towns and cities that were carried out almost entirely by young men of Pakistani heritage and Muslim faith (Carling et al., 2004; Macey, 2005; see also Ballard, 2007, and Malik, 2009, for general accounts). In many cases, the men's families originated from rural, rather than urban, Pakistan and lived in residentially and socially separated communities in Britain. This is particularly striking in cities like Bradford, West Yorkshire, which was the scene of the worst rioting for twenty years on mainland Britain, and to which (in a report written *before* the riots) Sir Herman Ouseley (2001) applied the term 'parallel lives' to describe the lack of interaction between ethno-religious communities. An inquiry into violent public disorder in Bradford in 1995 had already flagged up separation as a contributory factor (Allen and Barrett, 1996; see also Macey, 1999b). Official investigations after 2001 highlighted this factor in all the towns and cities involved (Cantle, 2001; Clarke, 2001; Denham, 2001; Ritchie, 2001), and the concept of 'community cohesion' was born.

Community cohesion, then, was a response to public disorder and the perceived role of lack of integration in this – and was greeted by denial and accusations of racism. For example, Phillips et al. (2002) and Simpson (2004) disputed the reality of residential and social separation, while Amin (2002), Robinson (2005) and Ballard (2007) questioned its assumed effects. Earlier work, however, had noted that segregation can shift into polarisation (Modood et al., 1997), that lack of interaction across ethnic boundaries can strengthen already conservative community traditions (Parekh, 2000a) and that lack of contact between ethnic groups can lead to defining outsiders as not sharing in the moral community, with potentially lethal results (Horowitz, 2002).

Cohesion became government policy with amazing speed, or, some might suggest, unholy haste. A mere year after the disturbances, the Local Government Association (LGA) had issued detailed guidance to local authorities and other public bodies on how they should promote (and measure) cohesion (LGA, 2002). Subsequently, there has been a broadening of the range of agencies assigned key roles in this process (Flint and Robinson, 2008), including education and housing (Department for Children, Schools and Families [DCSF], 2006; 2007a; Housing Corporation, 2007). And in the community and voluntary sector (CVS), projects applying for funding are now required to demonstrate that they involve working *across* ethnic boundaries (Community Development Foundation, 2007).

In 2007, the report of a Commission on Integration and Cohesion was published (Singh, 2007). Perhaps unsurprisingly, the reference to 'integration' proved provocative to some, who responded with accusations of retreating from multiculturalism and promoting assimilation (Baubock, 2002; Burnett, 2004; 2008; Rattansi, 2005; Bourne, 2007). We would argue, however, that these critics overestimate the extent to which cohesion breaks away from multiculturalism; indeed, we believe that it remains firmly rooted in multicultural thinking. First, the concept of cohesion is derived from the same kind of social psychological theories which underpinned early multiculturalism, that is, the notion that contact between different groups necessarily facilitates positive interaction (Adorno et al., 1950; Tajfel, 1970; Dozier, 2002). This assumption may not be true (Amin, 2002), and so the 'cohesion' approach may be simplistic in some respects, but it remains within a recognisably multicultural paradigm. Second, Cantle's statement of 'active' commitment to the maintenance of cultural diversity and minority languages (2005: 148; 2007: 94) establishes the distance of 'cohesion' from any assimilationist view. A third example is provided by Singh's encouragement of transnational identities (2007: 35), which he claims have been shown to promote social integration, though he does not provide details of this research. In any case, an emphasis on integration is not inconsistent with some versions of multiculturalism, and Singh's acceptance of the salience of transnational (and other aspects of) identities remains within a multicultural framework.

Cohesion is, nevertheless, associated with an upbeat tone that may have something to do with its origins as an official doctrine of government. For example, Hazel Blears (then Secretary of State for Communities and Local Government) states in her foreword to the Cohesion Delivery Framework Overview that:

> In Britain, we have learnt to celebrate the talents and contributions to our society of people from different backgrounds, races and faiths.

We are becoming more comfortable in our differences and confident in our shared values. The latest data from the Citizenship Survey shows that 92 per cent of people feel that individuals from different backgrounds get on well in their area. (Blears, 2009: 3)

Other surveys have also shown that large majorities of British citizens (around 80%) get on well together in their local areas (Attwood et al., 2004; Kitchen et al., 2006; MORI, 2007).

However, this official optimism deserves to be qualified in several respects. First, the facts of residential and educational separation between ethno-religious groups remain a matter of concern. High levels of separation between some groups make constructive engagement more difficult and contain the potential for polarisation, even though – in theory at least – separation does not pre-ordain the quality of relationships in particular areas (Carling, 2008). Easy optimism is also challenged by the growth of support for such far-right parties as the BNP, alongside the relative ease of access of young Muslims to *jihadi* Islamist influences through the Internet, for example. Because of the geographical concentration of minority religions noted in Chapter 2, the key issue is the quality of local relationships in a relatively small number of neighbourhoods within Britain, and this information may not be reflected adequately in large national surveys. An obvious question to ask the government is why, if people in Britain are thoroughly 'comfortable in our differences and confident in our shared values', it was thought necessary to spend £50 million in 2008 under the cohesion banner with a possible additional £8 million under 'connecting communities' in 2009 (Kitchin, 2008: 1–2). And many social inequalities of race, ethnicity and religion have persisted stubbornly, as outlined in Chapter 2, despite all the variations in official policy over the past half-century.

Overall, it seems fair to characterise 'cohesion' as an official variant of multiculturalism, developed by the government of the day as a specific response to the Northern Riots of 2001. Compared with its predecessors, cohesion tilts the balance slightly towards integration rather than separation within the policy spectrum of multiculturalism. It can be simplistic in its analysis and over-optimistic in tone. But it shares with multiculturalism generally a lack of clarity over the aims of policy and the principles that should regulate the relationships between groups. As we will see in the remainder of the chapter, this lack of clarity can have serious consequences for some of the more vulnerable members of minority ethnic and religious groups.

Multiculturalism and the law

As indicated in the previous chapter, there are two sides to the justice issue in relation to ethnic and religious diversity.

On the one hand, there are injustices faced by members of ethno-religious minorities in civil society and the delivery of public services as a result of their racial, ethnic or religious identities. Over the lifetime of the New Labour government since 1997, legislation covering these injustices was extended to religion or belief and consolidated in the Equality Act 2010. This Act also introduced an Equality Duty for religion or belief. There are also enactments that protect religious organisations in the practice of their faith, and the activities of FBOs. These measures include exemptions from the provisions of the law as it applies elsewhere. This body of legislation now provides extensive protection for members of ethno-religious minorities and their religious organisations.

On the other hand, there are injustices that arise as specific issues *within* ethno-religious communities in ways that are connected to the cultures which settlers bring with them from their homelands. These injustices particularly affect the more vulnerable members of communities, especially women and young people, in ways that both reflect and reinforce inequality and oppression. The difficulty arises when these practices violate established norms of equality or human rights, such as *sex selective abortion* (see Waldby, 2003, on Britain; Saharso, 2005, on the Netherlands; Puri, 2007, on the US; and Solomon, 2007, on Canada); *forced marriage* (see Uddin and Ahmed, 2000; Samad and Eade, 2002; Forced Marriage Unit [FMU], 2006; House of Commons Home Affairs Committee [HAC], 2008; Khanum, 2008); *female genital mutilation* (FGM) (see Ahlberg et al., 2004, on Sweden; Dorkenoo et al., 2006, on Britain; and Hilsdon and Rozario, 2006, on France), and so-called *honour-related violence*, up to and including murder (see Welchman and Hossain, 2005; Meeto and Mirza, 2007; HAC, 2008; Southall Black Sisters, 2008).

Multicultural policy and ideology has three concerns to address in relation to these practices. First, although most of them are not sanctioned by either the state or the cultural communities in which they occur, it can be argued that multiculturalism has created a climate of fear – of 'interfering in community affairs' and/or being accused of racism – which has facilitated their continuation (Johal, 2003; Burman et al., 2004; Meeto and Mirza, 2007). Second, to the extent that this has occurred, multicultural thinking has undermined equality and has impacted adversely on women and girl children especially (for a full discussion of the issues around multiculturalism and women see Okin, 1989; 1997; 1998; 1999; 2002; Macey, 2006; 2007a; 2008; 2009). Third, multiculturalism may have discouraged legislation in some of these areas, even though the wrongs committed against individuals are clear-cut, and in many cases devastating for their lives.

We examine these questions more closely in two of the cases above, forced marriage and FGM, before considering a third example of trans-racial adoption, which we include as an illuminating example of the impact of multiculturalism on policy and practice.

Forced marriage

The case for legislation on forced marriage has been put strongly by many minority ethnic women, as is illustrated by one worker in an agency specialising in helping victims:

> I think there is a need for a specific criminal offence. In this coun-try we have an offence against littering in the streets and yet we do not have a forced marriage criminal offence, and I say that because forced marriage leads to repeated rapes, et cetera, and horrific viol-ence. (Sanghera [Karma Nirvana], HAC, 2008: Ev.35)

It is difficult to imagine a clearer case of the violation of human rights than the 'statutory rape' (Idrus and Bennett, 2003) entailed in forced marriage. Yet the government has consistently refused to make forced marriage a criminal offence. Indeed, for many years, it simul-taneously maintained the stance that it was not known how many such marriages take place, but that there weren't many (and therefore no policy was needed). More recently, it has raised the age at which transnational marriages can take place, from eighteen to twenty-one, although this may prove counterproductive. It could result in wors-ening the position of young British girls taken abroad, married there and then left until they reach the legal age to return. This exposes them to 'greater risk of violence, rape and sexual abuse ... [and] by the time they can seek redress, they are usually pregnant or have young children' (Patel and Siddiqui, 2010: 112). Research commissioned by the Home Office and carried out by Hester et al. (2008) raised similar (and additional) concerns, concluding with the recommenda-tion that the age for transnational marriage should *not* be raised. The fact that this research was not published raises serious issues about the fate of independent research whose findings do not conform to funders' expectations (or desired outcomes?). We are aware of similar cases where publication has been suppressed, or made difficult. And a related example is the case of the Muslim Parliament of Great Britain, whose 2006 call for a national register of UK Madrasas to avoid child abuse has been largely ignored by both state authorities and other Muslim organisations. Such distortions of the research process are significant not just from an academic perspective, but because they act to reinforce the neglect of social harms.

Though the government's establishment of a Forced Marriage Unit[3] and the introduction of the Forced Marriage (Civil Protection) Act 2007 are viewed as a step in the right direction, many do not regard them as going far enough (HAC, 2008). Recent information suggests that the scale of the problem is much more serious than previously assumed, running into several thousands a year. In 2006, the FMU dealt with 5,000 enquiries and 300 cases of forced marriage (HAC, 2008). In Luton, Khanum (2008) reports that there are over 300 approaches annually to various CVS groups for advice on forced marriage, suggesting that several thousand such marriages may take place every year. In Bradford, the police, who are often the last port of call for women, recorded 191 cases of forced marriage in 2005 and say that the numbers are increasing every year – though they are sometimes 'hidden' under the heading of domestic violence (Bhatti, 2007). Karma Nirvana, though only a small community-based project, deals with over 15 new cases of forced marriage and 'honour' related violence *every week* (780 per year) (in HAC, 2008: Ev.238). In 2007, 11,022 spouse settlement applications were issued in Pakistan and 3,216 refused (HAC, 2008),[4] and in 2006, the immigration service reported that 47,000 spouses entered the UK on settlement visas (UK Border Agency, 2007). We are not suggesting that all these entail forced marriages, but it is likely that a significant proportion of those between British and South Asian citizens are not freely undertaken (Macey, 2008; 2009; Muslim Arbitration Tribunal [MAT], 2008).

To the above statistics should be added what Khanum (2008) calls 'false' marriages, that is, those marriages that do not need to involve force because they are based on deception in relation to the partner's attributes, such as educational qualifications, criminal background, drug addiction or disabilities. Khanum notes that such marriages impact particularly on brides from overseas where the marriage has taken place outside Britain without the groom being present. She cites one case in which the husband's physical disabilities were such that '[the bride] was forced by the groom's family to consummate the marriage in an unthinkable manner' (Khanum, 2008: 47). It is worth noting in this context that among the 407 cases referred to the Consular Immigration Link team in Pakistan in 2007 were 193 cases of forced marriage and 86 of 'vulnerable adults', that is people with a severe mental or physical disability (FCO in HAC, 2008: Ev.439).

Forced marriages are conventionally portrayed in the literature as the polar opposite of arranged marriages – the former being viewed as 'wrong' (Uddin and Ahmed, 2000: 4), the latter being seen as a 'respectable cultural practice' (Gupta, 2003: 69). However, a number of writers question the distinction between arranged and forced marriages. Bhopal, for example, says: 'I feel that in practice there is very little difference between arranged and forced marriage' (1997: 58). Bhatti's (2007) research, as well as her personal experience, leads her to conclude that almost all the marriages between a partner from Bradford and one from Mirpur are forced, not arranged. And the MAT states:

> The reality is that in over 70% of all marriages that take place, where the spouse is an English citizen and the other spouse is a foreign national from the Asian sub-continent, there is an element of force or coercion before the marriage takes place. ... These figures reflect the crisis that has loomed within the Muslim community without being noticed or dealt with for the past two decades. The figures that are reported to the authorities are only the tip of the iceberg. (2008: 9)

The point that all these writers are making is that while there is a distinction between forced and arranged marriage in theory, in reality this is often not the case, particularly in relation to transnational marriages. At one level, the reasons for this are self-evident: why would a young woman born and brought up in England, say, and educated to degree standard *choose* to marry an uneducated, unskilled young man from a village in Mirpur, with whom she has nothing in common – not even a shared language (Beckett and Macey, 2001)? At another level, they are complex, and involve deep cultural differences regarding the meaning attached to marriage. Among most social groups in Britain, marriage is seen to be about personal happiness and love between two *individuals*; among traditional Pakistani Muslims, it is a contractual agreement between two *families* and involves social structures and status, communal identity, culture and religion. This means that the individual's desires, needs, interests and happiness are secondary to those of the family and community (Shaw, 2001; Zaidi and Shuraydi, 2002).

Bhopal comments:

> [Arranged marriage] helps maintain the social stratification system in the society (caste), it gives parents control over family members, it enhances the chances to preserve and continue the ancestral line, it provides opportunities to strengthen the kinship group, it allows the consolidation and extension of family property and enables the elders to preserve the principles of endogamy. (1997: 58)

And Shaw notes:

> The choices that are made have a far-reaching impact upon the parents, their siblings, and their siblings' children, and a range of other relatives, affecting the futures and socio-economic positions of a much wider range of kin than just parents and children. For this reason, decisions about marriage are a matter of corporate, not individual concern. (2001: 325)

We would stress at this point that we are not suggesting that multiculturalism *causes* forced marriage, but we believe that it plays a part in its facilitation through processes both internal and external to communities. Internally, it encourages transnational orientations and maintenance of the traditions of the 'homeland'. Externally, it discourages inquiry into the prevalence of the practice and the investigation of specific cases.

Female genital mutilation

The terminology around FGM is contested: some prefer 'cutting' or 'circumcision' to avoid offending those who practise it or because this is the term that they use (Ahlberg et al., 2004). Some, notably those who have experienced FGM, dispute its categorisation as a tradition: '[FGM] is the most cynical form of child abuse and a crime that has to be punished' (Dirie in Kerbaj, 2009).

Sweden was the first Western European country to implement specific legislation against FGM (1982), followed by Britain (1985), and it is now illegal in most EU countries (as well as in Australia, Canada, the US and a number of African and Asian countries). Despite this, there is clear evidence that FGM is still taking place across the world, including in Europe, on a significant scale and on children as young as three months old (Leye and Deblonde, 2004; Leye et al., 2006; Poldermans, 2006). (See also Munanie, 2001, British Medical Association, 2004, and Dorkenoo et al., 2006, on Britain; Gallard, 1995, Weil-Curiel, 2002, and Hilsdon and Rozario, 2006, on France; and Ahlberg et al., 2004, on Sweden.) And though the British legislation was strengthened in 2003 to prevent girls being taken overseas for FGM, *The Independent* reports that 'cutters' are flown into Britain to perform FGM at 'parties' of up to twenty girls to reduce costs (Lakhani, 2009).

The practice of FGM raises several questions about the use of the law to prevent unacceptable behaviour. The first is whether it is effective in eliminating practices that are rooted in strongly held cultural traditions which have far-reaching consequences for the lives of the individuals involved. The second is whether the law is actually implemented, rather than being symbolic, because there have been very few prosecutions in Europe. Sweden and Italy have brought two prosecutions (Poldermans, 2006), though neither systematically takes cases through the criminal courts (Miller, 2004). Britain has brought no prosecutions, despite the Prohibition of Female Circumcision Act having been on the statute books since 1985 and the stronger Female Genital Mutilation Act having been law since 2003.

France is the exception to the general pattern of lack of legal action. Initially, as elsewhere, there was a view that Westerners should not intervene in minority community affairs (Gallard, 1995). However, in 1982, France embarked on the criminal proceedings route that it has systematically maintained since then. This was a reaction to pressure from African women's associations, who argued that failure to act against FGM constituted racism; it was also because of public outrage at the deaths of two little girls that year due to FGM – one a three-month-old baby (Poldermans, 2006). Notwithstanding this, as at 2004, less than 50 prosecutions for FGM had gone to criminal court (Weil-Curiel, 2002), a number that is widely held to represent the tip of the iceberg (based on demographic analysis of both France and the countries of origin of settlers and the incidence of FGM there).

Lack of prosecution for FGM may, as for 'honour' killings, be linked to the problem of amassing sufficient evidence: 'people will not give evidence against perpetrators, sometimes because they support what they're doing...and, even if they don't support it, they feel it would be against the honour of their community to stand out against it' (Mornington, who is a district judge and chairs the Northern Circuit Domestic Violence Group, cited in S. Malik, 2005). It is also possible that FGM is so much the norm in some communities that, like domestic violence, it is not defined as a problem (Akhter and Ward, 2004).

It may also be the case that the dominance of multiculturalism is implicated in both the continuation of FGM and the lack of prosecutions for it. To what extent might doctors be influenced by cultural relativism not to report cases, or even to feel that it is better for them to carry out the operation than for unqualified people to do so? (See Stewart, 1998, for a discussion of demands for FGM to be carried out through the National Health Service.) Leye and Deblonde (2004) report that doctors are unwilling to report cases of FGM for fear of being accused of racism, and a similar point may apply to police investigation of the practice, given that this fear applies in other areas of 'community affairs' (Mahoney and Taj, 2006; Raz, 2006; Meeto and Mirza, 2007). Some support for this suggestion comes from Puri's (2005) research in the US and Britain, which shows that GPs' treatment of South Asian women suffering domestic violence has been significantly influenced by multiculturalism.

It is also the case that multicultural theory can be – and is – used to support the practice of FGM through cultural relativism and the principle of non-interference. And while it is unlikely that many proponents of multiculturalism would openly support FGM, and some, such as Kymlicka, would utterly oppose it, the writing of others, such as Kukathas, lends itself to the defence of the practice (Margalit and Halbertal, 1994). Feminism has shown a similar ambivalence about human rights, where 'feminists of color' have challenged Western assumptions about the distinction between FGM and cosmetic surgery. For a discussion of this issue, see Kalev (2004) and Chambers (2004). FGM illustrates how prioritising the rights of the group over those of its individual members can result in the suffering of the most vulnerable members. This raises fundamental questions about approaches to equality to which we return later.

Transracial adoption

The story of 'transracial' adoption is a telling one in relation to a number of topics in this chapter. For a long period from the 1970s onwards, transracial adoptions were regarded as 'out of bounds' in Britain. Although the government eventually stressed that race was to be treated as only one aspect of a child's needs, this was not before thousands of children's lives had been ruined by their long-term experience of the care system. Nor, despite official criticism of a dogmatic 'same race' placement policy, has the practice been eliminated (Macey, 2007). This illustrates several aspects of a situation that has developed in Britain over time: first, the tendency to emulate the US irrespective of major differences between the two countries; second, a lack of confidence in responding to accusations of racism; and third, the dominance of ('politically correct') ideology over theoretical/conceptual accuracy and empirical research. Thus, when the US imposed a ban on transracial adoption – in response to such statements as that by the Association of Black Social Workers and Allied Professionals that placing black children in white homes constituted 'a blatant form of race and cultural genocide' (1972, cited in Simon and Alstein, 1987: 143) – the anti-racist movement here put pressure on the authorities to follow suit. And this they did – despite the facts that (a) there was a crucial shortage of substitute families for children who were labelled black but were, in reality, of mixed parentage (most often with white mothers), and (b) that there was strong empirical evidence that transracial placements were highly successful (Simon, 1974; Simon and Alstein, 1987; Bartholet, 1991; 1993; 1994; Simon et al., 1993; Aldridge, 1994; Gaber, 1994; Macey, 1995a; 1996; 1998).

This topic also provides one particularly graphic illustration of the consequences that can accrue from prioritising the rights of the group over those of the individual. This is Simon et al.'s (1993) example of a Native American woman who left the reservation on which she lived to give birth to a child whom she placed for adoption with a non-Indian family. The Mississippi Supreme Court, however, used the 1978 Indian Child Welfare Act to rule the adoption void. This Act prohibits the transracial adoption of Indian children and gives tribal courts exclusive jurisdiction over child custody proceedings. The court stated that tribal authority over children born to the reservation's domiciliaries must be protected, even where a parent sought to avoid it. This is a salutary warning of the dangers of defining rights at the group, rather than the individual, level, and one that assumes a high level of immediacy as multiculturalists in this country argue for minority ethnic and religious rights to be institutionalised in the public arena. For it is not inconceivable that similar situations could occur in Britain, whereby group (community) rights – generally determined by men – supersede those of women and children.

The case of transracial adoption also illustrates how policy approaches that are influenced by multicultural assumptions can become the professional norm in the public services, without ever being endorsed formally as government policy. This raises some fundamental questions about the evolution of policy, which apply in different ways to both multiculturalism and community cohesion. Multiculturalism itself was never official state policy, but its assumptions still dominated policy and practice across the public arena in Britain. Community cohesion, on the other hand, *is* official policy and all public sector institutions are required to implement it. The criticism of both of these developments is

that they sacrifice equality to diversity by encouraging – or at least failing to challenge – separatism, and by leaving power within communities in the hands of older men, too often at the expense of the interests of women, young people and other 'minorities within the minority'.

In addition, multiculturalism and community cohesion were developed without a broad process of consultation or democratic engagement, and it is a moot point whether such a process would have endorsed these approaches. Although we are not aware of any British data that bears directly on this topic, surveys in Australia, Austria, Canada, Germany and the Netherlands indicate that the general population is far from supportive of multiculturalism (see Betts, 1996, on Australia; Sniderman and Hagendoorn, 2007, on the Netherlands; Poulter, 1998, and Barry, 2001, on Canada; and Hjerm, 2000, for a comparison of Australia and Canada, and Austria and Germany). As we argue next, there is much less doubt about what the verdict on multiculturalism would be if the consultation were confined to women in minority communities.

Women speak out

The most damning indictments of the effects of multiculturalism in practice come from minority ethnic women, both secular and religious, academics and practitioners (as many of our references in this book indicate). 'Ordinary' women, too, have expressed their anger that abuses within their communities are ignored by wider society. Muslim women who took part in consultations in England (Raz, Muslim Women's Network, 2006) and Wales (Mahoney and Taj, The Saheli Project, 2006) raised such issues as women as young as eleven and as old as sixty-five disappearing; forced marriage; domestic violence; 'honour'-related violence, including murder; paedophilia in the community; sexual abuse in homes and mosques; incest; rape; attitudes and actions towards LGBT people, and the difficulty of obtaining divorces.

The women also suggested a number of ways in which the government and professionals (police, social workers and teachers) enabled violence and oppression to continue. These included treating culture as constituting a mitigating circumstance for violence; restricting so-called community consultation to male (often self-styled) 'leaders'; failing to understand the concept of *izzat* (honour) and its impact on women; failing to investigate incidents of abuse adequately, and failing to intervene in communities for fear of being accused of racism, or allowing 'political correctness' to take precedence over women's, children's and young people's human rights.

It is frontline professionals who are responsible for translating policy into practice. Doctors, teachers, social workers and the police are in key (proactive and reactive) positions with respect to the victims and potential victims of abuse. Unfortunately, and for a variety of reasons, the track record of such professionals is not always good. There is evidence of doctors reporting back to parents in cases of forced marriage and to husbands and community 'leaders' in cases of domestic violence (Puri, 2005). Police officers have sometimes treated women fleeing forced marriage as 'teenage runaways' and returned them to their families (Allen, who is the spokesperson on forced marriages for the Association of Chief Police Officers, in Sawyer, 2008; Khanum, 2008). Teachers have been tricked by parents into making contact with escapees, and social workers have used family mediation in cases of forced marriage (Khanum, 2008). All these actions quite literally put women's lives at risk, as the murder of Banaz Mahmod in 2007 shows – after her appeals to the police for help were ignored (Marshall, 2007).

Some of the above practices stem from ignorance, some from having bought into the multicultural edict of non-intervention and some from fear of being accused of racism. But sometimes minority ethnic men *choose* to prioritise the interests of parents and the community over those of victims. Imams, community 'leaders' and local councillors are widely distrusted on this dimension, and there is evidence that this distrust is well-founded (Keighley Domestic Violence Forum [KDVF], 1998; Gores, 1999; Macey, 1999a,b; Rehman-Sabba, 1999; Samaroo, 2005; Mahoney and Taj, 2006; Raz, 2006; Khanum, 2008). In other cases, workers in benefits offices and job centres have revealed personal information that has enabled families and 'bounty hunters' to trace escapees from domestic violence and forced marriage (Macey, 1999a; Allen, in Sawyer, 2008) and police officers have passed information back to communities.

We have advanced a number of criticisms of multiculturalism in practice, which suggest that it sometimes acts to conceal and thereby exacerbate injustices that occur within minority communities, especially as these affect women. We should emphasise, however, that the focus in this chapter on injustices within communities is not intended to negate concerns on the other side of the justice question – about external racism and discrimination, for example, or the persistence of inequality for some ethno-religious groups (as covered in Chapters 2 and 3). We will return to the question raised by the need to balance concerns over the two sides of the justice issue after drawing out some of the main characteristics of the ideology of multiculturalism, as this affects both policy and practice.

The ideology of multiculturalism

The analysis of multicultural practice suggests the existence of a number of problematic assumptions that underpin the multicultural enterprise as a whole and which comprise a distinctive multicultural ideology. Key among these are racialisation (or ethnicisation) and essentialism; a static conception of culture and identity; the prioritisation of the group over the individual, and cultural relativism.

Racialisation and essentialism. In a sense, multiculturalism was racialised from the outset, since it developed as an approach to dealing with the diversity in society that was seen to be a feature (and a problem) only of people who were *visibly* different to the majority population. It thus focused on a single aspect of identity – ethnicity or race, the two sometimes being elided. We have already noted that this flies in the face of social science theory that identities are not singular, static or all-encompassing, but multiple, dynamic and variable by situation/context (Sen, 2006). And in a globalised world, identities can also be hybrid and hyphenated due to national, transnational and international influences, both real and virtual (Kymlicka, 1995; 2001b; Bhabha, 1999; Anthias, 2002). This perspective is reinforced by the empirical findings for hyphen-groups discussed in Chapter 2.

Barth's definition of ethnic categories as 'organisational vessels that may be given varying amounts and forms of content in different socio-cultural systems' sounds a cautionary note on the dangers of over-emphasising the concept of ethnicity. He warns that '[ethnic categories] may be of great relevance to behaviour but they need not be; they may pervade all social life, or they may be relevant only in limited sectors of activity' (1969: 14). Unfortunately, Barth's warning is not heeded by multiculturalism, which reduces people to a single, all-encompassing *ethnic* identity that apparently dominates all aspects of life. This is not only theoretically inaccurate but also an essentialising and racialising process, as Stanfield notes with reference to the US:

> the reproduction of a singular monolithic identity as objectified reality is a must if people of color are to remain oppressed second- and third-class citizens. To recognize that people of color have ranges of identities is to acknowledge their humanity in a way that is threatening to the status quo, in that it disturbs the social, political, and economic arrangements of the dominant group. (1993: 21)

Bannerji raises similar concerns about Canadian multiculturalism, which, she suggests, poses 'Canadian culture' against 'multiculturalism', so that 'An element of whiteness quietly enters into cultural definitions, marking the difference between a core cultural group and other groups who are represented as cultural fragments' (2000: 10).

These issues are not merely matters of theoretical debate or analysis; they raise questions and have impacts at the societal and grassroots levels – the latter especially for less powerful categories such as women, children and young people. For essentialism – treating groups as undifferentiated – ignores the fact that the interests of, for example, women and young people not only differ from those of older men, but may sometimes be in conflict with them (Macey, 1999b; Mahoney and Taj, 2006). And the multicultural assumption that self-styled 'leaders' constitute ethnic spokespersons who are able to legitimately speak for whole communities has facilitated their control over such communities (Yalçin-Heckman, 1997; Macey, 1999a,b; 2005; 2006; 2007a; 2008; Puri, 2005; Baxter, 2006; Mahoney and Taj, 2006; Raz, 2006; McKerl, 2007). Patel comments:

> What multi-culturalism does (in return for information and votes) is to concede some measure of autonomy to community leaders to govern their communities. In reality this means that community leaders have most control over the family, women and children. Together with the state, community leaders define the needs of the minority communities then limit and separate progressive voices on the grounds of these being inauthentic and westernised. More radical elements of our community are labelled as extremists. This is the result of multi-cultural policies. They have had an enormous and devastating impact on women's autonomy and rights. (1998: 22)

This raises fundamental and far-reaching questions about the concept of 'community' – the group level at which multiculturalism generally operates. Puri comments:

> What goes unquestioned...are the politics of determining who is given the power to define a community, to name and define its 'different needs', as well as to guide physicians and other social service providers to the presumed 'right course of action'. (2005: 417)

This question refers not only to who *within* communities has the right to define its needs but also to who *outside* them does so. Who, for example, constructs the 'cultural awareness' criteria used to select police recruits? Or the curricula used to teach 'cultural competences' in social work? How accurate are the definitions of 'community needs' that (generally white) educators and trainers inculcate into future professionals? And what is the impact of all this on frontline professionals' ability and/or willingness to take effective action against the abuses that take place *within* communities? This point also has implications for the kind of polity recommended by Parekh (2000b) as 'a community of communities'.

Culture and identities. Just as racialisation and essentialism are linked within a multicultural framework, so, too, are culture and identities. Watson defines culture as:

> a process of the constant adaptation of people to historical circumstances which require them, as a condition of their own survival, to engage sympathetically with new ways of understanding the world and responding to it. ... any attempt to define, or worse, to legislate for a culture is doomed to failure. (2000: 109)

The problem here is the mismatch between theory and practice, rhetoric and reality, for there are two aspects of multiculturalism in the real world that militate against Watson's (accurate) statement of theory. First, in encouraging the continuous reproduction of the culture of the homeland, multiculturalism removes the onus from minority groups of 'engaging sympathetically with new ways of understanding the world and responding to it'. In this, it acts against the natural dynamism of cultures and pushes them into an even more static mould than is temporarily the case in the early stages of the migration process. Second, multiculturalism *does* legislate for culture through both policy and practice, as noted above with respect to the 'cohesion' agenda. Thus, multiculturalism can lock people into rigid, and often reactionary, cultural and religious categories, whether they want this or not – and there is no doubt that many young people do *not* want to be forced into some fixed and unchanging version of their parents' or grandparents' culture.

One of the most basic problems with multiculturalism is that it operates on the assumption that there are significant differences *between* minorities and the majority, but does not consider differences *within* either category. In practice, intra-group differences will always exist in various respects and to varying degrees, but the multicultural literature assumes, on the contrary, that inter-group differences are (a) real, (b) static and (c) apply equally to all members of the group. Indeed, this is the only way that multiculturalism *can* operate, since to question the reality of differences within and between minorities and majorities would be to question the need for its own existence! One of the most confusing aspects of the literature, however, is the propensity for multi-cultural theorists to claim that they take cognisance of diversity, whilst not actually doing, as, for instance, in Modood's reference to 'a variety of ways of being Sikh or African-Caribbean' (2007:106).

No matter how often multiculturalists refer to diversity *within* cultural and/or identity groups, they continue to prioritise ethnic and/or religious identity over all other aspects of the person. For the entire edifice of multicultural theory and practice is directed specifically towards essentialised minority ethnic groups, and this is done with few – if any – attempts at justification, other than generalised references to discrimination, exclusion, inequality and oppression. This suggests either that multiculturalists retain a static and essentialised view of the concept of identity – at least as it applies to minority groups – or that they are operating on a hierarchical model of oppressions within which racial or ethnic minorities are seen to be more oppressed than women, older people, disabled people and so on. Indeed, Modood explicitly adopts this stance, stating that 'the *most important* cultural racism is Islamophobia' (2001: 9, emphasis added). Whether this is actually the case is highly questionable, particularly since it is unclear how the relative importance of different racisms is to be ranked empirically. If anything, the evidence considered in Chapter 3 suggests that old-fashioned racism (the racial kind) creates more injustice than any 'cultural racism'. And the incidence of religious injustice, including Islamophobia, is certainly less widespread than is generally believed to be the case.

All this is linked to the concept of identity, which holds as central a place in multicultural theory as that of culture – and both are theoretically problematic, particularly in relation to the issue of essentialism and the question of change. Fisher refers to 'strategic essentialism', which involves the tendency of multiculturalists to deny that culture and identities are singular, fixed or static, but then to proceed as if they were (2005: 112). However, as noted above, it is difficult to see how else multiculturalism could operate, since culture must be the axis around which multiculturalism turns theoretically.

Another problematic usage of the concepts of identity and culture (or cultural identities) is in relation to their role in achieving equality. Omi and Winant (1994), Goldberg (1990; 1993; 1994) and Raz (1994) see minorities as being located in an alien web of cultural meanings, the difficulties of which are exacerbated by the racist definition of minority cultures as inferior. This is said to affect people's self-respect deeply (Margalit and Halbertal, 1994; Honneth, 1997; Muir et al., 2004). Multiculturalism is seen as necessary to mitigate this deficit because people can exercise meaningful agency only by tapping into their own cultures (Herr, 2004). Group identities then become a means of attaining justice and an important source of resistance to cultural imperialism (Young, 1990). From this viewpoint, multiculturalism is essential to self-respect and agency, a bulwark of resistance against external threats to cultures *and* a key resource in the struggle for racial/ethnic equality and justice.

We would make two points here. First, it is difficult to see how or why multiculturalism should (or could) be an effective means of achieving equality. For in encouraging minority communities to maintain the language, culture and religion of the homeland, multiculturalism may exacerbate inequality in that there are some aspects of some cultures that militate against the achievement of at least economic equality.

Second, the people who settled in Britain before the era of multiculturalism seem to have managed to maintain chosen aspects of their cultures and religions, while integrating into wider society in ways that have enabled them to benefit from the opportunities this has offered. Because the levels of religious injustice are lower than is widely believed, it follows that the elimination of religious injustice will have less impact on religious inequality than is widely anticipated. This reinforces the importance of factors such as education in achieving religious equality. Nor is there any evidence that Polish and Jewish people, for example, are bereft of agency, have experienced loss of identity or cultural genocide, or suffer from lack of self-respect or self-esteem – as multiculturalists suggest with reference to the groups that they see as being in need of 'protection'.

It is not without irony that these two elements of multicultural ideology, which essentialise and prioritise culture, are precisely those failings with which early multiculturalism taxed its anti-racist predecessor, as noted above.

The group versus the individual. In a sense, multiculturalism's focus on the ethnic collective rather than the individual is more in tune with the orientation of the groups at which it is directed, many of whose cultures are communitarian rather than individualistic. However, a number of the infringements of human rights that we have highlighted in this chapter are a direct result of this and are rooted in the homeland cultures which multiculturalism seeks to maintain. Migration itself also pushes communities towards resisting change and ossifying cultures as they existed at the point of migration, and this puts particular pressures on women as the 'bearers' of cultural and religious traditions (Anthias and Yuval-Davis, 1992; Afshar, 1994), which are sometimes expressed through increased violence against them (Akpinar, 2003).

It is highly likely that concerns to maintain the culture and traditions of the homeland unchanged would, left to their own devices, be relatively short-lived. For provided that the boundaries between ethnic groups are permeable, interaction with wider society 'naturally' brings about change (Wallman, 1986; Macey, 2007a). But multiculturalism operates against change, sometimes in conjunction with communities which seek to remain residentially and socially separate from others. This raises a number of questions in relation not only to members of minority communities but also to wider society and liberal democracy itself. These points are taken up in Chapter 6.

Cultural relativism is the view that no culture is better than any other, which is justified on the basis that there are no transcendent criteria by which cultural differences can be evaluated (Watson, 2000). At first sight, this seems like an eminently liberal proposition, geared towards encouraging acceptance of the cultural and religious diversity that now characterises Western liberal democracies. There are, however, a number of problems with relativism – or the 'anything goes' approach to diversity.

First, there is a contradiction between the cultural relativism on which multiculturalism is based and the universalism which characterises liberalism and increasingly underpins human rights in a globalised world (Kalev, 2004; Malik, 2005b). Second, the logical consequence of the 'all cultures are equal' approach is to propose that the Nazi and apartheid regimes are not open to criticism, or that there is no difference between FGM (including that performed on babies) and cosmetic surgery. Thus, cultural relativism can provide no resistance to human rights violations. Third, there are pragmatic difficulties (if not impossibilities) in trying to maintain the value-free stance that is a requirement of cultural relativism, especially in contemporary societies in which we are directly confronted with the reality of its effects on vulnerable people. Fourth, as Fisher argues, even if we *could* maintain such a stance, we should not do so: 'such appraisals [judgements] are arguably our shared philosophical and moral responsibilities – and we are all too familiar with the potential consequences, in a variety of historical and cultural contexts, of not saying anything' (2005: 118). Fifth, the implication of cultural relativism is that some British citizens (notably minority ethnic or religious women) are not entitled to the same rights or protection as majority ones. Spinner-Halev actually states that 'avoiding the injustice of imposing reform on oppressed groups is often more important than avoiding the injustice of discrimination against women' (2001: 86). And Kukathas extends this to children when he argues for the primary importance of non-intervention in minority cultural practices:

> Perhaps toleration of the cultural practices of ethnic groups includes allowing ritual acts to be carried out upon children, because these can be an essential part of the culture, and allow parents to educate and raise their children according to their cultural laws. (1986: 99)

As is clear from these two examples, cultural relativism does not provide any way around the requirement to make ethical judgements about competing claims, since any choice in the situations outlined above will either involve sacrificing the rights and interests of women and children, or it will not. The choice itself is inescapable. And it is difficult to see how cultural relativism can provide any guidance in the task of creating a legal and ethical framework for regulating the relationships between social groups with differing values. Any such framework must appeal to some values or other, and in order for the framework to succeed in its regulatory task, the values must gain some measure of acceptance from the regulated groups. This common ground will necessarily transcend the cultural differences between groups, and to this extent invalidate cultural relativism. But the task of creating such a framework is precisely the political and legal demand raised by the existence of a multicultural society. It follows that multiculturalism as a doctrine can either espouse cultural relativism or contribute to the functioning of a just multicultural society in which the human rights of *all* citizens are protected. It cannot do both.

This argument has been made well by Pierre Sané, who is the Assistant Director-General of the Social and Human Sciences section of UNESCO. He points out that the guiding principles for multicultural democratic societies laid down in the *Universal Declaration of Cultural Diversity* (UNESCO, 2001) are based on the idea that 'only when cultural diversity is in balance with social cohesion, can we find ways of democratic participation and peaceful co-existence' (2007: xi). Gitlin makes a similar point in a critique of multiculturalism:

> Democracy is more than a licence to celebrate (and exaggerate) difference. ... It is a political system of mutual reliance and common moral obligations ... If multiculturalism is not tempered by a stake

in the commons, then centrifugal energy overwhelms any commitment to a larger good. This is where multiculturalism has proved a trap even – or especially – for people in the name of whom the partisans of identity politics purport to speak. (1995: 236)

The trouble with multiculturalism

The trouble with multiculturalism as a policy is that the multicultural label names a range of options whose overall vagueness provides very little guidance regarding the appropriate aims of policy in and for a multicultural society. This vagueness may help to explain the popularity of multiculturalism, but it raises the possibility that the invocation of multiculturalism can act as a cover, or as a shield, for policies that are inimical to equality and human rights.

An examination of multiculturalism in practice suggests that this danger is a real one, and that multiculturalism can act to conceal or to exacerbate the inequalities or injustices suffered by vulnerable individuals, especially women and girls, within minority ethnic or religious communities.

Multiculturalism is driven by an ideology with characteristic elements or themes. As in the cases examined in previous chapters, these are 'ideological' in part because of the lack of balance in their approach. Thus, the significance of ethnic and religious identities is undeniable. But multicultural ideology makes these a privileged reference point compared to other aspects of social identity, and it prioritises the claims of religion and culture over those of gender, age, class and so on. In the same way, the ideology privileges the claims of the group over the individual, and cultural relativism acts to undermine the protection to which individuals are entitled as British citizens and, indeed, as persons who possess inherent human rights. And though multicultural ideology does not *cause* abuses of individual rights, it legitimises a climate that allows abuses to continue – and thus contributes to the commission of much suffering and harm.

5
The Problem with Religion

Introduction

This chapter focuses specifically on religion(s) within the complex of 'race, ethnicity, culture and religion'. It describes the sociological character of religion and locates this in the context of globalisation, migration and multicultural/multi-faith societies and a growing emphasis on religion on the part of both governments and academics. This stems not only from diversity, but also from the assertion of a global resurgence of religion which is paralleled by a theoretical/ideological shift that challenges secularisation and, indeed, Enlightenment thinking and claims a place for religion in the public arena. Yet in the context of ethnic diversity, religion may create or exacerbate social tensions and is itself responsible for inequality and oppression on a number of dimensions which we explore in this chapter.

Religion and sociology

Sociological approaches to religion fall broadly into the categories of consensus and conflict, though Weber (1961; 1966) added neo-phenomenological insights to the study of religion, and Berger (1967; 1969) contributed a full-fledged phenomenological perspective on it.

The *Consensus* approach to religion is widely thought to stem from the Latin verb *religare*, 'to bind things closely together' (Bowker, 2004: 6), and it was this aspect of religion that was the focus of early sociologists, such as Durkheim (1915) and later Parsons (1944; 1951), who viewed religion as providing a kind of social glue or cement which binds individuals and groups into a communal order (Turner, 1991). Though this approach was developed in the West and focused on Christianity, it underpins the New Labour government's approach to religion in a multicultural, multi-faith context.

The *Conflict* perspective focuses on one of two aspects of religion – the use to which it is put in controlling (and oppressing) people and thereby maintaining the status quo (Marx, 1957 [1844]), or the role of religion in creating, or exacerbating, conflict between groups of people. It is this latter perspective on which we focus in a book on religion and ethnicity, for, as Gutmann (2003) and Joppke (2004) observe, the fact is that in multicultural societies, the hard cultural conflicts tend to be religious.

The long-standing association of religion with conflict (cruelty and warfare) is surprising, given that the major world faiths share a central commitment to peace, justice, tolerance and respect for all human beings. However, it is less surprising given that religious beliefs are particularly strongly held because they are concerned with some of the most fundamental questions about the meaning of life and the universe. Another reason is that the mark of religion is to be exclusive (Zolberg and Long, 1991) and 'Religion often binds people into alternative and competing social groups or collectivities' (Turner, 1991: ix). Historically, this sometimes led to conflict when differing religious worldviews came into contact, but this was relatively rare; in the contemporary globalised world, the potential for conflict is considerably more immediate as people with competing religious views live as neighbours. And now, as in the past, religion is sometimes used to justify violence.

Two further sociological perspectives come from the interpretative school of thought. *Phenomenology* focuses on the role of religion in providing *meaning* at both the societal and individual levels, and in analysing how religion relates to existential questions, insights may be gained into its association with conflict. In diverse societies, the link between religion and ethnicity comes into play, for though these are conceptually separable, in reality they often combine. And in the context of migration for settlement, this can also contribute to conflict as people seek to resist real or perceived threats to some of their most cherished beliefs.

Postmodernism is a sociological perspective that has had a major influence on current debates in the sphere of religion, and underpins the challenge to secular ways of thinking, particularly the view that scientific reasoning and knowledge is superior to other forms, including (or even particularly) religious ones. The popularity of postmodern thinking is at least partially explicable in that it 'fits' with wider disenchantment with modernity and the power of science to transform human existence on the ideological, material and social levels. Some writers trace this to a 'loss of innocence' brought about by the use of advanced science and technology during WWII to bring about death and destruction on a huge scale (see Bauman, 1989, on modernity and the holocaust and Esposito et al., 2002, on the role of science in ending the hatred and bloodshed supposedly caused by religion).

The development of postmodern thinking was also significantly influenced by challenges from the black movement in the US and Britain during the 1960s and 1970s (Seidman, 1992), and sociology's growing attention to race and ethnic relations in the 1980s (Allen and Macey, 1994). The re-emergence of a women's movement in the 1960s and 1970s in the US, Western Europe and elsewhere was a further influence on postmodernism, as was the development of feminist theory in this area.

The rise of postmodernism as a 'flight from science' has coincided with claims and counter-claims about the resurgence of religion, which we consider next.

Secularisation or religious resurgence?

Secularisation was built into sociology from its inception via the evolutionary empiricism of its founding father, Auguste Comte, who believed that religion was a primitive stage in human development that would inevitably be replaced by secularisation/secular societies. This involved the dominance of scientific, rational thinking based on logical presuppositions, experiment and evidence, so that science would become the new religion of society (Comte, in Lenzer, 1975). This would be in contrast to the 'blind and irrational faith immune from falsification' that is supposedly involved in religious belief:

> Religious beliefs fail the test of propositional truth because they float free of evidence and reason, taking refuge in an internal coherence that is immune to falsification by new knowledge and events. Science, on the other hand, represents our most committed effort to verify that our statements about the world are true (or at least not false). (Harris, 2006: 75–6)

A linked (not necessarily competing) thesis saw the development of modern democratic societies as leading to secularism, as the integrative role of religion is transferred to what Habermas terms 'communicative reason', whereby 'the authority of the holy is gradually replaced by the authority of an achieved consensus' (1987: 77, cited in Habermas, 2010). Whatever the specific focus, the belief that secularisation was an inevitable and ongoing process continued to dominate sociological approaches to religion until relatively recently (Wilson, 1966; Berger, 1967; Bruce, 2002; 2006), though there were always dissenting voices (see Davie, 2001; 2002; 2004; 2006). Now, however, the secularisation thesis is undergoing a strong global challenge: Berger (1999; 2007) talks of 'de-secularisation'; Kepel (1994) refers to the 'resurgence' of religion, and Esposito et al. (2002) suggest that religion has defied the countless theorists who predicted its demise.

The basis on which claims that secularisation continues (in the West) are clear insofar as they rest on such measurable religious practices as church attendance, prayer and so on, contrasted with self-identification, which is *not* accompanied by such action. As discussed in Chapter 1, this is our position with reference to Britain; it is also that of Norris and Inglehart (2007) in relation to the US and a number of Western European countries. What, for instance, are we to make of the young men who define themselves as 'Muslim', while simultaneously stating that they are 'not religious', do not attend mosque, do not fast or pray, and/or breach religious edicts to abstain from alcohol, drugs and tobacco (Khan, 1997; Archer, 2001; Macey, 2005; 2007b; Billings and Holden, 2007; Mirza et al., 2007)? The only thing that seems clear in such cases is that self-identification by religion tells us very little about religiosity!

What is *not* clear to us is the basis on which the claim is made that we are witnessing a global resurgence of religion, for this seems to be more assumed than demonstrated, with writers moving rather rapidly from statement to explanation. Kepel, for instance, links the growth in religion from the mid-1970s to Islamic criticisms of 'failed modernism' being a consequence of separation from God. This, he says, has subsequently spread all over the world, always taking the form of setting itself against 'crises' in society and involving the 'Islamisation of modernity' (1994: 2). It is not only Islam, suggests Kepel, but all the Abrahamic faiths that have reacted in apocalyptic terms to the loss of communism as a messianic ideology, the spread of AIDS, pollution and the energy crisis, and this has resulted in the spread of religious movements (1994: 191).

Furbey links religious resurgence to globalisation and uncertainty, suggesting that 'much of this...is associated with separation and conflict, reflecting a defensive reaction to the uncertainties and risks of a globalised and "liquid" world' (2009: 120). We are not questioning the logic of this; indeed, it follows older approaches to understanding the different trajectories taken by religion in times of rapid change and uncertainty, from the radical to the reactionary (Neilsen, 1984; Robinson, 1988; Macey, 1991; Yuval-Davis, 1991; Allen and Macey, 1994). But none of these writers suggested that de-secularisation was occurring, and it is the accuracy of this of which we are unconvinced. Eisenstadt (2000) also locates the resurgence of religious movements in the context of globalisation, pointing to their challenges not only to the secularisation process but to Enlightenment thinking and, indeed, to the hegemony of Western definitions of modernity itself.

Casanova (2007), on the other hand, does not question the secularisation process to date but suggests that 'immigrant religions' present a challenge to this, a view supported by Kaufmann, as discussed in Chapter 1. However, as a whole (and with the exception of Kaufmann), the 'counter secularisation thesis' is not grounded in empirical research, whilst there is strong evidence – at least with respect to traditional Christianity in the West – for the secularisation thesis in the steady decline in religious practice over time. And while it would be unwise to conclude from this that 'God is Dead' (Nietzsche, 1992; Bruce, 2002), it seems to us that it would be equally unwise to conclude that 'secularisation is dead'. The main grounds for this contention seem to be that belief has become privatised (Davie, 2002), or that there is a growth in different forms of *spirituality*, such as NRMs (Heelas, 2001; Heelas and Woodhead, 2005). Writers can also sustain the thesis by defining 'religion' so broadly that the term becomes conceptually vacuous. Surprisingly, this is the direction taken by the Equality and Human Rights Commission – the body responsible for developing and overseeing the religion and belief legislation, which (under the heading 'Defining religion and belief') states: 'Religion is a word analogous to "politics" or "society". It is not a "thing" with uniform characteristics, but a collective term for a range of different dimensions' (Woodhead, 2009: iii). It will be interesting to see how the term is operationalised in research and how claims of religious discrimination are adjudicated within the EHRC's perspective.

It may be that a number of variables have combined to give a spurious impression of growing religiosity across the globe and, by definition, that the secularisation process has slowed or stopped. A major factor could be the non-European migration and settlement which has turned Western societies into multicultural ones, in that (a) perceived problems with this have led governments to adopt multicultural strategies for managing diversity, many of which afford religion a central place;

(b) human rights legislation has developed over time to include religion (and belief) because it is assumed that minorities are highly religious; (c) post-WWII migrant workers have now lived in Europe long enough to make demands on governments for special treatment – often based on the cultural interpretations of religion imported from 'the home-land'. A further aspect is the vast literature that has been generated since the Islamist terrorism in the US and Europe in the 2000s. This latter, however, represents a challenge to the secularisation thesis with which we have no quarrel in that, rather than suggesting an increase in religiosity, it points to the significance of religion as a social phenom-enon becoming more clearly apparent from a global perspective (Reder and Schmidt, 2010).

The reality is that we do not know the extent to which ethno-religious minorities *are* religious in terms of practice. As noted previously, there appears to be a tendency for religiosity to become more variable within each religious tradition, so that a general tendency towards secularisa-tion is accompanied by a sharp reassertion of conservative identity by a minority within the minority (Mirza et al., 2007). And, crucially, as also noted, we do not know the extent to which defining oneself by religion is a signifier of a separatist, political identity (Macey, 2007), or whether in some cases – such as with some Christians in Britain – it might be a reaction against multiculturalism's stress on minority ethno-religious groups (Macey et al., 2010). Yet there are a number of reasons for needing to know considerably more than we do about the importance of religion to minority ethnic groups. One of these concerns the potential of reli-gion – especially when combined with ethnicity – to exacerbate, or even cause, conflict, including violence, which we discuss next. Another relates to the oppressive impact that religion can have on both believers and non-believers and the implications of this for equality and human rights. Together these raise questions about the legitimacy of multicultural claims for religious recognition in the public realm which we explore later.

Religion and conflict

A number of the writers cited above express concerns that the resur-gence of religion could increase conflict, though most do not view this as inevitable. Kepel (1994), however, says that though Christianity, Judaism and Islam share a rejection of secularism (based on the belief that only a religious transformation will cure society's ills), they have nothing else in common. Thus, their visions of what society 'should be' both diverge and become deeply antagonistic – and this carries with it 'a potential for bitter conflict in which none of their versions of truth can afford to compromise on pain of losing followers' (Kepel, 1994: 192). This is a deeply pessimistic interpretation of the role of religion in conflict and one that it might be suggested pre-empts Huntington's (1996) 'clash of civilisations' thesis – which is totally rejected by, for instance, Eisenstadt (2007). It is a matter of some concern, however, that writing in the 1990s, Kepel accurately predicted that 're-Islamization movements have the greatest potential' (1994: 193), for certainly this has proved to be the case in relation to Muslim involvement in violence on a global scale, as we discuss below.

Religion, ethnicity and violence

Terrorism is currently the most extreme example of the involvement of religion in violence, and the clearest illustration of the disjunction between religious teaching and its (ab)use in practice. We do not intend to explore the issue of Islamist terrorism in detail in this book (see Bergesen and Lizardo, 2004, on the characteristics of contemporary international terrorism; Pape, 2005, on suicide bombing; and Abbas, 2007, on Islamic political radicalism in Europe). However, we would note that Islamist terrorism has a considerably longer history than 9/11, and has been occurring on a global scale since the 1970s (Cohen and Kennedy, 2007).

The phenomenon of international terrorism suggests that some young Muslims have prioritised the 'religious' aspect of their identity over others and that they have a global, rather than a local, orientation in which loyalty to the *ummah* takes precedence over commitment to their own societies. And it is this latter aspect of the bombings in Spain, 2004, and England, 2005, which has led to an unprecedented interest in the role of religion in conflict. As noted previously, this concern with minority religions is not restricted to academics but, in Britain and other parts of Western Europe, extends to governments, and in the context of 'the war on terror' includes 'the war for Muslim minds'. Kepel (2004) suggests that Al Qaeda is also engaged in this 'war' and that this is part of the reason for 9/11.

Whatever the reasons for young Muslim men being willing to kill themselves and their fellow citizens, the international nature of the enterprise points *away* from explanations that focus on individual societies or cultural interpretations of Islam. Thus, 'the same tired old explanations' (Alibhai-Brown, 2001) that were produced at the time of the 'Northern Riots' – deprivation, social exclusion and racism – together with the newer Islamophobia and the Far Right (McGhee, 2005), are of questionable relevance. For the common and consistent denominators in Islamist terrorism are religion, age and gender – and access to a global identity and *jihadi* ideologies via the Internet (Kepel, 2004). A focus on these would raise questions of a different order – about the weakness of national identity (Barry, 2001), young male masculinities (Dwyer, 2000; Archer, 2003), the way that Islam is taught (Ramadan, 2004; Lewis, 2006) or even Islam itself (Manji, 2005) and how these might encourage violent extremism. We suggest that the failure to address such issues in Britain is at least partly to do with the dominance of a brand of multiculturalism that silences genuine debate in the interests of 'political correctness'. But, as Hirsi Ali comments: 'some things must be said, and there are times when silence becomes an accomplice to injustice' (2007: xii), or, we would add, murder. However, few academics in Britain are willing to acknowledge that global Islamist terrorism is religiously inspired, though Awan says:

> A cursory reading of the biographies of many of the individuals implicated in... terrorist acts points to one glaring, inescapable commonality: their political radicalisation, culminating in terrorism, is somehow inextricably linked to, or perhaps even contingent upon, the complex phenomenon of sudden or increasing religiosity... it remains an indelible sociological fact that these individuals considered themselves to be Muslim, and indeed Islam provided (at least in their minds) the *raison d'être* for their acts of terrorism and even self-immolation. (2007: 208)

Public disorder and riot. In 1995 and 2001, images were circulated around the world of young Asian men violently attacking the police while the city of Bradford burned. The two incidents shared many features, including the religion, ethnicity and gender of the perpetrators (almost entirely Muslim, Mirpuri and male); the numbers involved (300–400); the groups targeted (not only the police but also non-Muslim civilians); the violence involved (throwing missiles – stones, rocks, roof tiles, fireworks and petrol bombs); the destruction of property (smashing shop and pub windows; looting; wrecking and burning buildings and cars); the erection of burning barricades and issuing death threats at knife point to innocent people trying to escape. The only real difference between the two events was the scale of damage and injury, with the 2001 riot being viewed as the worst rioting on mainland Britain for twenty years, injuring 326 police officers and taking over 1,000 staff from nine forces to bring under control (see Allen and Barrett, 1996, on the 1995 disorder and Carling et al., 2004, and Macey, 2005, on the 2001 disorder and riot). It is interesting to note that the 'explanations' put forward for the Bradford riots did not (with the exception of Parekh, 2003) include religion, despite the fact that the perpetrators were almost entirely Muslim men who claimed religion as the key element of their identities (Macey, 2005). This provides another example of the ideological tendency to stress external factors (in the social environment of communities) at the expense of internal (community) factors in the treatment of outcomes for members of minority religions.

Protests and demands. In Western Europe, Muslims have been to the forefront in a number of instances of violent protest involving a clash between religious sensitivities and the values of liberal, secular states. A British example of this is 'the Rushdie Affair', which began with the publication of Salman Rushdie's novel *The Satanic Verses* in 1988. This was greeted by Muslim demands that the book be banned as blasphemous – a demand supported by such violence as ritual book burnings, bombings and burnings of book shops, and Ayatollah Khomeni's issue of a *fatwa* calling on all good Muslims to kill Rushdie and his publishers or point him out to those who *could* kill him. Rushdie was forced into hiding under police protection, a situation that lasted for over a decade, and the protest spread around the world, resulting in the injury and death of many people – some through assassination, others during rioting (see Pipes, 2003).

A comparable incident took place in Denmark in 2005, where Muslims expressed outrage at the publication of a series of cartoons of the Prophet Mohammed in the newspaper *Jyllands-Posten*. Initial protests were peaceful, consisting of demand for withdrawal of the cartoons, but subsequent rioting was justified on the grounds of religious offence. By 2006, newspapers in other countries had published the cartoons and the issue went global, with a number of Muslim countries publicly condemning the cartoons – accompanied by the burning of national flags and embassies and rioting which resulted in loss of life. Much of the Muslim anger in 2006 followed a visit to the Middle East by a delegation of Danish imams, during which the imams had added three extra, highly inflammatory, cartoons *not* produced by the *Jyllands-Posten* cartoonists (BBC, 2009).

The Danish cartoon incident is ongoing, as many of the artists remain in hiding or have round-the-clock police protection – which has not prevented two assassination attempts in 2010: one in Denmark and one in Ireland (BBC, 2010a,b). And at his trial in March 2010 a Chicago man (of mixed white [American] and Pakistani heritage) admitted that among other offences (including the Mumbai bombings), he had been involved in an assassination plot against staff at *Jyllands-Posten*. He stated that he had been told by the Pakistani terrorist organisation with which he was involved to behead captives and throw their heads out of the building 'to heighten the response from Danish authorities' (Korecki, 2010).

Despite the cartoons not being published in Britain, their impact continues on a number of levels. A Saudi Arabian lawyer is threatening to use the British courts to overturn the Danish free-speech ruling (Waterfield, 2010), which is made possible by Britain's membership of the EU and the strength of our libel laws. And though these are currently under review, their potential use in blocking freedom of speech raises serious questions for liberal democracy (see Bleich et al., 2006, for a discussion of freedom of speech). It is also possible that stereotypical images of Muslims have been reinforced by protesters outside the Danish Embassy in London brandishing such placards as 'Slay [butcher/massacre/behead/exterminate] those who insult Islam'; 'Europe is the cancer and Islam is the cure', and 'Europe will pay, your 9/11 is on its way' (Hansen, 2006: 10).

Two examples of threatened or actual killings on the grounds of religious offence occurred in the Netherlands in 2004 when the filmmaker, Theo van Gogh, was murdered and the politician, Ayaan Hirsi Ali, was threatened with assassination because they had made a film criticising Islam's treatment of women. After shooting and slitting his throat, van Gogh's murderer used a knife to pin a five-page letter in the form of a *fatwa* addressed to Hirsi Ali to van Gogh's chest. This opened with the words 'In the name of Allah Most Gracious Most Merciful' (Hirsi Ali, 2007: 322) and provides clear confirmation that the murder was religiously motivated and corresponds to a worldview which is incomprehensible to most people.

Two examples of more limited violence occurred in Bradford during Muslim demands for special treatment on the basis of religion. The first, in 1983, was a campaign for the provision of *halal* meat in schools; the second, in 1995, was a campaign against prostitution in what had become a majority-Muslim residential area. Both began as legitimate democratic protest, but were turned into violent public disorder by young men who used Islam to rally support for their objectives, which were achieved successfully in both cases. We would raise four issues at this juncture: first, it is not only Muslims who have engaged in public protest on the grounds of religious offence; so, too, have Christians, Hindus and Sikhs, though not generally using violence; second, such protests are sometimes directed at followers of the religion; third, failure to achieve their aims may lead to a sense of grievance and the belief that government favours one ethno-religious group over another; and finally, it may be that protest by a religious group which achieves its aims encourages further protest by this, and other, groups.

An example of Christian protest was that directed at the award-winning musical *Jerry Springer: The Opera*, which ran in London from 2003 to 2005 before touring Britain and being screened on BBC television in 2006. The show is notorious for profanity and the irreverent treatment of Judeo-Christian themes, and some fundamentalist (Evangelical) organisations threatened to bring prosecutions for blasphemy – attracting considerable criticism from both secular and Christian groups. Street demonstrations took place as well as thousands of protest letters being sent to the BBC.

A different kind of protest was that carried out by Hindus against the slaughter of the sacred bull, Shambo, at a Welsh temple (and the sacred cow, Gangotri, at an English one) in 2007. Shambo's slaughter was ordered because he had tested positive for bovine tuberculosis, but Hindus used European law on freedom of religion to try to prevent this on the grounds that their religious beliefs prohibit the taking of life. The High Court ruled in their favour, but the Welsh Assembly government's appeal against the decision was upheld. Hindu protesters gathered at the temple but failed to prevent the removal of the bull for slaughter. This case illustrates the feeling that religious communities are not treated equally in Britain, as illustrated by the unanimous resolution from Hindu organisations that the 'Government has failed the British Hindu community'. The President of the National Council of Hindu Temples claimed:

> This Government has no regard for the needs of communities that do not shout... If this had been some other community, the Government would have rushed to find a solution. Just because Hindus are quiet, we are ignored, isolated and sidelined. (Hindu Forum of Britain, 2008)

In 2004, there was a Sikh protest against the staging of the play *Behzti* (Dishonour) which caused offence because it contains scenes of rape, physical abuse and murder set in a *gurdwara*. Both local and national Sikh organisations protested outside the theatre and violence broke out. As with the case of the Jerry Springer show, criticisms of the protest came from inside, as well as outside, the religion, and the Sikh Federation was condemned as 'militants' (Bassey, 2005). But the really significant aspects of this protest – other than the fact that it achieved its aim of having the play cancelled – are that (a) the play was written by a Sikh woman, and (b) comments made by young Sikh protestors suggest that their use of violence emulated that of Muslims. Grillo reports: 'Only when protests turned violent, militants claimed, did anyone listen'; '[When they burned *The Satanic Verses*], that soon put a stop to it'; 'if some fool thinks he/she can mock our religion, mock our faith, use our faith as a joke and to humiliate us, then they got another think coming, mate', and '[Muslims] hit hard anything that makes a mockery of them, so much so that people are afraid to tackle issues involving Islam' (2007: 13). This incident, and the views of its perpetrators, raise a broader question:

> If you had to write a theatrical pitch for what Birmingham has just witnessed over the play Behzti, you could do it in seven words: play offends community, community protests, play cancelled. But that simple three act performance conceals a far more complex drama about how we all share the same space in a pluralistic society. (Casciani, 2004)

In sum, the material covered in this section highlights some serious issues in relation to how liberal democratic societies can (or should) accommodate divergent worldviews that are sometimes expressed in violent action and justified in the name of religion. This has implications for the multicultural demand that religion should move into the public arena; indeed, it has implications for the multicultural enterprise itself (Entzinger, 2003; Joppke, 2004). If religion is going to be given explicit recognition in the public sector, it is very important to know which interpretation(s) of religion will be recognised in this way, and which individuals or organisations are regarded as representative of their traditions. Recognition of religions will also have potential consequences for the equalities agenda, as we explore next.

Religion and equality

Over the past few years, the most frequently asked question in relation to religion and equality has been whether people of faith – particularly Muslims – are discriminated against on the basis of religion. We examined the evidence for this in Chapters 2 and 3, highlighting the difficulty of separating religion from ethnicity, and the distinction between perception and reality, and assessing the independent impact of religion on disadvantage. In this section, therefore, we concentrate on a question which is much less commonly asked – that relating to the inequality and discrimination which may result from religious belief, or be practised by people of faith against both believers and non-believers. Before moving on to this, however, it is relevant to note that few of the protests mentioned above are due to mainstream society's refusal to make allowances for religious needs, as discussed below.

Religion and civil law

Until the implementation of an increasing range of equalities legislation, Britain's response to requests for change to the law to accommodate minority religions tended towards the *ad hoc,* taking the form of extensions to, and exemptions from, legal requirements (Phillips, 2003; Phillips and Dustin, 2007). For example, Sikhs are exempt from laws on offensive weapons and health and safety to enable them in to carry the *kirpan* (ceremonial dagger) and not to wear safety helmets on building sites or when riding motorcycles. But Parekh's comment that 'The Sikh's turban no longer remains a cultural symbol, which is what it largely is, and becomes a religious requirement' (1998: 208) raises the issue of the distinction between religion and culture and whether the latter is sometimes confused with the former. These changes, however, are not generally seen as contentious in a multi-faith, liberal democratic context, though our next two examples are.

The exemption of Jews and Muslims from the law on humane animal slaughter to enable the practise of *halal* and *kosher* (*sheshita*) killing is controversial because there is clear evidence that this causes unnecessary suffering to animals (Singer, 1991). The government's independent advisor, the Farm Animal Welfare Council, has called for the practice to be banned: 'Council considers that slaughter without pre-stunning is unacceptable and that the Government should repeal the current exemption' (FAWC, 2003: 36). This raises several questions: (a) on what basis are expert recommendations *and* the accepted norms (and laws) of the majority overturned at the demand of minorities? (b) since ritual slaughter is banned in Iceland, Norway, Sweden and Switzerland, is it absolutely essential to the practise of Islam and Judaism? and (c) is there any justification for inflicting unnecessary pain on animals?

The second contentious issue is that of Muslim multiple marriages – which in secular law constitute bigamy and are illegal. However, not only are Muslim men allowed more than one wife (provided that additional marriages are contracted outside England) but full welfare benefits are paid to additional wives and families (Wynn-Jones, 2008). This seems to us to take multiculturalism too far in that (a) having more than one wife is an option within Islam, *not* a religious requirement; (b) it is questionable whether living off state benefits fulfils the Islamic requirement for multiple marriage of being able to provide equally for all wives, and (c) this exemption from the law impacts negatively on first wives.

The most controversial example, which crosses the civil/religious divide in relation to the law, is the existence of religious courts/councils/tribunals in Britain, such as the Jewish *Beth Din* and Muslim *Shar'ia* Councils and Arbitration Tribunals. Though the government did not instigate these, neither has it challenged them, despite their constitution of separate jurisdictions for Jews and Muslims. This raises some fundamental issues in relation to liberal democratic society and what Patel and Siddiqui term 'shrinking secular spaces' (2010: 102). It is noteworthy that one of the foremost proponents of multiculturalism has stated: 'Britain cannot allow separate legal systems for different communities without violating the fundamental principles of common citizenship before the law' (Parekh, in Grillo, 1999: 204).

Jewish religious courts have operated in Britain for over a hundred years and deal with disputes in a range of arenas – from divorce to partnerships in private companies. In all cases, both parties must be Jewish and have agreed to a *Beth Din* ruling. *Shar'ia* Councils have existed in England since the early 1980s, and, like the *Beth Din*, rule on a range of issues, but act principally as mediators in marriage disputes and divorces (Bano, 2010). Neither Jewish courts nor Muslim councils have any official standing in secular law, so that concerns about them are mitigated by their restriction to the religious sphere.

The Muslim Arbitration Tribunal, however, has significantly changed this situation through what it describes as 'exploitation of a loophole' in the 1996 Arbitration Act – which enables decisions made under *shar'ia* law to be enforced through secular judicial channels:

> MAT will operate within the ADR [Alternative Dispute Resolution] framework of England and Wales thereby ensuring that any determination reached by MAT can be enforced through existing means of enforcement open to normal litigants. Although MAT must operate within the legal framework of England and Wales, this does not prevent or impede MAT from ensuring that all determinations reached by it are in accordance with one of the recognized Schools of Islamic Law. *MAT will therefore, for the first time, offer the Muslim community a real and true opportunity to settle disputes in accordance with Islamic*

> *Law with the knowledge that the outcome as determined by MAT will be*
> *binding and enforceable within the English jurisdiction.* (MAT, 2007: 3,
> emphasis added)

These tribunals have been in operation since August 2007, though this
became public knowledge only in 2008 (Taher, 2008), by which time
they had ruled on over 100 cases – including a number of criminal
offences. It is worth noting that the introduction of *shar'ia* law has considerable support among Muslims according to opinion poll findings:

> two-fifths would not respect British law if it interfered with Islamic
> belief and practice, three-fifths favour the introduction of Sharia
> courts into Britain to resolve civil cases between Muslims, two-
> fifths want Sharia law introduced into predominantly Muslim areas,
> just under a third want to live completely under Sharia rather than
> British law and a fifth are prepared to move to a country governed by
> Sharia law rather than to stay in Britain. (Field, 2007: 467, from five
> different polls conducted during 2004–6)

Given the potential implications of allowing what comes close to a parallel legal system based on religion to operate in Britain, it is worth
looking more closely at some of MAT's decisions. For though they cannot, supposedly, break the law of the land, some of their judgements
certainly run counter to secular equalities legislation.

For example, in the six cases of domestic violence heard by the courts
in their first twelve months of operation, the ruling was that the abus-
ers should undergo anger management classes! It is noteworthy that all
the women withdrew their complaints to the police – an outcome that
is viewed as positive by the MAT because 'marriages were saved and
couples given a second chance' (Siddiqui, cited in Taher, 2008). And
while this interpretation is not surprising, given Islamic attitudes to
divorce and the emphasis on mediation (Bano, 2010), in cases of violence against women it is extremely dangerous. An example of a different kind of case dealt with by the MAT is that of a disputed inheritance
between three women and two men in which – and in accordance with
shar'ia law – the latter were awarded twice as much as the former.

One of the main justifications of religious courts is that they are voluntary, though the concept of choice can be questioned in cultures
where there are (particularly) large disparities in the power of men and
women and in which women are socialised into accepting a subordin-
ate role (Okin, 1997; Bhatty, 1998; Bhopal, 1999; Bhatti, 2007; Macey,
2007a; 2009). This is not to deny diversity in minority communities

or in interpretations of *shar'ia* law; nor is it to deny women agency. However, it *is* to suggest that the outcomes of the tribunals cited above make it difficult to see any logical reason why women would *choose* to be judged under religious rather than secular law. It is important here to distinguish clearly between arbitration tribunals and councils, for a study of the latter found that women using their mediation services had done so freely, that is without pressure from male family members (Shah-Kazemi, 2001). Bano (2010) observes that councils can help women who are having difficulty in obtaining divorces, though she criticises their emphasis on mediation – structured as it is by the centrality of gender relations, the stress on reconciliation as a moral duty, and the religious obligation to preserve the sanctity of the family.

All this raises some important issues in relation to (gender) equality, but before examining the effects of religious doctrine and tradition on this, we look at some examples of secular social policy that have been developed in response to pressure from religious groups.

Religion, social policy and practice

As with the law, a number of the changes that have been made to British social policy and practice are indicative of acceptance of the multi-faith nature of society, and similar comments apply here as to the law. In addition, a number of the examples of multicultural policy and practice given in the previous chapter are relevant to religion as well as ethnicity, but will not be discussed here.

As with earlier multicultural and anti-racist initiatives, much of the current concern with cohesion centres on schools. At one level, this is not surprising since from a sociological point of view education has always been used by the state to both maintain *and* change the social system. At a different level, various interest groups – of, for example, class or religion – look to the education system to maintain, or improve, *their* interests (and sometimes survival). This supports Flint's comment that 'schools are sites where wider social, economic and cultural forces play out rather than schools themselves being the sole, or even primary drivers of these forces' (2009: 177). However, it can be suggested that never before have schools been faced with as many conflicting ideological demands as they are today. On the one hand, competition and educational attainment are emphasised (measured by standardised attainment tests and examination results that are published in national league tables to which funding is tied). On the other hand, the education system operates within a multicultural framework within which diversity is valorised and the promotion of cohesion is a legal requirement. And within this complex, inequality of educational outcomes by social class (with which race, ethnicity and religion are linked) remains as stubbornly resistant to change as ever.

It is in this context that schools are faced with demands for change to take account of religious sensibilities (though we would suggest that some of these are more clearly grounded in culture, rather than religion). These demands include the provision of single-sex secondary schools; government-funded faith schools; separate lessons for boys and girls in some subjects within mixed schools; the provision of *halal* food; exemption from sex education and religious lessons and assemblies, and exemption from uniform requirements for girls.

Britain has accommodated some of these demands through formal policy (as with the right of parents to withdraw their children from religious education lessons and assemblies), but more commonly, it has operated pragmatically – quietly making changes in practice. In areas with large Muslim populations, for example, local education authorities frequently provide separate secondary schools for boys and girls, and *halal* food. Notwithstanding schools' efforts to accommodate religious diversity, some research found widespread support among Muslim parents for Islamic secondary schools (Bristol City Council/MORI, 2004), and there are a number of areas of conflict that have been 'settled' only through the legal system, and some that remain unresolved. An example of the former is the demand that Muslim girls be exempt from school uniform requirements, to which British schools generally responded by modifying their uniform requirements so that girls could, for instance, wear trousers instead of/in addition to skirts. Most schools have also allowed the *hijab* (or scarf) to be worn, but have drawn the line at the *niqab*, *jilbab* or *burqa* on both health and safety and pedagogical grounds – the former because they prevent recognition; the latter because they interfere with the teaching/learning process. This has resulted in a number of court (including high court) cases which we will not detail here, other than to say that the courts have supported the schools' ruling on staff as well as student dress. Lack of space prevents further discussion of the complexities involved in, and diverse opinions on, the issue of female dress, as became clear when the French government banned 'conspicuous' religious symbols in schools (but see Hoodfar, 1993, El-Solh and Mabro, 1994, Moghadam, 1994, Bullock, 2002, Ruby, 2004, Hamdan, 2007, Macey, 2007a, 2009, and Macey et al., 2010).

If the issue of school uniform is a bone of religious contention, it pales into insignificance relative to that of separate faith schools, where the debate is frequently coloured more by strong feeling than empirical evidence. This is particularly the case since the New Labour government's reiteration of its commitment to faith schools in 2007, citing historic reasons for a 'dual' system of education and arguing that parents have the right to choose schools in accordance with their religious beliefs (DCSF, 2007a). The ECHR also gives parents the right to an education for their child 'in conformity with their own religious and philosophical convictions', while British equalities legislation affording equal weight to religious and non-religious beliefs has added to the complexity, as has the duty placed on schools to promote cohesion, which Zolberg and Long (1999) suggest is a source of potential conflict with the inherently exclusive nature of religious affiliation. It will be interesting to see how this issue plays out with the Coalition government's stated intention to encourage groups of parents to establish their own state-funded schools.

The subject of separate faith schools generates a number of claims and counter-claims that can only be touched on here, many demonstrating the dominance of multicultural and cohesion thinking. These debates have gone on in Europe for centuries (MacCulloch, 2003), illustrating concerns about the relationship between civil society and religion and the divisive potential of the latter. In Britain, they have been given a new impetus in recent times by Muslim demands for parity of treatment with Christians and Jews in the funding of separate faith schools. We suspect that some of the anxieties expressed rest on stereotypes of Islam and Muslims, but they also reflect concerns about the link between ethno-religious separation and violence, with sectarianism in Northern Ireland and Scotland, and ethnic rioting in England providing ready examples. The growth in the number of Evangelical (fundamentalist) Christian schools and, for example, their alleged teaching of creationism *instead of* evolutionary theory (Randerson, 2006) is a further source of concern. This might be defended on multicultural grounds, or even on grounds of equality of religion or belief.

Judge (2001; 2002) raises one of the most basic questions about faith schools in asking whether, in a society already divided on the bases of ethnicity and religion, the government should be contributing to the funding of faith-based schools at all. This appears to assume, however, that faith schools are divisive, which is by no means clear. The composition of Christian schools is more diverse than that of non-denominational ones (T. Phillips, 2006). This is because they draw from wider residential catchment areas and also because they attract a number of minority religious children, perhaps because they are generally academically successful (Judge, 2001; Allen and West, 2007; Butler and Hamnett, 2007) and are seen to have high levels of discipline and good standards of behaviour (Flint, 2007). Despite this, some accuse faith schools of failing to teach tolerance (Valins, 2003; Meer, 2007), though others argue that their ethos and practice promote both tolerance of ethnic diversity and respect for other religions (Miller, 2001; Grace, 2003; Association of Muslim Social Scientists, 2004; Billings and Holden, 2007).

Other aspects of the operation of faith schools have also been criticised. Frean (2007) says that some minority religious schools operate more stringent admissions policies than their Christian counterparts – which means that they prioritise their own religion. Valins (2003) suggests that some Orthodox Jewish schools aim to preserve a distinctive way of life by 'fixing' children's religious, cultural and social identities; he also notes that though academic standards are of key importance to parents, so, too, is a Jewish ethos. Pennell et al. (2007) accuse both Christian and Jewish schools of selecting pupils on the basis of socio-economic status and conclude that if community cohesion is to be achieved, all schools need to be inclusive of all religions and none.

Some of these criticisms are rather peculiar. For example, surely the prioritisation of children of the religion involved is a logical consequence of the very existence of faith schools? It may also be parental choice, rather than selection bias, that skews intake profiles. Similar comments apply to the transmission of a distinctive way of life in Orthodox Jewish schools, in that this is surely what they were established to do, and what parents opt for in choosing such schools. And social class bias in selection procedures is hardly surprising in a 'market place' context demanding academic success (Grace, 2002), though here again, it may be parental choice, rather than school policy, that is the driving force.

Arguably, however, it is Pennell et al.'s comment on the need for all schools to be inclusive of all religions and none that illustrates some of the confusions in the discussion surrounding faith schools. Since the whole purpose of faith schools is to provide education with a religious ethos, a point will presumably come at which demands for 'inclusiveness' render the concept of 'faith' schools meaningless. And since the facts of residential separation by social class, race and/or ethnicity mean that no schools in Britain are, or ever have been, truly inclusive, on what basis are faith schools any different from non-denominational schools? This raises deeper issues about how, or whether, education can be used in the search for social cohesion.

Religious inequality, discrimination and oppression

In this section, we look at some examples of discrimination practised by religions themselves and the inequality and even oppression that this can inflict on both adherents of the faith and those outside it. We have chosen to limit our discussion to gender and sexuality because in all religions it is women and homosexuals – lesbian, gay, bisexual and transsexual (LGBT) people – who are the principal victims of oppression. Two issues, which we cannot develop fully here, involve the denial of legitimacy by mainstream religions to particular denominations/interpretations of faith, and the negative responses to individuals' desire to leave a religion. Examples of the former are Judaism's rejection of Messianic Jews (Kollontai, 2004) and Islam's rejection of Ahmadis. An example of the latter comes from Islam, in which apostasy is so strongly condemned that it carries the death penalty in some parts of the world and has resulted in serious harassment in Britain – including death threats and physical assaults (Meral, 2008).

In focusing next on gender and sexuality, we would stress at the outset that religions reflect most societies across the world (including Britain) in their unequal treatment of women and LGBT people, extending to physical violence. Thus, though religion is certainly used to legitimise homophobia and misogyny, it cannot be said to cause them.

Religiously based inequality – gender

Turner (1991) suggests that the patriarchal nature of the Abrahamic faiths and its permeation of their theologies and practices is at the root of the tension between religion and women's equality. de Ferrari points to the 'persistence of an anthropology that assigns a "special nature" to women' (2000: 25–6), and Lerner observes that a basic gender assumption of patriarchy is that:

> Men and women are essentially different creatures, not only in their biological equipment, but in their needs, capacities and functions. Men and women also differ in the way they were created and in the social function assigned to them by God. (1993: 4)

All religions have clearly defined gender roles which carry prescriptions for behaviour. Brown observes that the concept of 'complementarity' is central to an Islamic understanding of male–female relations as operating in harmony with the skills and natural attributes of men and women. This asserts that biological differences determine how to be a good Muslim, and that society should be ordered for the fulfilment of men's 'regency on earth' (2006: 424). This leads to women being defined *in relation to* men (as daughters, sisters, wives and mothers), rather than as autonomous beings, and it is this aspect of Islam that

Moghissi (2000), Manji (2005) and Hirsi Ali (2006) see as underpinning discrimination against women:

> No amount of twisting and bending can reconcile the Qur'anic injunctions and instructions about women's rights and obligations with the idea of gender equality. Regardless of the interpretation of the Qur'an and the Shar'ia, if the Qur'anic instructions are taken literally, Islamic individuals or societies cannot favour equal rights for women in the family or in certain areas of social life ... The Shar'ia is not compatible with the principles of equality of human beings. (Moghissi, 2000: 140–1)

The particular focus on women is perhaps because their key involvement in reproduction is not only biological but also cultural and religious. As the bearers and principal socialisers of children, it is important that women remain sexually and religiously 'pure', and men sometimes go to extreme lengths to 'police' women's appearance and behaviour, as noted in relation to Islam in Britain (Afshar, 1989; Alibhai-Brown, 1998; Scott, 2003). This extends to physical violence, including murder – euphemistically termed 'honour' killing (Afshar, 1994; Macey, 2007a; 2008; Meeto and Mirza, 2007; HAC, 2008). The concept of *izzat* (honour) is deeply rooted in cultures in which 'purity' is central and can determine economic as well as social status (Khanum, 1992; Bhatty, 1998; Moghissi, 2005; Bhatti, 2007). In such cultures it is women who carry responsibility for the honour of the entire family, so that 'any transgression denotes a failure, not only of the women, but also and particularly of their menfolk and hence the entire family' (Afshar, 1994: 134). And this is where religion comes into play, as noted by a participant in the government-funded consultation with Muslim women in England: 'Men in all societies may control women, however they don't use religion as a justification, the way it is wrongly used by Muslim men within the community' (cited in Raz, 2006: 49).

Religions other than Islam also seek to control female sexuality, sometimes in the process constructing boundaries between themselves and wider society (see Aune and Sharma, 2007, on a white Evangelical community in Britain and Hunt and Lightly, 2001, and Hunt, 2002, on a black Pentecostal church). This raises questions about religion and cohesion, particularly in the light of the government's re-turn to religion as a means of involving 'hard to reach' communities in regeneration and other community and voluntary sector (CVS) activities (Farnell et al.,

2003). The role of religion in gender inequality is not restricted to sexuality, but, as noted above, permeates all aspects of all religions, from the formal (doctrinal) to what Glick and Fiske (2001) term 'benign sexism'. An example of the former is the Catholic Church's prohibition on women becoming priests, Orthodox (but not Reform) Judaism's ban on female rabbis, and Islam's insistence that imams are male (though this is not universal). Even the Anglican Church, which admits women to the priesthood, did not allow them to become bishops until 2008. And the issue of women priests remains such a major source of conflict within the wider Anglican Communion that Sani and Reicher (2000) and Crockett and Voas (2003) talk of the danger of schism.

Numerous examples of institutionalised sexism are provided by FBOs. Here, despite the fact that women are over-represented in voluntary work, they are rarely found in positions of leadership or decision-making, a situation summarised by a senior national community development professional who said: 'The activity that is faith based is also in our view misogynist' (in Farnell et al., 2003: 34). Another example from the same research is the response of the committee member of a Hindu temple to a question about the involvement of women in running the temple: 'Every day women look after the kitchen very well, and wherever there is need, they are there. General maintenance, cleaning and hoovering' (in Farnell et al., 2003: 34). While superficially humorous, this comment is deeply revealing of the extent to which taken-for-granted assumptions about women's roles permeate thinking – both men's and women's. This may go some way towards explaining not only women's lack of advancement but also their involvement in the oppression of other women (through, for example, FGM and forced marriage). It also raises concerns about the potential impact of the practice of subcontracting public services to FBOs (British Humanist Association, 2007).

Our focus so far in this section has been on the public arena, but it can be argued that it is in the private sphere of home and family life (marriage, children, divorce) that gendered inequality, discrimination and oppression have most impact on women's lives. Yet family law is seen by multiculturalists as the most appropriate arena in which to allow religious freedom and self-governance (see Nussbaum, 1999; 2000, Shachar, 1998; 1999; 2001, and Deveaux, 2000; 2002, for a discussion of the potential impact of this on women). And it is here that multiculturalism's ceding of community control to male 'leaders' (Patel, 1998) is so significant and where a faith-based approach reinforces unequal gender and other power relationships within minority communities.

A consultation with Muslim women held in Bolton, Lancashire, high-lighted their under-representation in the public sphere, and difficulties of childcare, transport and poverty. The problems posed by male 'gate-keepers' to the community were also aired (Woolaston, 2008). Brittain et al. (2005) observe that minority women have no effective political representation and no power to challenge the hegemony of the religious establishment. This is why Patel and Siddiqui (2010) stress that secular spaces are a necessary precondition for women's struggles for freedom in the personal and public spheres. They also make two further points that are worthy of note: the first relates to the links between 'moder-ates' and 'extremists'; the second raises the question of the impact on wider society of what goes on in 'faith' communities. An example of the former is the establishment of Muslim Arbitration Tribunals and their introduction of *shar'ia* law into Britain, which Patel and Siddiqui say are 'doubly dangerous' because they are supported by highly influential liberal establishment figures such as the Archbishop of Canterbury and Lord Justice Phillips:

> In the rush to be tolerant or sensitive to religious differences, they create the space for the most reactionary and even fundamentalist religious leaders to take control of minority communities. (Patel and Siddiqui, 2010: 120)

An example of the second point relates to the potential impact of a faith-based approach on cohesion and is summed up in the comment:

> The struggle for community representation... has largely been won by predominantly fundamentalist and conservative male dominated groups who usually have exclusionary if not extremist political agen-das. It is precisely these groups that have become more prominent under the new 'faith'-based approach. (Patel and Siddiqui, 2010: 105)

We now look briefly at a number of issues in the private arena which can usefully be assessed in light of (a) their tension/conflict with con-temporary civil law and wider social attitudes, and (b) Barry's con-tention that when the state turns a blind eye to private coercion, this brings about much the same result as if it had formally delegated legal decision-making power, so that 'Public tolerance is a formula for creat-ing a lot of private hells' (2001: 143).

Perhaps the most fundamental of Barry's 'private hells' relates to not having a choice to remain single and/or not having a choice of marriage partner. For while all religions see heterosexual marriage as the only acceptable way of expressing sexuality, some – such as Islam and Judaism – see it as the only 'natural' way of living, and in Islam marriage is virtually a requirement for becoming a 'full' Muslim. It is this, together with an extreme emphasis on chastity outside marriage, that underpins pressures towards early marriages, which are permissible from puberty in Islam and have certainly taken place at very young ages between British and Pakistani citizens (FMU, in HAC, 2008). The centrality of marriage in Islam may influence the forced marriages of people with mental disabilities (Brandon and Hafez, 2008; Khanum, 2008). It may also be linked to the belief in some Muslim communities that marriage can cure both disabilities (Channabasavanna et al., 1985; O'Hara, 2003) and sexual 'deviance' (Yip, 2004; Raz, 2006).

'Mixed' marriages, that is between members of different faiths and none, are generally disapproved of by most religions, though the extent and expression of this varies. Orthodox Judaism refuses to accept the validity of marriage outside the faith, while Islam regards those between Muslims and non-Muslims as highly transgressive, though it allows men (but not women) to marry 'people of the book', that is Christians and Jews (Al-Yousuf, 2006).

Women (and men) are protected by law from violence within marriage, but the *Qur'an* permits the 'limited physical chastisement' of women (Mather, 1998), and Kapoor and Crossman (1996) comment on the contemporary popularity of the ancient Hindu saying 'A drum, a vessel, a donkey and a woman are all worthy of being beaten.'

A woman's right to refuse sex within marriage is protected by the law against rape, though the 'conjugal exemption' was not repealed in a number of European countries until the 1990s (Romito, 2008). However, secular law is no protection for Muslim women who are expected to be sexually available on demand: 'A wife may not deny herself to her husband' (Kidwai and Huda, 2007: 35). Here, Levitt and Ware's research with religious leaders in the US is illuminating and is summed up by the imam who said that it would be unwise for a woman to refuse sex with her husband since he might then decide to remarry (2006: 35).

Whether to have children, and how many, is influenced by cultural and religious expectations and rulings on contraception, with Catholic, Jewish and Muslim family size being affected by this.

Different cultures and religions have varying attitudes towards divorce, though no religions encourage it. In Britain, the right to divorce is institutionalised, but it remains unacceptable in Catholicism and allowed only through men in Judaism and Islam, though Muslim women can sometimes instigate divorce. Custody of children following divorce is usually awarded to the mother, but in Islam men have the right to custody of children who have been weaned. And while this is unlikely to impress secular courts, the development of *shar'ia* tribunals could impact negatively on women in this sphere. Religious attitudes towards divorce can also place mothers in extreme financial difficulty because in secular law child maintenance is paid not on separation, but on divorce – which is not always available to religious women (Chantler, 2004). In addition, some interpretations of Islam deny alimony payments to women after three months following divorce (Nasir, 1990), which needs to be read in the context of Muslim women having a very low rate of labour market participation (EOC, 2006a,b; Platt, 2007b). All this means that religious women, especially Muslims, are in an extremely vulnerable position in relation to their ability to gain even minimal economic independence (Shachar, 2001), let alone exercise the 'right of exit' so beloved of multiculturalists (Galston, 1995; Kukathas, 1997; Spinner-Halev, 2001). As with child custody decisions, the potential impact of Muslim Arbitration Tribunals on women's ability to leave even violent relationships is a matter of considerable concern.

In all these ways, religion is implicated directly in the maintenance of inequality and the violation of human rights.

Religiously based inequality – sexuality

Much of what we have written about gender inequality and oppression is relevant to sexuality, though considerably less is known about the latter than the former, partly because homosexuality is a relatively recent addition to legality and an even later one to the equalities legislation. This means that there is a serious shortage of statistics with respect to inequality or even violence and hate crime, and that such information as we have is likely to significantly underestimate the actuality of this. However, Stonewall's 1999 national survey of 2,656 LGBT people found that two-thirds of them had been the victim of at least one homophobic incident (National Advisory Group, 1999). And in the twelve months to January 2006 the Metropolitan Police alone recorded 1,359 incidents of homophobic hate crime, but estimate that as much as 90% of such crime goes unreported (Home Office, 2006).

All the world faiths condemn homosexuality, and in limiting the expression of sexuality to heterosexual marriage, all promote heterosexism, which may contribute to homophobia, as over 90% of the respondents in Yip and Keenan's survey of lesbian and gay Christians suggested (Yip, 2002b). And that all the Abrahamic faiths can produce fundamentalist readings of their holy books to support this makes it unsurprising that they are having most difficulty with the sexual orientation element of equalities legislation, though the extent of this varies by religion. In Christian terms, the Anglican and Catholic Churches are probably at opposite ends of the liberal–conservative spectrum, though within the Anglican tradition, the growth of Evangelicals and Pentecostals noted in Chapter 1 is a potential threat to the liberal agenda.

In addition, Crockett and Voas (2003) see the Anglican Church as suffering from a crisis around homosexuality, which in their view mirrors a lack of consensus on sexual morality in British society. They suggest that the general trend towards acceptance of gay sex masks a growing gulf between liberal and conservative views in the population as a whole, involving ideological, gender and generational divisions. Gilliat-Ray (2001) and Yip and Keenan (2004) agree that there is a crisis around homosexuality, locating this in the international context and noting the potential influence of non-European members of the Anglican Communion. For instance, 17.5 million Anglicans are Nigerian, a country strongly influenced by non-liberal attitudes towards homosexuality, and similar considerations apply to the Catholic Church, in which liberal priests and laity have concerns about the traditional orientation of the Nigerian church hierarchy (Utti, 2006). And in the context of international migration and settlement, these global features of religion impact on the local, as is illustrated by the growth of black Pentecostal churches in Britain.

While the above seems to support Crockett and Voas' warning to avoid 'the liberal temptation to suppose that homosexuality is now condemned by only a small minority' (2003: 3.2), there are individuals and groups whose voices support a more optimistic interpretation of the current state of play. For example, Stonewall's survey of nearly 3,000 people, far from supporting the suggestion that Christians are prejudiced against lesbians and gay men, found that the vast majority want to see all forms of homophobia stopped (by law where appropriate) and – despite religious teaching – do not believe that homosexuality is always wrong (strikingly, the *lowest* indicator of support for LGBT rights was 84%) (Cowan, 2007). And no less a figure than the South African Archbishop (Emeritus) Desmond Tutu has accused the Church of having an 'obsession' with gay priests, saying that the Gospel message is being undermined by 'extreme homophobia':

> God must be weeping looking at some of the atrocities that we commit against one another. In the face of all of that, our Church,

especially the Anglican Church, at this time is almost obsessed with questions of human sexuality. (2007)

However, Yip's 1998 survey of LGB Christians in Britain showed their growing confidence to challenge the Church on both its theology and practice (Yip, 2002b), so that any temptation by the Anglican Church to retreat from a liberal stance on sexual orientation would be vigorously challenged.

As far as practice is concerned, while some research suggests that religious organisations and individuals discriminate against LGBT people, the majority of it is *ad hoc*, rather than systematic. It also has to be remembered here that religions are exempt from some aspects of the law prohibiting discrimination on the grounds of sexuality. Nevertheless, ACAS reports that between January 2004 and September 2006, 470 cases were brought which alleged discrimination on the grounds of sexuality (Savage, 2007). Information is not provided on the track record of religious organisations relative to secular ones with respect to sexual orientation, though there have been accusations that religious organisations are abusing the legislation (see Stonewall, 2010).

There is clearer evidence with respect to schools, where 30%–50% of children report homophobic bullying, compared with 10%–20% who experience 'normal' bullying (House of Commons Education and Skills Committee, 2007; see also Stonewall/DfCSF, 2007). Hunt and Jensen (2006) cite a figure of 65% of children experiencing homophobic bullying but say that this rises to 75% in faith schools, where victims were less likely to report it and teachers were implicated by both commission and omission: 'It's a Catholic school...we are told "gay people will go to hell because the Bible condemns it"...It's horrid, you just want to go and cry at some of the remarks made by teachers. It's just not fair' (cited in Hunt and Jensen, 2006: 10). And 62% of children who reported homophobic bullying to teachers said that it was ignored and that 50% of teachers do not respond when they hear homophobic language. Commenting on this research, Hartnell – who experienced extreme homophobic bullying at a school run by Benedictine monks – says that this means that 143,000 secondary school pupils suffer name-calling; 64,000 are physically attacked and 26,000 experience death threats. He notes that teachers often join in the 'joke', or ignore incidents: 'Ears all too often turn deaf; eyes turn blind' (Hartnell, 2007). The figures given in these sources are extremely high, and if they truly reflect the scale of the problem, they must give rise to very serious concerns.

Another example of religiously based homophobia comes from Hicks' analysis of the writings of a Christian organisation on lesbian and gay parenting, which he, says, construct homosexuality as diseased and dangerous to produce a 'Christian homophobic discourse' that is part of a broader anti-gay agenda being promoted by some British and US Christians (2003: 1.1, 1.2). Though Hicks' work refers to a specific organisation that would generally be viewed as fundamentalist, it is not only such groups that are opposed to 'same-sex' child adoption placements. Other faith-based charities hold similar views which are rooted in deeply held religious convictions. For example, the Catholic Children's Rescue Society stopped providing adoption services, rather than conform to the requirements of such legislation as the 2007 Equality Act (Sexual Orientation). This matter is by no means resolved, since Catholic Care has recently won its high court appeal against being required to consider same-sex couples for adoption (Pitcher, 2010). Whatever one's views on this, it is a clear illustration of the inevitability of conflict in some spheres of the religion and belief legislation, for when 'man-made' laws are seen as being in opposition to God's law, many believers will feel that they have no option but to oppose the former.

It should be noted, however, that the sphere of sexuality provides clear examples of the diversity that exists *between individuals* and *within religions* and illustrates people's capacity for negotiating religious prohibitions. For despite the ban on homosexuality by all the major world faiths, lesbian and gay people who subscribe to a religious belief find ways of negotiating their identities in relation to religious doctrine, the public and the private, and – in the case of South Asian Muslims – the intersection between culture and religion (Yip, 2002b; 2004). Yip's participants had developed widely varying strategies for coping with the dissonance between their sexuality and Islamic teaching, and the demands of family, community and mosque. These sometimes differed by context and often involved drawing on both their own and Western cultural traditions (Bose, 2000; Roald, 2001). Thus, despite the power of religious doctrine *and* cultural ideology to structure both attitudes and actions, individuals retain the ability to resist these and to negotiate, instead, their own definitions of reality. And this applies even when they are forced into marriage to 'cure' their (Western acquired) 'deviance' (though there are clear gender differences here).

The problem with religion

The most basic problem with religion in relation to the current equalities agenda arises from a number of examples discussed above. This concerns the question of what happens when secular and religious laws are in conflict – a dilemma that is clearly articulated in Fredman's comment that:

> An individual's religious values cannot be overridden by a mere assertion of dominant values. However, religion cannot in itself be used to justify an infringement of the equal rights and dignity of others, in particular, in respect of women, children or gay, lesbian or bisexual people. (2002b: iv)

Thus far, in the relatively short time that the Religion and Belief legislation has been operative in Britain, what has happened has been a typical British 'fudge' insofar as religions have been granted certain temporary exemptions from the law. However, short of God announcing a change of mind (simultaneously to all the world faiths and branches thereof), it is difficult to see how the contradictions inherent in such an approach can be maintained.

This highlights a more fundamental problem, which is that historically, the liberal solution to religious conflict was to locate religion in the private sphere; now we are confronted by the multicultural proposal to bring it back into the public arena. But the research we have reviewed in this chapter suggests that this exacerbates conflict because it forces a direct confrontation between strongly held transcendental beliefs which are in contradiction with each other *and* the law of the land.

Jurgen Habermas (2010) has challenged secular reason to clarify its relation to religious experience and to engage religions in a constructive dialogue because, he suggests, nothing is more dangerous than the refusal to communicate that we are seeing today in various forms of religious and ideological fundamentalism. But, far from buying into multiculturalism, Habermas imposes two liberal democratic conditions on this dialogue: (1) religion must accept the authority of secular reason as the fallible results of the sciences and the universal egalitarianism in law and morality, and (2) secular reason must not set itself up as the judge of the truths of faith. We argue in the final chapter that these two principles provide useful guidance for the place of religion in diverse societies.

6
Towards Equality of Religion or Belief

The changing landscape of religion or belief

The landscape of religion is changing in Britain in ways that are reasonably clear, even if the details of the process often cry out for further investigation. There has been a continuing movement of secularisation, with declining observance in organised (mainly Christian) religions, and an accompanying shift 'from forms of religion that are imposed or inherited to forms of religion that are primarily chosen' (Davie, 2005: 281). Davie regards this shift 'from obligation to consumption' as characteristic of Northern Europe as a whole, and not just the UK. These processes have left a situation in which those who practise religion actively make up a small minority of the population – no more than 20% in Britain, even on the most generous assumptions about what counts as practice of the Christian religion. The majority of the population occupy a variety of different positions within an alternative spectrum of spiritual, agnostic and secular belief that has very little connection with any organised religion, at the levels of either (accepted) religious practice or (conventional) religious belief. Although Stark and Finke have claimed that 'it seems time to carry the secularization doctrine to the graveyard of failed theories', their obituary notice is premature, since secularisation is alive and well in nearly all developed countries (2000: 79, cited in Norris and Inglehart, 2007: 32).

At the same time, and in a contrary movement, there has been a reassertion of religion in several different areas. First, immigration and settlement over the past half-century has markedly extended the range of religions practised by significant numbers within Britain, and created distinctive minority ethno-religious communities in particular parts of the country (especially London and a relatively small number of English provincial towns and cities). As a result of this process, Britain is and will remain a multi-faith society, as well as being a multicultural society, characterised by a huge variety of racial and ethnic groups. Second, there has been a revival of Christian practice in specific localities and forms, sometimes relating to particular ethnic groups, and especially involving Evangelical branches of Christianity such as Pentecostalism. These (re)assertions of a religious presence are not, however, taking place on a scale that challenges the overall tendencies away from organised religion within the population at large. Indeed, the growth in Evangelical Christianity is in part a reflection of Davie's shift from obligation to choice in the forms of religious observance. We can suggest overall that whilst the everyday religious landscape has continued to flatten out, it has also become punctuated by a number of relatively isolated yet dramatic peaks.

In addition, there has been an upsurge of interest in (and concerns regarding) the claims of religion and religious identity across the whole range of cultural and political institutions, from the media and academic research through government, politics and law. The appearance of a spate of works making root-and-branch attacks on religion from an Atheist standpoint has paid a backhanded compliment to this new place of religion in the discourse of public life (Grayling, 2004; Dawkins, 2006; Dennett, 2006; Harris, 2006; Hitchens, 2007). Speaking very broadly, religion has become politicised over the recent past, in a process that has often responded to national and international incidents – especially terrorist attacks that have been religiously inspired – and to broader international conflicts, including the wars joined by Britain in both Afghanistan and Iraq, and the continuing conflict in the Middle East.

The result of these developments, taken together, is thus a striking *disjunction* between the place of organised religion in the spheres of politics, culture and the law, and its place in people's lives. Whilst this book is concerned primarily with issues of religious inequality and religious injustice, it is this background that creates much of the interest (and difficulty) in its subject matter. Given the assumptions that have dominated the national conversation about religion and equality, it is a moot point how much the heightened public discussion has advanced constructive or viable solutions to the problems of 'religion and society'.

Religious inequality

We have been concerned with religious inequality and injustice mainly in relation to the minority (non-Christian) religions, and the factual picture is reasonably clear in basic outline, though (once again) crying out for further investigation in certain specific respects.

Religious inequalities persist on a number of different dimensions of social wealth and well-being, including education, economic participation, socio-economic status (social class), housing conditions, and health and disability. On the one hand, these findings show that 'religion makes a difference' to social position in Britain, so that 'religion' should normally be included as an independent variable in empirical research. On the other hand, the social effects of religious identity are usually combined with other aspects of social identity, especially ethnicity, race, gender, disability and/or social class. It might be said that what makes the difference in social terms is not religious identity per se, but 'religion plus' identities.

This combination of factors makes for a fascinating (and quite complex) picture that is worth summarising briefly here. Quantitative analysis suggests that the causes of social inequality relate both to the external circumstances of the relevant groups in the British context and to the internal characteristics of groups, including skills, economic resources and a range of cultural and social factors. These are often tied to specific histories and trajectories of migration. Some particular groups emerge consistently as the most disadvantaged, especially Pakistani and Bangladeshi Muslims, and to a slightly lesser extent, Sikhs. This does not apply to all Muslim groups, however, since Indian Muslims tend to be placed in a better position than other Muslims. Nor is minority religious status always associated with social disadvantage, because Jewish and Buddhist groups in particular are placed above the average on a number of indicators. There is a general pattern of findings in which the operative social entities appear to be hyphen-groups which combine ethnic and religious identity (such as Indian Muslims, for example). At the same time, the (relatively positive) experiences of Jewish and Buddhist groups, considered alongside the (relatively negative) experiences of groups such as black Christians, suggest that racial factors may play an important role, rather than religious factors per se. It appears necessary to bear in mind the influence of a communal identity that combines racial with ethnic and religious elements, and not to allow the new focus on religion and culture to overshadow the continued importance of race. We have drawn attention to the combined 'RER' identity with this point in mind.

However, the connection of religious identity with other facets of social identity does not end at this point. The pattern of findings on some indicators such as housing conditions and long-term health suggests that religious inequalities can be caused by social class differences, which are correlated with religious identity. The incidence of disability in some of the poorest ethno-religious groups raises concerns about the role of ethnic and religious cultures on this dimension of inequality. And the findings suggest that it is very difficult to consider the unequal position of women in some ethno-religious communities apart from their gender identities. Thus, the employment profiles of Pakistani and Bangladeshi Muslim women are very sharply distinct from those of Pakistani and Bangladeshi Muslim men and from those of women of other ethnic or religious groups, including Indian women. Here, it is ethnicity *and* religion *and* gender (and possibly race also) that makes the difference. And these findings from quantitative work about the importance of gender are strongly reinforced by the discussion of cultural and religious factors in the previous chapter.

This complex picture has important implications for policy. It means on the one hand that the reduction of religious inequality needs to be addressed by a large range of different measures, relating to education and the provision of skills, and the reduction of poverty. On the other hand, it is not obvious that measures that are related to religious identity per se will make the required difference, since it may be factors relating to gender, or race, or ethnicity (as distinct from religion) that are responsible for the religious inequalities observed. This implies that one might go a long way towards ameliorating religious inequality with very little reference to religious identity. How far this is true will depend in part on the extent of religious injustice, which forms the next part of the story.

Religious injustice

There are a number of areas in which justice issues arise in relation to religion. First, there are the unjust harms that members of minority religions experience in civil society or at the hands of the state as a result of their religious identity. The main evidence suggests that religious discrimination – especially against Muslims – is commonly believed to be widespread in Britain, whereas the actual incidence of discrimination is much less frequent than it is generally believed to be. This gap between the *perception* and the (self-reported) *experience* of religious injustice is a striking feature of the contemporary scene. It applies not only to Muslims in Britain, but (in slightly different ways) to Catholics in Scotland (see Chapter 3, and Bruce et al., 2005). This implies that the elimination of religious discrimination, which is now backed by law, will have less effect on the reduction of inequality than is commonly anticipated. This reinforces the point made at the end of the previous section.

The evidence regarding hate crime is strongest in relation to anti-semitic attacks, thanks to the work of the CST. In addition, there are reports giving rise to concern about attacks directed against individuals identified as Muslim, especially women, but these are not backed by the same quality of investigation. It is noteworthy, nevertheless, that, whilst the level of such attacks responds to national or international incidents, there is little evidence of an increasing trend.

It is remarkable that there is almost no comprehensive or systematic work on the topic of Islamophobia, despite the fact that this concept has dominated recent debate on issues of religion and justice. There has been a steady increase in the media coverage of Muslims and Islam over the past decade, which is perhaps not surprising, given the participation of Muslims in terrorist attacks. Much of this coverage has been negative, again unsurprisingly, but it is reassuring that there has not been a deterioration in the general social attitude towards Muslims over the same period, with only a minority (of around 20%) expressing an unfavourable attitude towards Islam and Muslims. Overall, this aspect of the justice issue does not present as gloomy a picture as it is commonly believed to do, and the areas of main concern are now covered by law. As Malik (2005b) contends, the negative effects of Islamophobia may arise from the belief in it among Muslims, with a corresponding sense of victimhood, as much as from the experience of Islamophobia itself within social relationships.

Second, there is another side to the issue of religion and justice, which concerns the commission of injustice by religious groups, FBOs or iso-lated individuals acting in the name of religion. Religiously motivated violence by Muslims falls into this category, but the category is much broader. It includes attempts at the suppression of free speech, and the effects of religion in either shielding or endorsing violations of the principles of equality and human rights. One issue here involves the exemptions to the equality laws, which have the effect of permitting (what would otherwise be) discrimination on the grounds of gender and sexual orientation especially.

Our conclusion is that a balanced perspective on religion and justice must take account of both sides of the justice issue. We reject the posi-tion that there is a hierarchy of oppressions, in which the elimination of one form of injustice takes precedence over another. We see no con-tradiction in arguing for the elimination of religious discrimination and religious hate crime on the one hand and arguing at the same time for the elimination of human rights abuses that are connected directly or indirectly with religion or culture. Injustice is injustice, wherever it appears.

The impact of ideology

In the course of reaching these conclusions, we have had to wrestle with, and struggle through, a large body of literature that generates very different impressions. This discrepancy between the evidence in the field and the received opinions of the ostensible experts became so marked and so striking that we began to sense that something more systematic was at work. We began to see that (and how) a prevailing ideology exerts a profound effect on the way that issues are approached, and policies conceived.

This ideology has two branches. On the one hand, there is what we have called *the ideology of religious injustice*. The hallmark of this branch of the ideology (covered in Chapter 3) is conceptual inflation, whereby concepts with normative implications are stretched beyond their appropriate range of application. Examples of conceptual inflation include the assumptions that all inequality is caused by external factors; that all inequality results from injustice; that hate crimes can be nominated as such by any observer; that anti-religious attitudes (and even 'indifference or ignorance about religion') count as 'cultural and attitudinal discrimination' (Woodhead, 2009: 15); that all unfavourable attitudes constitute prejudice, and that the perception of discrimination is equivalent to the experience of discrimination. 'Islamophobia' participates in this ideology through the implication that opposition to a particular religion is a type of mental illness.

The other branch of the ideology is connected with 'multiculturalism', which is the dominant approach to the question of diversity within a multicultural society, and as a result has obvious implications for the question of religious diversity (see Chapter 4). The leading characteristics of multicultural ideology are racialisation and essentialism; the prioritisation of culture and identity; the prioritisation of the group over the individual, and cultural relativism. Multicultural ideology cannot be understood simply as a response to cultural and religious diversity, but needs to be seen against the background of the 'subjectivist turn' within Western culture more generally, linked especially to the rise of postmodernism, and the emphasis on an identity politics of recognition, at the expense of a material politics of distribution. The emphasis on subjectivity in both branches of the ideology has given us the subtitle of our book.

The combined effect of these two ideologies can be traced both at the level of perception and at the level of practice. The cognitive effect of the ideology of religious injustice is to 'turn up the volume' on the state/civil society side of the justice issue, and to exaggerate the incidence of injustice experienced by members of minority religions. This is accompanied sometimes by deliberate exaggeration, such as we have documented in relation to the MCB. The practical effect of the ideology is to strengthen the argument for the recognition of religious injustice by government and in law. The most remarkable example of the influence of this ideology is that the law was extended to religion or belief in Britain in the absence of evidence that social wrongs existed on a scale that might justify legislative intervention. Given that religious discrimination could have been addressed by other means, there is even an argument from the Southall Black Sisters, which we will not pursue further here, that calls implicitly for the repeal of this aspect of the law (Patel and Siddiqui, 2010).

The cognitive effect of the multicultural branch of the ideology is to 'turn down the volume' on the community side of the justice issue, which is often, though not exclusively, concerned with the position of women (and LGBT individuals). It does this partly by erecting normative barriers around the community, so that non-members feel unable to concern themselves with anything defined as 'community business', and partly by undermining the basis of cross-cultural judgement through the commitment to cultural relativism. The practical effect of the ideology is to shield activities within the community from external scrutiny. This creates a free (or at least a freer) space in which cultural practices with some religious legitimation can proceed at the expense of equality and/or human rights. It is crucial to note here that consultations with minority religious women tend to bring the latter issues to the fore (as noted in Chapters 4 and 5), and that the women concerned express astonishment (and anger) that the experts seem so reluctant to criticise, and the authorities so reluctant to intervene.

The combined effect of the two ideologies, by turning up the volume in one area and turning it down in another, is to leave an unbalanced impression about the two sides of the justice issue: it tends to overplay the injustices experienced by men especially in civil society and downplay the injustices experienced by women (and LGBT individuals), either in civil society or in community life. This conclusion relates to a straightforward and familiar argument that policy initiatives are unlikely to work effectively if their foundations of analysis involve inaccuracy, systematic misrepresentation or distortion (Miles, 1989). So there is a very general interest in 'seeing through' the effects of this ideology, and in restoring an appropriate balance to the discussion.

Equality of religion or belief

Even though the legislation on religion or belief may have been passed 'before the facts' (as we argued above), the existence of the legislation, coupled with the form that it has taken, may have long-term consequences for the relationship between religious organisations within Britain, and for their relationships with the state. This is because it establishes, in effect, a new model of settlement for religion within the liberal democratic state, which we have called 'equality of religion or belief'. We argued in Chapter 3 that the legislation rested implicitly on three distinct principles of equality, and we are concerned here with the two principles we called *equal advantage of religion or belief* and *strand equality* respectively.

Equal advantage of religion or belief gives equal recognition to all religions and belief systems. It insists only that there is equal recognition but leaves open the level of recognition itself. To give one example, if there are state-funded faith schools which are Christian or Jewish, it offends against the principle if there are no state-funded schools that are Muslim (or Atheist). But the principle can then be honoured either by closing all the Christian and Jewish schools or by opening (a requisite number of suitably funded) Muslim (and Atheist) schools alongside them. Equal advantage does not therefore imply secularism but is consistent with it. The two authors take slightly different positions on this issue, and, perhaps surprisingly, the author who is personally more 'religious' is also more inclined to advocate a secular solution. But we are not embarrassed by this difference, because the principle of equal advantage is consistent with both of our positions.

Strand equality comes into play because the legislation on religion/belief is part of a broader equalities framework, and strand equality insists that religion/belief should take an equal place within that framework.

We do not propose to deal here with all the questions raised by these two principles of religious equality, which draw in a very wide range of historical, philosophical and indeed theological issues. We are nonetheless concerned in the rest of this chapter to take the discussion further than in Chapter 3, and to map out the terrain in a preliminary way, to see where this conception might be leading.

The first point is that 'equality of religion or belief' is intended for deployment within the framework of a liberal democratic state, and a state, moreover, with a long history, a settled population and deep traditions of its own, both religious and secular. It arises in the first instance as a means of accomplishing the social inclusion of minority religions within this context, but it is worth bearing in mind that this requirement applies to a very small minority of the population – of around one in twenty (5%), who will vary in their religious commitments in any case. The principle of equal advantage also addresses the situation of the majority of the British population, who are no longer religious in any conventional sense and yet live under a political system with an established church.

The second point involves the contrasting approaches of equality of religion or belief and multiculturalism towards the classical dilemma of liberal toleration: to what extent can (or should) liberalism/liberal democracy tolerate (let alone actively encourage) groups/communities whose cultures are intolerant and non-democratic? Deveaux asks: 'Are the intolerant to be tolerated?' (2002: 503; and see especially McKinnon, 2006).

Multiculturalists are deeply divided on this question. Kymlicka (1995) says that rights should be denied to cultural or religious groups which overtly discriminate against women. Raz (1994) states that such cultures should only be supported if their oppressive aspects can be neutralised or compensated for. Kymlicka has recently gone further and placed multiculturalism squarely within the framework of equality and human rights:

> the human rights revolution is a two-edged sword. It has created political space for ethnocultural groups to contest inherited hierarchies. But it also requires groups to advance their claims in a very specific language – namely, the language of human rights, civil rights liberalism, and democratic constitutionalism, with their guarantees of gender equality, religious freedom, racial non-discrimination, gay rights, due process and so on. The leaders of minorities can appeal to the ideals of liberal multiculturalism to challenge their historic exclusion and subordination, but those very ideals also impose the duty on them to be just, tolerant, and inclusive. (2007: 92–3)

On Kymlicka's account, there is no contradiction between multiculturalism and equality of religion or belief. Indeed, strand equality is built into the conception, and multiculturalism becomes the name for the extension of the equalities framework to address cultural and religious diversity. But the key point is that the term 'multiculturalism' is qualified by the word 'liberal', and this qualification turns out to be highly significant. For here is Parekh, who has produced a masterpiece of equivocation (and masculine imagery) on this very point:

> The dialogically constituted multicultural society both retains the truth of liberalism and goes beyond it. It is committed to both liberalism and multiculturalism, privileges neither, and moderates the logic of one by that of the other. It neither confines multiculturalism within the limits set by liberalism and suppresses and marginalises non-liberal values and cultures, nor confines liberalism within the limits of multiculturalism and emasculates its critical and emancipatory thrust. (2000b: 340)

Kukathas (1992; 1997; 2001) is a third proponent of multiculturalism, who has argued much less equivocally than Parekh, and directly contrary to Kymlicka, that cultural and religious groups should be left to live by their own norms and values without intervention from the state. And Kukathas (1986) is perhaps the most consistent advocate of an unreconstructed (or perhaps franker) multiculturalism, who comes closest to defending such practices as FGM in the name of cultural difference. Others have argued that liberal democracy is incapable of dealing with the tensions and potential conflicts that accompany cultural and religious diversity (Tully, 1995; Parekh, 2000b; Kelly, 2002). Still others state that it is inappropriate to impose Western liberal democracy on people from non-Western backgrounds who subscribe to different moral systems (Young, 1990; Taylor, 1994; Panniker, 1996; Steiner and Alston, 1996; Herr, 2004; Byrnes, 2005). The more radical of these arguments are undoubtedly influenced by postmodern and feminist critiques of Enlightenment thinking, which have informed the cultural relativist perspective that is central to multiculturalism. There is a general argument, sketched at the end of Chapter 4, that no plausible framework of law or politics for regulating cultural diversity can depend on cultural relativism. So equality of religion or belief is almost certainly at odds both with a wide range of multicultural policy positions and with one of the main features of its underlying ideology.

Thus far, we have compared equality of religion or belief to other positions, but not produced any positive arguments directly in its favour. In what follows, we are not necessarily advocating equality of religion or belief as our own favoured position, but sketching an argument as to how the defence might go.

The case for equality of religion or belief

In general, there are (only) three ways in which differences of religion or belief can be handled: separation, assimilation or accommodation. *(a)*

Separation (at the level of the state) is ruled out by the terms of our problem, which is to create a framework for the regulation of religion within, and for, an existing political system, with a unified jurisdiction. We have expressed concern in Chapter 5 about whether separation is taking place at the local level through the development of minority religious courts, for example, that claim some element of separate jurisdiction over family matters, but this does not affect developments at the level of the state, which are at issue here. And Parekh has made clear that his proposal for 'a community of communities', which might be thought to have separatist implications, does not go so far as to delegate jurisdiction and legal power to distinctive ethno-religious communities within a single state. Parekh is not advocating 'community autonomy' in that sense (although a number of Muslim writers do take this step, by arguing for the introduction of *shar'ia* law for Muslim communities within Britain).

We are left then with the two options of assimilation and accommodation, which are both ways of integrating minority religious or ethnic groups into a liberal democratic state. But assimilation is ruled out of *(b)* court for a variety of different reasons. This was the assumption that underpinned the earlier phases of British government policy towards ethnic (and therefore religious) diversity for much of the 1950s and 1960s. It was always unrealistic to suppose that ethnic, and perhaps especially religious, difference would become progressively attenuated and eventually absorbed into an undifferentiated Britishness. However, the fact that previous groups of settlers (such as Jews and Poles) have maintained their cultures, languages and religions whilst simultaneously integrating into mainstream society raises questions – not least about the public versus private spheres. Nevertheless, the assimilationist (and, indeed, integrationist) approach foundered on the experience of persistent difference from the 1970s onwards, and became increasingly difficult to sustain in the face of a renewed emphasis on cultural identity, and the increasing politicisation of religion, especially among Muslims.

This leaves accommodation (in some form) as the only viable alternative *(c)* for the management of religious diversity. Accommodation is sufficiently multicultural to recognise that religious and cultural difference will persist. It implies, moreover, some form of mutuality or intercommunication across the differences.

Accommodation could come about in a variety of different ways, with a range of different outcomes. If we envisage a process of (implicit or explicit) negotiation between religious groups and state authorities (including the occasional episode of 'bargaining by riot'), the result could involve a wide variety of different 'places within the constitution' for particular religious groups, reflecting national traditions or histories, the relative size of groups and so on. But if we impose a criterion of justice or fairness on the outcome, the range of admissible solutions narrows considerably. The basic contention here is that all groups of religion or belief must be treated equally because there is no good reason to treat any of them differently. This is the essential argument in favour of the principle of equal advantage.

A variety of philosophical considerations might lead to this conclusion. If religious or other worldviews are incommensurable in principle, then this might be the only basis on which to create a framework to contain them all. Or this might simply be a pragmatic response to the difficulties of reaching a workable consensus among the different perspectives on 'religion or belief'. This applies as much to the relationships between Christians and Atheists as it does to the relationships of, say, Muslims with Sikhs. This argument implies that the primary responsibility of the state in this field is not to intervene in any of the controversies surrounding religion or belief, but to stand back from the differences and to hold the ring for diversity. This secures the safety of the space in which cultural exchange – argument, dialogue and the elaboration of new socio-cultural forms – can take place. We should note in this connection that diversity is increased not just when a new religious tradition is added to a national scene, through migration and settlement. It is increased when the blank spaces between the traditions already present within a country are filled in with mixed, or hybrid, cultural forms, combining elements of two or more traditions.

But we can now appreciate the appeal of the two requirements put forward by Habermas and quoted at the end of the previous chapter. The suggestion that secular reason must not set itself up as the judge of the truths of faith creates (or justifies) the social space for different traditions to exist side by side, and to follow their own approaches to the truth; so much is guaranteed by the principle of equal advantage. But the balancing (or countervailing) suggestion is that religion must accept the authority of secular reason in areas such as science, and universal egalitarianism in the spheres of law and morality. And the latter point implies that religions should accede in practice to something like the principle of equality of religion or belief, which is the application of the universal value of impartiality to the issues of religious diversity.

This position leaves many questions open. As we have emphasised above, it leaves open in particular how far the (equal) recognition of religion and belief will extend within the public arena, and how much, if any, formal participation of religion there will be within the institutions of state, or funded by it. At least in principle, it is possible to imagine a range of solutions, from French secularism on the one hand to (an equalised) version of British religious inclusion on the other – a kind of establishment of every faith or belief. There is scope here for an argument about how far it is reasonable to expect the constitution of a democratic state to change in order to accommodate the requirements of a very small percentage of the population, especially when the majority has little connection with organised religion of any kind. A judgement along these lines would weigh in favour of secularism. But the important point is that, unlike the policies of multiculturalism, the principle of equal advantage offers guidance about the general forms of relationship within the state and supplies a significant constraint on their realisation.

There is clear guidance, too, in the matter of strand equality, and the necessary limit placed upon toleration within this framework. Here, we will simply conclude with the position put forward by Fredman, as cited above:

> An individual's religious values cannot be overridden by a mere assertion of dominant values. However, religion cannot in itself be used to justify an infringement on the equal rights and dignity of others, in particular, in respect of women, children or gay, lesbian or bisexual people. (2002b: iv)

Statistical Appendix

All data are derived from the 2001 Census

Tables

Table 1 UK population by self-identified religion or belief

Religion or belief	Number	%
Christian	42,079,417	71.6
No Religion	9,103,727	15.5
Muslim	1,591,126	2.7
Hindu	558,810	1.0
Sikh	336,149	0.6
Jewish	266,740	0.5
Buddhist	151,816	0.3
Other Religion	178,837	0.3
Total religion or belief	54,266,622	92.3
Not stated*	4,522,572	7.7
Total	58,789,194	100.0

* 'Not stated' includes 'No Religion' in Northern Ireland.

Source: Weller, 2004.

Table 2 Followers of 'other religions' by self-identification, England and Wales

Other religion	Number (thousands)
Spiritualism	32
Paganism	31
Jainism	15
Wiccan	7
Rastafarianism	5
Bahaí'ísm	5
Zoroastrianism	4
Other	52
Total	151

Source: ONS, 2004.

Table 3 Minority religious population by socio-economic classification (social class) and gender, England and Wales

	Managerial and professional occupations (%)	Intermediate occupations (%)	Semi-routine and routine occupations (%)
Men			
Jewish	68	26	6
Buddhist	53	31	17
Hindu	50	30	20
Sikh	35	36	29
Muslim	32	34	33
All men	**42**	**34**	**24**
Women			
Jewish	57	31	11
Buddhist	47	29	24
Hindu	38	33	29
Sikh	31	33	36
Muslim	35	33	32
All women	**38**	**33**	**29**

Source: ONS, 2006.

Table 4 Non-Christian religious population, nations of the UK and selected English cities

Place	Non-Christian religious population (thousands)	Proportion of total population (%)
London	1244	17
Birmingham	196	20
Bradford	86	18
Leicester City	86	31
Luton	35	19
Slough	33	28
Blackburn	28	20
England	**2940**	6
Wales	**44**	2
Scotland	**95**	2
Northern Ireland	**5**	<1

Source: ONS, 2003.

Figures

Figure 1 Religion by ethnicity, England and Wales

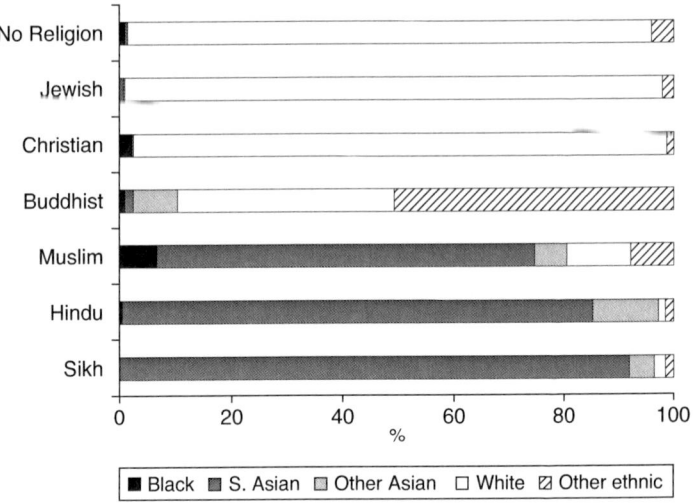

Source: ONS, 2003.

Figure 2 Ethnicity by religion, England and Wales

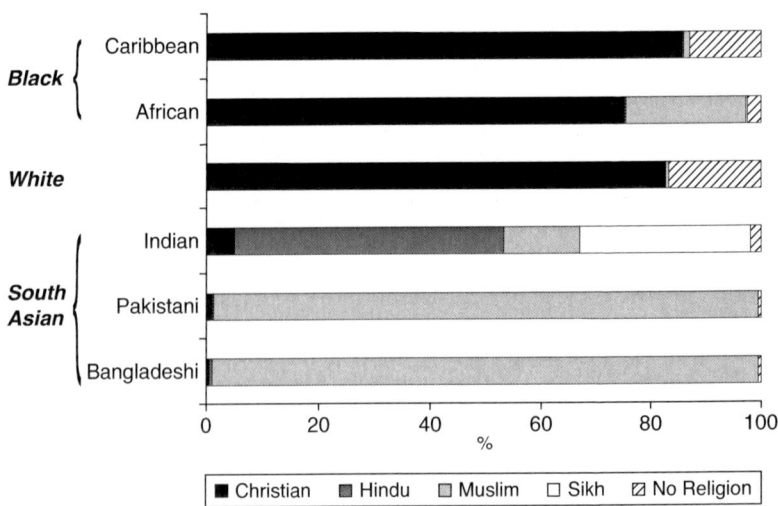

Source: ONS, 2003.

Figure 3 Minority religious population by religion, nations of Britain and selected English cities

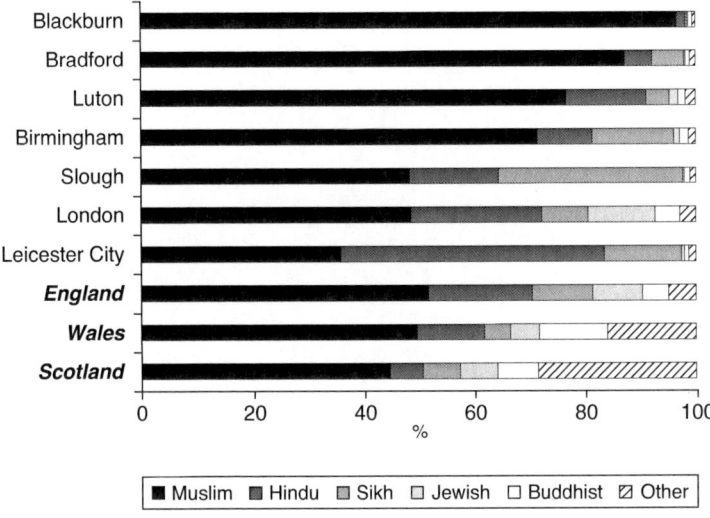

Source: ONS, 2003.

Figure 4 Religion of household reference person by housing tenure, Britain

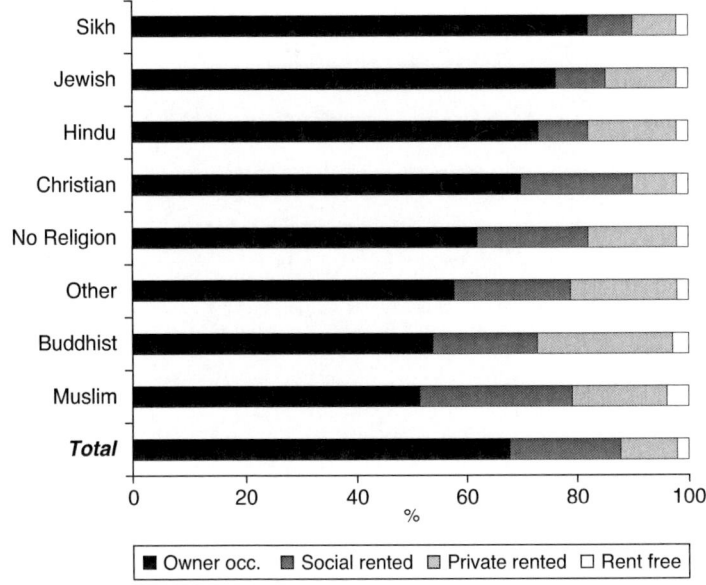

Source: ONS, 2006.

Figure 5   Age-standardised limiting long-term illness or disability by religion and gender, Britain

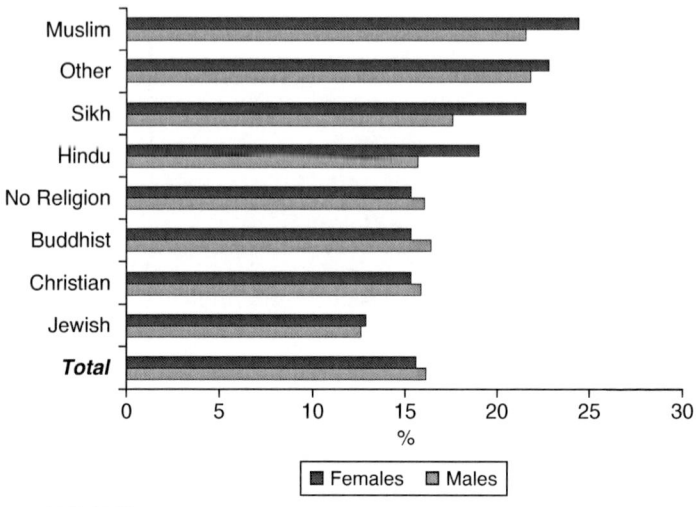

Source: ONS, 2003.

Figure 6   Adults with no listed qualification by age and religious group, Scotland

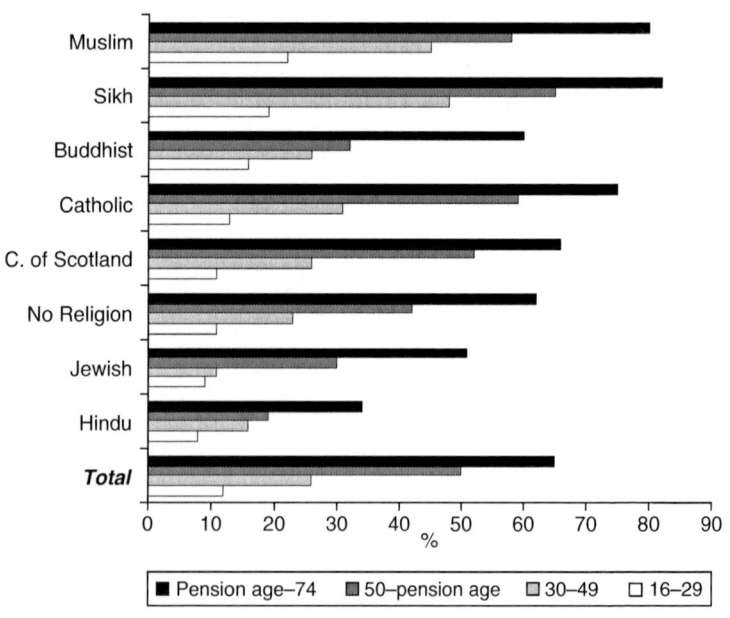

Source: Scottish Executive, 2005.

Notes

1. The term 'caste' is a rather peculiar one to introduce in the British context, given that it is the term for the Indian stratification system and, unlike the Western 'class' system, does not permit mobility. This is because it is rooted in the Hindu belief in reincarnation, which can be used to justify discrimination, based on one's behaviour in a previous incarnation. The Indian constitution has now outlawed such discrimination, but it continues particularly in rural areas. The concept has also found its way into South Asian Muslim usage.
2. Considerable confusion is caused by a tendency in the literature to use the term *hijab* for a wide range of Muslim dress. The *hijab* is a headscarf; the *niqab* is a veil that covers the face below the eyes; the *jilbab* is a full-length loose garment like a coat that is worn over other clothes, and the *burqa* is a garment that covers the woman from head to foot with an opening for the eyes, sometimes covered with mesh.
3. The Forced Marriage Unit is a joint initiative between the Foreign and Commonwealth Office (FCO) and the Home Office which offers advice and help to victims or potential victims of forced marriage. It also advises front-line professionals who might come into contact with cases of forced marriage, produces multi-agency guidelines, information packs and posters, and is involved in rescuing British citizens overseas.
4. Entry visas can be refused when it is suspected that sponsors are 'reluctant', as in forced marriage. However, around a third of the cases that go to appeal are won by appellants, largely because the sponsor is unwilling to make a public statement of her reluctance (Sedwell, Director of UK Visas, in HAC, 2008).

References

Abbas, T. (2002) 'The Home and the School in the Educational Achievements of South Asians', *Race, Ethnicity and Education*, 5 (3): 291–316.

Abbas, T. (2003) 'The Impact of Religio-cultural Norms and Values on the Education of Young South Asian Women', *British Journal of Sociology of Education*, 24 (4): 411–28.

Abbas, T. (2005) 'Recent Developments to British Multicultural Theory, Policy and Practice: The Case of British Muslims', *Citizenship Studies*, 9 (2): 153–66.

Abbas, T. (ed.) (2007) *Islamic Political Radicalism: A European Comparative Perspective*, Edinburgh: Edinburgh University Press.

Abrams, D. and Houston, D.M. (2007) *Equality, Diversity and Prejudice in Britain: Results from the 2006 National Survey*, London: Cabinet Office.

Adams, M. and Burke, P.J. (2006) 'Recollections of September 11 in Three English Villages: Identifications and Self-Narrations', *Journal of Ethnic and Migration Studies*, 32 (6): 983–1003.

Adogame, A. (2007) 'HIV/AIDS Support and African Pentecostalism: The Case of the Redeemed Christian Church of God', *Journal of Health Psychology*, 12 (3): 475–84.

Adorno, T.W., Frenkel-Bruswik, E., Levinson, D. and Sanford, N. (1950) *The Authoritarian Personality*, New York: Harper and Row.

Afshar, H. (1989) 'Women and Reproduction in Iran', in F. Anthias and N. Yuval-Davis (eds) *Woman – Nation – State*, London: Macmillan.

Afshar, H. (1994) 'Muslim Women in West Yorkshire: Growing Up with Real and Imaginary Values amidst Conflicting Views of Self and Society', in H. Afshar and M. Maynard (eds) *The Dynamics of 'Race' and Gender: Some Feminist Interventions*, London: Taylor and Francis.

Ahlberg, B.M., Krantz, I., Lindmark, G. and Warsame, M. (2004) ' "It's Only a Tradition": Making Sense of Eradication Interventions and the Persistence of Female "Circumcision" within a Swedish Context', *Critical Social Policy*, 24 (1): 50–78.

Ahmad, F. (2006) 'British Muslim Perceptions and Opinions on News Coverage of September 11', *Journal of Ethnic and Migration Studies*, 32 (6): 961–82.

Ahmad, W.I.U. (1995) 'Consanguinity and Related Demons: Science and Racism in the Debate on Consanguinity and Birth Outcome', in C. Sampson and N. South (eds) *The Social Construction of Social Policy: Methodologies, Racism, Citizenship and the Environment*, Basingstoke: Macmillan.

Ahmad, W.I.U., Darr, A. and Jones, L. (2000) ' "I Send My Child to School and He Comes Back an Englishman": Minority Ethnic Deaf People, Identity Politics and Services', in W.I.U. Ahmad (ed.) *Ethnicity, Disability and Chronic Illness*, Buckingham: Open University Press.

Aitsiselmi, F. (2006) 'North African Immigrants in France', in A.H. Carling (ed.) *Globalization and Identity: Development and Integration in a Changing World*, London: I.B. Tauris.

Akhter, R. and Ward, K.B. (2004) *Knowledge and Attitudes towards Domestic Violence: Listening to Bangladeshi Women's Voices*. www.allacademic.com

Akpinar, A. (2003) 'The Honour/Shame Complex Revisited: Violence against Women in the Migration Context', *Women's Studies International Forum*, 26 (5): 425–42.

Alam, Y. and Husband, C. (2006) *British-Pakistani Men from Bradford: Linking Narratives to Policy*, York: Joseph Rowntree Foundation.

Aldridge, A. (2000) *Religion in the Contemporary World*, Cambridge: Polity Press.

Aldridge, A. (2006) 'Religion', in J. Payne (ed.) *Social Divisions*, 2nd Edition, Basingstoke: Palgrave Macmillan.

Aldridge, J. (1994) 'In the Best Interests of the Child', in I. Gaber and J. Aldridge (eds) *In the Best Interests of the Child: Culture, Identity and Transracial Adoption*, London: Free Association Books.

Ali, Z., Fazil, Q., Bywaters, P., Wallace, L. and Singh, G. (2001) 'Disability, Ethnicity and Childhood: A Critical Review of Research', *Disability and Society*, 16 (7): 949–68.

Alibhai-Brown, Y. (1998) 'God's Own Vigilantes', *The Independent*, 12 October.

Alibhai-Brown, Y. (2001) 'Bradford's Burning', *The Independent*, 10 July.

Allen, C. (2004) *Review of the 2004 Commission on British Muslims and Islamophobia Report*, Stoke on Trent: Uniting Britain Trust/Trentham Books.

Allen, C. (2007) *The 'First' Decade of Islamophobia: 10 Years of the Runnymede Trust Report 'Islamophobia: A Challenge for Us All'*, West Midlands: Allen.

Allen, C. and Nielsen, J. (2002) *Summary Report on Islamophobia in the EU after 11 September 2001*, Vienna: EUCM.

Allen, R. and West, A. (2007) 'Religious Schools in London: School Admissions, Composition and Selectivity?' Cited in Flint (2009).

Allen, S. (2008) in P. Sawyer, 'Forced Marriage Victims Betrayed by Doctors', *The Telegraph*, 29 June.

Allen, S. and Barrett, J. (1996) *The Bradford Commission Report*, London: HMSO.

Allen, S. and Macey, M. (1990) 'Race and Ethnicity in the European Context', *British Journal of Sociology*, 41 (3): 375–93.

Allen, S. and Macey, M. (1994) 'Some Issues of Race and Ethnicity in the "New" Europe: Rethinking Sociological Paradigms', in P. Brown and R. Crompton (eds) *The New Europe: Economic Restructuring and Social Exclusion*, London: UCL Press.

Allen, S., Bentley, S. and Bornat, J. (1977) *Work, Race and Immigration*, Bradford: University of Bradford.

All Faiths for One Race (1982) *Talking Chalk: Black Pupils, Parents and Teachers Speak about Education*, Birmingham: AFFOR.

Allison, M. (2006) 'Global Begins at Home: Women, Parity and France', in A.H. Carling (ed.) *Globalization and Identity: Development and Integration in a Changing World*, London: I.B. Taurus.

All London Teachers Against Racism and Fascism (1984) *Challenging Racism*, London: ALTARF.

Al Sadaawi, N. (1991) 'Women in Islam', Paper presented to the Women in Society Seminar Series, Bradford: University of Bradford.

Al-Yousuf, H. (2006) 'Negotiating Faith and Identity in Muslim-Christian Marriages in Britain', *Islam and Christian-Muslim Relations*, 17 (3): 317–29.

Ameli, S.R., Elahi, M. and Merali, A. (2004) *British Muslims' Expectations of the Government – Social Discrimination across the Muslim Divide*, London: IHRC.

Ameli, S.R., Ahmed, S., Seyfeddin, K. and Merali, A. (2007) *British Muslims' Expectations of the Government – The British Media and Muslim Representation: The Ideology of Demonisation*, London: IHRC.

Amin, A. (2002) 'Ethnicity and the Multicultural City: Living with Diversity', *Environment and Planning*, 34 (6): 959–80.

Anderson, J. and Doyal, L. (2003) 'Psychological and Socio-medical Aspects of AIDS/HIV', *AIDS Care*, 16 (1): 95–105.

Anderson, P. (1991) *Imagined Communities*, London: Verso.

Annette, J. and Creasy, S. (2007) 'Individual Pathways to Participation', *Mapping the Public Policy Landscape*, London: ESRC/NCVO Seminar Series.

Ansari, H. (2002) *Muslims in Britain*, London: Minority Rights Group International.

Anthias, F. (2002) 'Beyond Feminism and Multiculturalism: Locating Difference and the Politics of Location', *Women's Studies International Forum*, 25 (3): 275–86.

Anthias, F. and Yuval-Davis, N. (1992) *Racialized Boundaries: Race, Nation, Gender, Colour and Class and the Anti-racist Struggle*, London: Routledge.

Anwar, M. (1979) *The Myth of Return: Pakistanis in Britain*, London: Heinemann Educational Books.

Archer, L. (2001) 'Muslim Brothers, Black Lads, Traditional Asians: British Muslims' Constructions of Race, Religion and Masculinity', *Feminism and Psychology*, 11 (1): 79–105.

Archer, L. (2003) *Masculinity and Schooling: Muslim Boys and Education*, Buckingham: Open University Press.

Association of Chief Police Officers (2005) *Guidance Principles for the Police Service in Relation to the Articulation and Expression of Religious Beliefs and Their Manifestation in the Workplace*, London: ACPO.

Association of Metropolitan Authorities (1985) *Housing and Race: Policy and Practice in Local Authorities*, London: AMA.

Association of Muslim Social Scientists (2004) *Muslims on Education: A Position Paper*, Richmond: AMSS.

Atkin, K., Ahmad, W.I.U. and Jones, L. (2002) 'Young Asian Deaf People and Their Families: Negotiating Relationships and Identities', *Sociology of Health & Illness*, 24 (1): 21–45.

Attwood, C., Trikha, S., Pennant, R. and Wedlock, E. (2004) *2003 Home Office Citizenship Survey: People, Families and Communities*, London: Home Office.

Aune, C. and Sharma, S. (2007) 'Sexuality and Contemporary Evangelical Christianity', in C. Beckett, O. Heathcote and M. Macey (eds) *Negotiating Boundaries? Identities, Sexualities, Diversities*, Newcastle: Cambridge Scholars Press.

Awan, A.N. (2007) 'Transitional Religiosity Experiences: Contextual Disjuncture and Islamic Political Radicalism', in T. Abbas (ed.) *Islamic Political Radicalism: A European Perspective*, Edinburgh: Edinburgh University Press.

Baker, C. (2007) *Religious Literacy, Faithful Capital and Language*, ESRC/NCVO Seminar Series, Anglia Ruskin University, 23 January.

Baker, J., Lynch, K., Cantillon, S. and Walsh, J. (2004) *Equality: From Theory to Action*, Basingstoke: Palgrave Macmillan.

Ballard, R. (1994) *Desh Pardesh: The South Asian Presence in Britain*, London: C. Hurst.

Ballard, R. (2002) 'The South Asian Presence in Britain and Its Transnational Connections', in H. Singh and S. Vertovec (eds) *Culture and Economy in the Indian Diaspora*, London: Routledge.

Ballard, R. (2004) *Remittances and Economic Development*, Memorandum submitted to the United Kingdom Parliament Select Committee on International Development, London: UK Parliament.

Ballard, R. (2007) 'Living with Difference: A Forgotten Art in Urgent Need of Revival?' in J. Hinnells (ed.) *Religious Reconstruction in the South Asian Diasporas,* Basingstoke: Palgrave Macmillan.

Banaji, S. and Al-Ghabban, A. (2006) '"Neutrality Comes from Inside Us": British-Asian and Indian Perspectives on Television News after 11 September', *Journal of Ethnic and Migration Studies,* 32 (6): 1005–26.

Bannerji, H. (2000) *The Dark Side of the Nation: Essays on Multiculturalism, Nationalism and Gender,* Toronto: Canadian Scholars' Press.

Bano, S. (2010) 'Shariah Councils and the Resolution of Matrimonial Disputes', in R.K. Thiara and A.K. Gill (eds) *Violence against Women in South Asian Communities: Issues for Policy and Practice,* London: Jessica Kingsley Publishers.

Barker, E. (2001) 'New Religious Movements', in N.J. Smelser, P.B. Baites and D.L. Sills (eds) *The International Encyclopedia of the Social and Behavioral Sciences,* Vol. 16, Amsterdam: Elsevier.

Barry, B. (2001) *Culture and Equality: An Egalitarian Critique of Multiculturalism,* Cambridge: Polity Press.

Barth, F. (ed.) (1969) *Ethnic Groups and Boundaries: The Social Organization of Culture Difference,* Oslo: Universitetsforlaget.

Bartholet, E. (1991) 'Where Do Black Children Belong? The Politics of Race Matching in Adoption', *University of Pennsylvania Law Review,* 139 (1163): 1207–26.

Bartholet, E. (1993) *Family Bonds: Adoption and the Politics of Parenting,* New York: Mathew Bonder.

Bartholet, E. (1994) 'Race Matching in Adoption: An American Perspective', in I. Gaber and J. Aldridge (eds) *In the Best Interests of the Child: Culture, Identity and Transracial Adoption,* London: Free Association Books.

Bassey, A. (2005) 'The Birmingham Rep Riot: Behind the Scenes', BBC Radio 4, 23 August.

Battu, H., Mwale, M. and Zenou, Y. (2003) 'Do Oppositional Identities Reduce Employment for Ethnic Minorities?', IZA Discussion Paper 721, Bonn: IZA.

Baubock, R. (2002) 'Liberal Pluralism under Attack: Reflections on Diversity and Cohesion from Austrian and European Perspectives', in *Cohesion, Community and Citizenship,* Conference Proceedings, London: The Runnymede Trust.

Bauman, Z. (1989) *Modernity and the Holocaust,* Cambridge: Polity Press.

Baxter, C. (1998) 'Learning Difficulties', in S. Rawaf and V. Bahl (eds) *Assessing Health Needs of People from Minority Ethnic Groups,* London: Royal College of Physicians/Faculty of Public Health Medicine.

Baxter, K. (2006) 'From Migrants to Citizens: Muslims in Britain 1950s–1990s', *Immigrants and Minorities,* 24 (2): 164–92.

Beckett, C. and Macey, M. (2001) 'Race, Gender and Sexuality: The Oppression of Multiculturalism', *Women's Studies International Forum,* 24 (3/4): 309–19.

Beckford, J., Gale, R., Owen, D., Peach, C. and Weller, P. (2006) *Review of the Evidence Base on Faith Communities,* London: ODPM.

Begum, N. (1992) '... Something to Be Proud Of ...' The Lives of Asian Disabled People and Carers in Waltham Forest,* London: Borough of Waltham Forest, Race Relations Unit and Disability Unit.

Belden, D. and Grayling, A.C. (2005) 'Is It Time for Humanists to Start Holding Services ... or Is That Just What We Could Do Without?' *New Humanist,* 120 (6): 12–13.

Berger, P.L. (1967) *The Sacred Canopy: Elements of a Sociological Theory of Religion*, New York: Doubleday.

Berger, P.L. (1969) *The Social Reality of Religion*, London: Pelican.

Berger, P.L (ed.) (1999) *The Desecularization of the World: Resurgent Religion and World Politics*, Washington, DC: Ethics and Public Policy Center/Grand Rapids: Eerdmans.

Berger, P.L. (2002) 'Whatever Happened to Sociology?' *First Things: The Journal of Religion, Culture and Public Life*, October. www.firstthings.com

Berger, P.L. (2007) 'Pluralism, Protestantization, and the Voluntary Principle', in T. Banchoff (ed.) *Democracy and the New Religious Pluralism*, New York: Oxford University Press.

Bergesen, A.J. and Lizardo, O. (2004) 'International Terrorism and the World System', *Sociological Theory*, 22 (1): 38–52.

Berry, J. (2004) 'Not the Way to Get the Balance Right', *Police Review*, 29 October.

Berthoud, R. (1997) 'Income and Standards of Living', in T. Modood, R. Bethoud, J. Lakey, J. Nazroo, P. Smith, S. Virdee and S. Beishon (eds) *Ethnic Minorities in Britain: Diversity and Disadvantage*, London: Policy Studies Institute.

Berthoud, R. (2000) 'Ethnic Employment Penalties in Britain', *Journal of Ethnic and Migration Studies*, 26: 389–416.

Bertossi, C. (2007) *Distant Neighbours – Understanding How the French Deal with Ethnic and Racial Diversity*, London: The Runnymede Trust.

Betts, K. (1996) *The Great Divide*, Sydney: Duffy and Snellgrove.

Bhabha, H.K. (1999) 'Liberalism's Sacred Cow', in J. Cohen, M. Howard and M.C. Nussbaum (eds) *Susan Moller Okin (with respondents) Is Multiculturalism Bad for Women?* Princeton, NJ: Princeton University Press.

Bhatti, M. (2007) *Victim of Tradition: My Painful Journey through a Forced Marriage*, MA Dissertation, Bradford: University of Bradford.

Bhatty, Z. (1998) *Socialising of the Female Muslim Child*, New Delhi: Orient Longman.

Bhopal K. (1997) *Gender, Race and Patriarchy: A Study of South Asian Women*, Aldershot: Ashgate.

Bhopal, K. (1999) 'South Asian Women and Arranged Marriages in London', in R. Barot, H. Bradley and S. Fenton (eds) *Ethnicity, Gender and Social Change*, London: Macmillan.

Billings, A. and Holden, A. (2007) *The Burnley Project: Interfaith Interventions and Cohesive Communities: The Effectiveness of Interfaith Activity in Towns Marked by Enclavisation and Parallel Lives*, Lancaster: University of Lancaster.

Bland, N., Miller, J. and Quinton, P. (2000) *Upping the PACE? An Evaluation of the Recommendations of the Stephen Lawrence Inquiry on Stops and Searches*, Police Research Series Paper 12. London: Home Office.

Blears, H. (2009) 'Foreword', in Communities and Local Government, *Cohesion Delivery Framework Overview*, London: CLG. www.communities.gov.uk

Bleich, E., Carens, J.H., Hansen, R., Modood, T. and O'Leary, B. (2006) 'The Danish Cartoon Affair: Free Speech, Racism, Islamism, and Integration', *International Migration*, 44 (5): 4–62.

Bolliver, V. (2006) *Social Inequalities of Access to Higher Status Universities in the UK*, London: Nuffield Education Seminar.

Bolognani, M. (2007) 'Community Perceptions of Moral Education as a Response to Crime by Young Pakistani Males in Bradford', *Journal of Moral Education*, 36 (3): 357–69.

Bose, R. (2000) 'Families in Transition', in A. Lau (ed.) *South Asian Children and Adolescents in Britain*, London: Whurr.

Bottomore, T. (1970) 'Foreword', in S. Zubaida (ed.) *Race and Racialism*, London: Tavistock Publications.

Bourne, J. (2007) *In Defence of Multiculturalism*, Institute of Race Relations Briefing Paper 2, London: IRR.

Bowker, J. (2003) *World Religions: The Great Faiths Explored and Explained*, London: Dorling Kindersley.

Bradby, H. and Williams, R. (2006) 'Is Religion or Culture the Key Feature in Changes in Substance Use after Leaving School? Young Punjabis and a Comparison Group in Glasgow', *Ethnicity and Health*, 11 (3): 307–24.

Bradley, J.M. (2006) 'Sport and the Contestation of Ethnic Identity: Football and Irishness in Scotland', *Journal of Ethnic and Migration Studies*, 32 (7): 1189–208.

Brandon, J. and Hafez, S. (2008) *Crimes of the Community: Honour-Based Violence in the UK*, London: The Centre for Social Cohesion.

Brennan, J. and McGeevor, P. (1987) *Employment of Graduates from Ethnic Minorities*, London: CRE.

Brierley, P. (ed.) (2000) *UK Christian Handbook, Religious Trends No. 2 2000/1*, London: Christian Research.

Brierley, P. (2005) *Religious Trends No. 5 2005/6: The Future of the Church*, London: Christian Research.

Brierley, P. (2006a) *Pulling Out of the Nosedive: A Contemporary Picture of Churchgoing*, London: Christian Research.

Brierley, P. (2006b) *Religious Trends No. 6 2006/7: Analyses from the 2005 English Church Census*, London: Christian Research.

Brierley, P. (2008) *Religious Trends No. 7 2007/8: British Religion in the 21st Century*, London: Christian Research.

Bright, M. (2006) *When Progressives Treat with Reactionaries: The British State's Flirtation with Radical Islamism*, London: Policy Exchange.

British Broadcasting Corporation, www.bbc.co.uk/religion/religions

British Broadcasting Corporation (2003) 'The Secret Policeman', BBC, Manchester, October.

British Broadcasting Corporation (2009) 'Swiss Voters Back Ban on Minarets', BBC News, 29 November.

British Broadcasting Corporation (2010a) 'Danish Cartoonist Remains Defiant', BBC News, 26 February.

British Broadcasting Corporation (2010b) 'Danish Paper Apologises for Publishing Muhammad Cartoon', BBC News, 26 February.

British Humanist Association (2007) *Quality and Equality: Human Rights, Public Services and Religious Organisations*, London: BHA.

British Medical Association (2004) 'Female Genital Mutilation. Caring for Patients and Child Protection: Guidance from the Ethics Department', London: BMA.

Brittain, E., Dustin, H., Pearce, C., Rake, K., Siyunyi-Siluwe, M. and Sullivan, R. (2005) *Black and Minority Ethnic Women in the UK*, London: The Fawcett Society.

Bromley, C., Sproston, K. and Shelton, N. (eds) (2005) *The Scottish Health Survey: Volumes 1–4*, Edinburgh: Scottish Executive.

Brown, C. and Gay, P. (1985) *Racial Discrimination: 17 Years after the Act*, London: Policy Studies Institute.

Brown, K. (2006) 'Realising Muslim Women's Rights: The Role of Islamic Identity among British Muslim Women', *Women's Studies International Forum*, 29: 417–30.

Brown, K.S. (2003) 'Reforming England's Blasphemy Law to Protect the Individual', *Islam and Christian-Muslim Relations*, 14 (2): 189–203.

Brown, M. (2000a) 'Quantifying the Muslim Population in Europe: Conceptual and Data Issues', *International Journal of Social Research Methodology*, 3 (2): 87–101.

Brown, M. (2000b) 'Religion and Economic Activity in the South Asian Population', *Ethnic and Racial Studies*, 23 (6): 1035–61.

Brown, R. (1995) *Prejudice*, Oxford: Blackwell.

Bruce. S. (ed.) (1992) *Religion and Modernization: Sociologists and Historians Debate the Secularization Thesis*, Oxford: Clarendon.

Bruce, S. (1995) *Religion in Modern Britain*, Oxford: Oxford University Press.

Bruce, S. (2002) *God Is Dead: Secularization in the West*, Oxford: Blackwell.

Bruce, S. (2006) 'Secularization and the Impotence of Individualized Religion', *Hedgehog Review*, 8 (1–2): 35–45.

Bruce, S. and Glendinning, A. (2003) *Religion in Modern Scotland: 2001 Scottish Social Attitudes Survey*, End of Award Report, Swindon: ESRC.

Bruce, S., Glendinning, T., Paterson, I. and Rosie, M. (2005) 'Religious Discrimination in Scotland: Fact or Myth?' *Ethnic and Racial Studies*, 28 (1): 151–68.

Bullock, K. (2002) *Rethinking Muslim Women and the Veil: Challenging Historical and Modern Stereotypes*, London: International Institute of Islamic Thought.

Bunzi, M. (2007) *Anti-semitism and Islamophobia: Hatreds Old and New in Europe*, Chicago: Chicago University Press.

Burgess, S. and Wilson, D. (2003) *Ethnic Segregation in England's Schools*, Centre for Market and Public Organisation Working Paper Series 03/086, Bristol: University of Bristol.

Burgess, S., Wilson, D. and Lupton, R. (2005) 'Parallel lives? Ethnic Segregation in Schools and Neighbourhoods', *Urban Studies*, 42 (7): 1027–56.

Burke, A. (1988) 'Psychic Function and Mental Illness: The Ethnic Minority Population', in S. Allen and M. Macey (eds) *Race and Social Policy*, London: ESRC.

Burman, E., Smailes, S. and Chantler, K. (2004) ' "Culture" as a Barrier to Service Provision and Delivery: Domestic Violence Services for Minoritized Women', *Critical Social Policy*, 24 (3): 332–57.

Burnett, J. (2004) 'Community Cohesion and the State', *Race and Class*, 45 (3): 1–18.

Burnett, J. (2008) 'Community Cohesion in Bradford: Neoliberal Integrationalism', in J. Flint and D. Robinson (eds) *Community Cohesion in Crisis?* Bristol: The Policy Press.

Burris, C.T. and Jackson, L.M. (2000) 'Social Identity and the True Believer: Responses to Threatened Self-Stereotypes among the Intrinsically Religious', *British Journal of Social Psychology*, 39 (1): 257–78.

Bush, J., Bhopal, R., Kai, J., Rankin, J. and White, M. (2003) 'Understanding Influences on Smoking in Bangladeshi and Pakistani Adults', *British Medical Journal*, 326 (7396): 962–5.

Butler, T. and Hamnett, C. (2007) 'The Geography of Education', *Urban Studies*, 44 (7): 1161–74.

Byrnes, S. (2005) 'Our Faith in Western Liberal Democracy, and Our Belief That It Possesses a Superior Moral Truth, Have Blinded Us to Countries with Other Traditions', *New Statesman*, 3 October.

Cantle, T. (2001) *Community Cohesion: A Report of the Independent Review Team,* London: Home Office.

Cantle, T. (2005) *Community Cohesion: A New Framework for Race and Diversity,* Basingstoke: Palgrave Macmillan.

Cantle, T. (2008) *Community Cohesion: A New Framework for Race and Diversity,* Revised and Updated Edition, Basingstoke: Palgrave Macmillan.

Carling, A. (2008) 'The Curious Case of the Mis-claimed Myth Claims: Ethnic Segregation, Polarization and the Future of Bradford', *Urban Studies,* 45 (3): 553–89.

Carling, A., Davies, D., Fernandes-Bakshi, A., Jarman, N. and Nias, P. (2004) *Fair Justice for All? The Response of the Criminal Justice System to the Bradford Disturbances of July 2001,* Bradford: Programme for a Peaceful City/Joseph Rowntree Charitable Trust.

Casanova, J. (2007) 'Immigration and the New Religious Pluralism', in T. Banchoff (ed.) *Democracy and the New Religious Pluralism,* New York: Oxford University Press.

Casciani, D. (2004) 'Birmingham Becomes Stage for Tragedy', BBC News, 13 September. news.bbc.co.uk.

Chahal, K. and Ullah, A.I. (2004) *Experiencing Ethnicity: Discrimination and Service Provision,* York: Joseph Rowntree Foundation.

Chambers, C. (2004) 'Are Breast Implants Better Than Female Genital Mutilation? Autonomy, Gender Equality and Nussbaum's Political Liberalism', *Critical Review of International Social and Political Philosophy,* 7 (3): 1–33.

Chambra, R., Ahmad, W.I.U. and Jones, L. (1998) *Improving Services for Asian Deaf Children – Parents' and Professionals' Perspectives,* York: Joseph Rowntree Foundation.

Channabasavanna, S.M., Bhatti, R.S. and Prabhu, L.R. (1985) 'A Study of Attitudes of Parents towards the Management of Mentally Retarded Children', *Child Psychiatry Quarterly,* 18: 85–92.

Channel 4 Dispatches/GfK NOP (2006) *Attitudes to Living in Britain – A Survey of Muslim Opinion,* London: GfK. www.gfknop.com

Chantler, K. (2006) 'Independence, Dependency and Interdependence: Struggles and Resistances of Minoritized Women within and on Leaving Violent Relationships', *Feminist Review,* 86: 27–49.

Chartered Institute of Personnel and Development (2003) *Religious Discrimination: An Introduction to the Law,* London: CIPD.

Chesler, P. (2005) *The New Anti-Semitism: The Current Crisis and What We Must Do about It,* San Francisco: Jossey Bass/Wiley.

Choudhury, T. (2007) 'Muslims and Discrimination', in S. Amghar, A. Boubekeur and M. Emerson (eds) *European Islam: Challenges for Public Policy and Society,* Brussels: Centre for European Policy Studies.

Christian Research (2005) *The 2005 English Church Census.* www.christian-research.org.uk

Christianson, A. and Modell, B. (2004) 'Medical Genetics in Developing Countries', *Annual Review of Genomics and Human Genetics,* 5: 219–65.

Church of England (2008) *Recent Surveys/Mapping Exercises Undertaken across the English Regions to Measure the Contribution of Faith Groups to Social Action and Culture.* www.urcsouthern.org.uk

CIMEL/INTERIGHTS (2001) *Roundtable on Strategies to Address 'Crimes of Honour',* Women Living Under Muslim Laws, Occasional Paper 12, London: CIMEL.

Clark, K. and Drinkwater, S. (2007) *Ethnic Minorities and the Labour Market: Dynamics and Diversity*, Bristol: The Policy Press.

Clarke, T. (2001) *Burnley Task Force Report on the Disturbances in June, 2001*, Burnley: Burnley Borough Council.

Cohen, R. (1988) *The New Helots: Migrants in the International Division of Labour*, Aldershot: Gower.

Cohen, R. and Kennedy, P. (2007) *Global Sociology*, 2nd Edition, Basingstoke: Palgrave Macmillan.

Coleman, P.G., Ivani-Challan, C. and Robinson, M. (2004) 'Religious Attitudes among British Older People: Stability and Change in a 20-Year Longitudinal Study', *Ageing and Society*, 24 (2): 167–88.

Coles, C. and Bonney, R. (2003) *Community Cohesion: Meeting the Needs of Muslim Pupils*, Conference Report, Nottingham: University of Nottingham.

Commission for Racial Equality (1987) *Living in Terror: A Report on Racial Violence and Harassment in Housing*, London: CRE.

Commission for Racial Equality (2004) *Annual Report of the Commission for Racial Equality 1 January 2003–31 December 2003*, London: CRE.

Commission for Racial Equality (2005a) *The Police Service in England and Wales: Final Report of a Formal Investigation by the Commission for Racial Equality*, London: CRE.

Commission for Racial Equality (2005b) *Race Equality in Prisons: A Formal Investigation by the Commission for Racial Equality into HM Prison Service in England and Wales, Part 2*, London: CRE.

Commission on Urban Life and Faith (2007) *Faithful Cities: A Call for Celebration, Vision and Justice*, London: Church House.

Community Development Foundation (2007) *Cohesive Communities: Cohesion and Community Development*. www.cdf.org.uk

Community Security Trust (2010) *Antisemitic Incidents Report 2009*. www.thecst.org.uk

Confederation of Indian Organisations (UK) (1987) *Asians and Disabilities*, London: CIO.

Connelly, N. (1987) *Social Services Departments and Race: A Discussion Paper*, London: Policy Studies Institute.

Conway, G. (1997) *Islamophobia: A Challenge for Us All: Report of the Runnymede Trust Commission on British Muslims and Islamophobia*, London: The Runnymede Trust.

Cowan, K. (2007) *Living Together: British Attitudes to Lesbian and Gay People*, Report of a YouGov survey carried out for Stonewall, London: Stonewall.

Crockett, A. and Voas, D. (2003) 'A Divergence of Views: Attitude Change and the Religious Crisis over Homosexuality', *Sociological Research Online*, 8 (4). www.socresonline.org.uk

Crockett, A. and Voas, D. (2006) 'Generations of Decline: Religious Change in Twentieth-Century Britain', *Journal for the Scientific Study of Religion*, 45 (4): 567–84.

Daily Telegraph (2008) 'Prince Charles to Be Known as Defender of Faith', 13 November.

Darr, A. (1997) 'Consanguineous Marriage and Genetics: A Positive Relationship', in A. Clarke and E. Parsons (eds) *Culture, Kinship and Genes: Towards Cross-cultural Genetics*, Basingstoke: Palgrave Macmillan.

Davie, G. (1994) *Religion in Britain Since 1945: Believing without Belonging,* Oxford: Blackwell.

Davie, G. (2001) 'The Persistence of Institutional Religion in Modern Europe', in L. Woodhead, P. Heelas and D. Martin (eds) *Peter Berger and the Study of Religion,* London: Routledge.

Davie, G. (2002) 'Praying Alone? Church-Going in Britain and Social Capital: A Reply to Steve Bruce', *Journal of Contemporary Religion,* 17 (3): 329–34.

Davie, G. (2004) 'Reply to Francis & Robbins', *Implicit Religion,* 7 (1): 55–8.

Davie, G. (2005) 'From Obligation to Consumption: A Framework for Reflection in Northern Europe', *Political Theology,* 6 (3): 281–301.

Davie, G. (2006) 'Is Europe an Exceptional Case?' *Hedgehog Review,* 8 (1–2): 23–34.

Davis, F. (2008) 'Moral, but No Compass – A Challenge to Every Politician', *Thinking Faith. Journal of the British Jesuits,* 9 June. www.thinkingfaith.org

Dawkins, R. (2003) *A Devil's Chaplain,* London: Weidenfeld and Nicolson.

Dawkins, R. (2006) *The God Delusion,* London: Bantam Press.

de Ferrari, P. (2000) *Proclaiming Justice: Women and Catholic Social Teaching: Shaping a New World,* Washington DC: NETWORK Education Program.

de Galembert, C. (2005) 'The City's "Nod of Approval" for the Mantes-la-Jolie Mosque Project: Mistaken Traces of Recognition', *Journal of Ethnic and Migration Studies,* 31 (6): 1141–59.

Denham, J. (2001) *Building Cohesive Communities: A Report of the Ministerial Group on Public Disorder and Community Cohesion,* London: HMSO.

Dennett, D. (2006) *Breaking the Spell: Religion as a Natural Phenomenon,* London: Allen Lane.

Denvir, A., Broughton, A., Gifford, J. and Hill, D. (2007) *The Experiences of Sexual Orientation and Religion or Belief Discrimination Employment Tribunal Claimants,* London: ACAS.

Department for Children, Schools and Families (2006) *The Education and Inspections Act 2006,* London: DCSF.

Department for Children, Schools and Families (2007a) *Faith in the System,* Nottingham: DCSF.

Department for Children, Schools and Families (2007b) *Guidance on the Duty to Promote Community Cohesion,* London: DCSF.

Department for Communities and Local Government (2006) *Managing for Diversity: A Case Study of Four Local Authorities,* London: DCLG.

Department for Communities and Local Government (2007a) *Face to Face and Side by Side: A Framework for Interfaith Dialogue and Social Action.* London: DCLG.

Department for Communities and Local Government (2007b) *What Works in Community Cohesion?* London: DCLG.

Department of Constitutional Affairs (2006) *A Guide to the Human Rights Act,* 3rd Edition, London: DCA.

Department of Education and Science (1985) *Education for All,* the Swann Report, London: HMSO.

Department of Health (2003) *NHS Chaplaincy Meeting the Religious and Spiritual Needs of Patients and Staff,* London: DoH.

Deveaux, M. (2000) *Cultural Pluralism and Dilemmas of Justice,* Ithaca, NY: Cornell University Press.

Deveaux, M. (2002) 'Political Morality and Culture: What Difference Do Differences Make?' *Social Theory and Practice,* 28 (3): 503–18.

Dinham, A., Furbey, R. and Lowndes, V. (eds) *Faith in the Public Realm: Controversies, Policies and Practices,* Bristol: The Policy Press.

Dirie, W. (2009) in Kerbaj, J. 'Thousands of Girls Mutilated in Britain', *The Times,* 16 March.

Dogra, N., Vostanis, P., Abuateya, H. and Jewson, N. (2005) 'Understanding of Mental Health and Mental Illness by Gujarati Young People and Their Parents', *Diversity in Health and Social Care,* 2: 91–7.

Dorkenoo, E., Morison, L. and Macfarlane, A. (2006) *A Statistical Study to Estimate the Prevalence of Female Genital Mutilation in England and Wales,* Summary Report, London: FORWARD.

Douds, A.C., Cox, M.A., Iqbal, T.H. and Cooper, B.T. (2003) 'Ethnic Differences in Cirrhosis of the Liver in a British City: Alcoholic Cirrhosis in South Asian Men', *Alcohol and Alcoholism,* 38 (2): 148–50.

Dozier, R.W. (2002) *Why We Hate,* New York: Contemporary Books.

Dummett, A. (1991) 'Europe? Which Europe?' *New Community,* 18 (1): 167–75.

Durkheim, E. (1915) *The Elementary Forms of Religious Life,* trans. J.W. Swain, London: Allen and Unwin.

Dwyer, C. (2000) 'Negotiating Diasporic Identities: Young British South Asian Muslim Women', *Women's Studies International Forum,* 23 (4): 75–86.

Dzi, B. (2009) *German Mosques: A Journey of Discovery.* www.IslamOnline.net

Echchaibi, N. (2007) 'Republican Betrayal: Beur FM and the Suburban Riots in France', *Journal of Intercultural Studies,* 28 (3): 301–16.

Edge, P. (2002) 'The Construction of Sacred Places in English Law', *Journal of Environmental Law,* 14 (2): 161–83.

Eisenstadt, S.N. (2000) 'The Resurgence of Religious Movements in the Processes of Globalisation – Beyond End of History or Clash of Civilisations', *International Journal on Multicultural Societies,* UNESCO, 2 (1): 4–15.

Eisenstadt, S.N. (2007) 'The Resurgence of Religious Movements in Processes of Globalization – Beyond the End of History or the Clash of Civilizations', in M. Koenig and P. de Guchteneire (eds) *Democracy and Human Rights in Multicultural Societies,* Aldershot: Ashgate.

El-Solh, C. and Mabro, J. (eds) (1994) *Muslim Women's Choices: Religious Belief and Social Reality,* Providence, RI: Berg.

Emerson, E., Azmi, S. and Hatton, C. (1997) 'Is There an Increased Prevalence of Severe Learning Disabilities among British Asians? *Ethnicity and Health,* 2 (4): 317–21.

Entzinger, H. (2003) 'The Rise and Fall of Multiculturalism: The Case of the Netherlands', in C. Joppke and E. Morawska (eds) *Towards Assimilation and Citizenship,* Basingstoke: Palgrave Macmillan.

Equal Opportunities Commission (2003) *Citizens Forum to Discuss Equality in Britain,* London: EOC.

Equal Opportunities Commission (2006a) *Facts about Women and Men in Great Britain, 2006.* Manchester: EOC.

Equal Opportunities Commission (2006b) *Glass Doors Not Just Glass Ceilings: Research into the Employment of Visible Minority Ethnic Women in Scotland (Focusing on African, Caribbean, Bangladeshi, Chinese, Indian and Pakistani Communities,* Glasgow: EOC.

Equal Opportunities Commission (2007) *Moving on Up? The Way Forward: Report of the EOC's Investigation into Bangladeshi, Pakistani and Black Caribbean Women and Work*, Manchester: EOC.

Esman, M. (2004) *An Introduction to Ethnic Conflict*, Cambridge: Polity Press.

Esposito, J.L., Fasching, D.J. and Lewis, T. (2002) *World Religions Today*, New York: Oxford University Press.

European Monitoring Centre on Racism and Xenophobia (2004a) *Manifestations of Antisemitism in the EU. 2002–2003*, EUMC. www.eumc.europa.eu

European Monitoring Centre on Racism and Xenophobia (2004b) *Perceptions of Antisemitism in the EU: Voices of the Jewish Community*, EUMC. www.eumc.europa.eu

European Monitoring Centre on Racism and Xenophobia (2006a) *Muslims in the European Union: Discrimination and Islamophobia*, EUMC. www.eumc.europa.eu

European Monitoring Centre on Racism and Xenophobia (2006b) *Perceptions of Discrimination and Islamophobia*, EUMC. www.eumc.europa.eu

Farm Animal Welfare Council (2003) *Report on the Welfare of Farmed Animals at Slaughter or Killing, Part I*, London: FAWC/Defra. www.fawc.org.uk

Farnell, R., Lund, S., Furbey, R., Lawless, P., Wishart, B. and Else, P. (1994), *Hope in the City? The Local Impact of the Church Urban Fund*, Sheffield: Centre for Regional Economic and Social Research, Sheffield Hallam University.

Farnell, R., Furbey, R., Shams-Al-Haqq Hills, S., Macey, M. and Smith, G. (2003) *'Faith' in Urban Regeneration? Engaging Faith Communities in Urban Regeneration*, Bristol: The Policy Press/JRF.

Field, C.D. (2007) 'Islamophobia in Contemporary Britain: The Evidence of the Opinion Polls, 1988–2006', *Islam and Christian-Muslim Relations*, 18 (4): 447–77.

Fisher, L. (2005) 'State of the Art: Multiculturalism, Gender and Cultural Identities', *European Journal of Women's Studies*, 11 (1): 111–19.

Flint, J. (2007) 'Faith Schools, Multiculturalism and Community Cohesion: Muslim and Roman Catholic State Schools in England and Scotland', *Policy and Politics*, 35 (2): 251–68.

Flint, J. (2009) 'Faith-Based Schools: Institutionalising Parallel Lives?' in A. Dinham, R. Furbey and V. Lowndes (eds) *Faith in the Public Realm: Controversies, Policies and Practices*, Bristol: The Policy Press.

Flint, J. and Robinson, D. (2008) 'Conclusions', in J. Flint and D. Robinson (eds) *Community Cohesion in Crisis?* Bristol: The Policy Press.

Forced Marriage Unit (FMU) (2006) *Forced Marriage: A Wrong Not a Right. Summary of Responses to the Consultation on the Criminalisation of Forced Marriage*, London: FCO.

Francis, L.J., Robbins, M., Lewis, C.A. and Barnes, L.P. (2008) 'Prayer and Psychological Health: A Study among Sixth-Form Pupils Attending Catholic and Protestant Schools in Northern Ireland', *Mental Health, Religion and Culture*, 11 (1): 85–92.

Franks, M. (2000) 'Crossing the Borders of Whiteness? White Muslim Women Who Wear the Hijab in Britain Today', *Ethnic and Racial Studies*, 23 (5): 917–29.

Frean, A. (2007) 'Hindu School's Admission Policy "Too Strict"', *The Times*, 29 November.

Fredman, S. (2002) *The Future of Equality in Britain*, Working Paper Series 5, Manchester: EOC.

Fredman, S. (2005) 'Changing the Norm: Positive Duties in Equal Treatment Legislation', *Maastricht Journal of European and Comparative Law*, 12 (4): 372–3.

Furbey, R.A. (2008) 'Beyond "Social Glue"? Faith and Community Cohesion', in J. Flint and D. Robinson (eds) *Community Cohesion in Crisis?* Bristol: The Policy Press.

Furbey, R.A., Dinham, A. and Farnell, R. with Finneron, D., Wilkinson, G., Howarth, C., Hussain, D. and Palmer, S. (2006) *Faith as Social Capital*, York. Joseph Rowntree Foundation.

Gaber, I. (1994) 'Transracial Placements: A History', in I. Gaber and J. Aldridge (eds) *In the Best Interests of the Child: Culture, Identity and Transracial Adoption*, London: Free Association Books.

Gale, R. (2004) 'The Multicultural City and the Politics of Religious Architecture: Urban Planning, Mosques and Meaning-Making in Birmingham UK', *Built Environment*, 30 (1): 18–32.

Gale, R. (2005) 'Representing the City: Mosques and the Planning Process in Birmingham', *Journal of Ethnic and Migration Studies*, 31 (6): 1161–79.

Gale, R. and Naylor, S. (2002) 'Religion, Planning and the City: The Spatial Politics of Ethnic Minority Expression in British Cities and Towns', *Ethnicities*, 2 (3): 387–409.

Gallard, C. (1995) 'Female Genital Mutilation in France', *British Medical Journal*, 310: 1592–3.

Galston, W.A. (1995) 'Two Concepts of Liberation', *Ethics*, 105 (3): 516–34.

Gatrad, A.R. and Sheikh, A. (2004) 'Risk Factors for HIV/AIDS in Muslim Communities', *Diversity in Health and Social Care*, 1: 65–9.

Gifford (Lord), Brown, W. and Bundey, R. (1989) *Loosen the Shackles: First Report of the Inquiry into Race Relations in Liverpool*, Liverpool: Liverpool Law Centre/London: Karia Press.

Gilliat-Ray, S. (2001) 'The Fate of the Anglican Clergy and the Class of '97: Some Implications of the Changing Sociological Profile of Ordinands', *Journal of Contemporary Religion*, 16 (2): 209–25.

Gilliat-Ray S. (2007) *Genetics, Religion and Identity: A Study of Bangladeshi Muslims in Britain*, End of Award Report, Swindon: ESRC.

Gilroy, P. (1982) 'Police and Thieves', in Centre for Contemporary Cultural Studies, *The Empire Strikes Back*, London: Hutchinson.

Gilroy, P. (1987) *There Ain't No Black in the Union Jack*, London: Hutchinson.

Gilroy, P. (1992) 'The End of Antiracism', in J. Donald and A. Rattansi (eds) *'Race', Culture and Difference*, London: Sage.

Gitlin, T. (1995) *The Twilight of Common Dreams: Why America Is Wracked by Culture Wars*, New York: Henry Holt.

Glick, P. and Fiske, S.T. (2001) 'An Ambivalent Alliance: Hostile and Benevolent Sexism as Complementary Justifications for Gender Inequality', *American Psychologist*, 56: 109–18.

Glock, C. and Stark, R. (1965) *Religion and Society in Tension*, Chicago: Rand McNally.

Goldberg, D.T. (1990) 'The Social Formation of Racist Discourse', in D.T. Goldberg (ed.) *Anatomy of Racism*, Minneapolis: University of Minnesota Press.

Goldberg, D.T. (1993) *Racist Culture*, Oxford: Blackwell.

Goldberg, D.T. (ed.) (1994) *Multiculturalism: A Critical Reader*, Oxford: Blackwell.

Gordon, P. and Newnham, A. (1985) *Passport to Benefits? Racism in Social Security*, London: The Runnymede Trust.

Gordon, P. and Newnham, A. (1986) *Different Worlds: Racism and Discrimination in Britain*, 2nd Edition, London: The Runnymede Trust.

Gores, B. (1999) *Domestic Violence in Asian Communities*, BA Dissertation, Bradford: University of Bradford.

Grace, G. (2002) *Catholic Schools: Mission, Markets and Morality*, London: Routledge Falmer.

Grace, G. (2003) 'Educational Studies and Faith-Based Schooling: Moving away from Prejudice to Evidence-Based Arguments', *British Journal of Educational Studies*, 51 (2): 149–67.

Graham, D. (2003) *Secular or Religious? The Outlook of London's Jews*, London: Institute for Jewish Policy Research.

Graham, D., Schmool, M. and Waterman, S. (2007) *Jews in Britain: A Snapshot from the 2001 Census*, London: Institute for Jewish Policy Research, 1.

Grayling, A.C. (2004) *What Is Good? The Search for the Best Way to Live*, London: Phoenix.

Grayling, A.C. (2007) 'Can an Atheist Be a Fundamentalist?' in C. Hitchens (ed.) *The Portable Atheist: Essential Readings for the Nonbeliever*, London: Da Capo.

Greater London Action for Race Equality (1987) *The Face of Injustice*, London: GLARE.

Greater London Association for Disabled People (1987) *Disability and Ethnic Minority Communities – A Study in Three London Boroughs*, London: GLAD.

Green, J. (1990) *THEM: Voices from the Immigrant Community in Contemporary Britain*, London: Secker and Warburg.

Grieve, J., Jochum, V., Pratten, B. and Steel, C. (2007) *Faith in the Community – The Contribution of Faith-Based Organisations to Rural Voluntary Action*, London: National Council of Voluntary Organisations.

Grillo, R.D. (1999) *Pluralism and the Politics of Difference: State, Culture and Ethnicity in Comparative Perspective*, Oxford: Clarendon Press.

Grillo, R.D. (2007) 'Licence to Offend? The Behzti Affair', *Ethnicities*, 7 (1): 5–29.

Gupta R. (2003) 'Walls into Bridges: The Losses and Gains of Making Alliances', in R. Gupta (ed.) *From Home Breakers to Jail Breakers*, London: Zed Press.

Gutmann, A. (2003) *Identity in Democracy*, Princeton, NJ: Princeton University Press.

Habermas, J. (2010) *An Awareness of What Is Missing: Faith and Reason in a Post-secular Age*, Cambridge: Polity Press.

Hamdan, A. (2007) 'The Issue of Hijab in France: Reflections and Analysis', *Muslim World Journal of Human Rights*, 4 (2): 1–27.

Hansen, R. (2006) 'The Danish Cartoon Controversy: A Defence of Liberal Freedom', *International Migration*, 44 (5): 7–16.

Harb, A. and Bessaiso, E. (2006) 'British Arab Muslim Audiences and Television after September 11', *Journal of Ethnic and Migration Studies*, 32 (6): 1063–76.

Harries, R. (2002) *God outside the Box: Why Spiritual People Object to Christianity*, London: SPCK.

Harris, S. (2006) *The End of Faith: Religion, Terror and the Future of Reason*, London: The Free Press.

Hartnell, S. (2007) *Tackling Hate Crime*, Schools Out. www.schoolsout.org.uk

Haugh, J.F. (1990) *What Is Religion?* New Jersey: Paulist Press.

Healthcare Commission (2007) *Results of the 2006 National Census of Inpatients in Mental Health and Learning Disability Services in England and Wales*, London: Commission for Healthcare, Audit and Inspection.

Health Education Authority (2000) *Black and Ethnic Minority Groups in England: The Second Health and Lifestyles Survey*, Abingdon: HEA.

Heelas, P. (2001) 'New Age Utopianism, Cultural Extremities and Modernity', in K. Flanagan and P. Jupp (eds) *Virtue Ethics and Sociology*, Basingstoke: Palgrave Macmillan.

Heelas, P. and Woodhead, L. with B. Steel, B. Szerszynski and K. Tuesting (2005) *The Spiritual Revolution: Why Religion Is Giving Way to Spirituality*, Oxford: Blackwell.

Heim, D., Hunter, S.C., Ross, A.J., Bakshi, N., Davies, J., Flatley, K.J. and Meer, N. (2004) 'Alcohol Consumption, Perceptions of Community Responses and Attitudes to Service Provision: Results from a Survey of Indian, Chinese and Pakistani Young People in Greater Glasgow, Scotland, UK', *Alcohol and Alcoholism*, 39 (3): 220–6.

Hepple, B. and Choudhury, T. (2001) *Tackling Religious Discrimination: Practical Implications for Policy-Makers and Legislators*, Home Office Research Study 221, London: Home Office.

Herr, R.S. (2004) 'A Third World Feminist Defence of Multiculturalism', *Social Theory and Practice*, 30 (1): 73–103.

Hester, M., Chantler, K., Gangoli, G., Devgon, J., Sharma, S. and Singleton, A. (2008) *Forced Marriage: The Risk Factors and the Effects of Raising the Minimum Age for a Sponsor, and Leave to Enter the UK as a Sponsor or Fiancé(e)*. www.bristol.ac.uk

Hewstone, M., Paolini, S., Cairns, E., Voci, A., Hamberger, J. and Neins, U. (2006) 'Intergroup Contact and the Promotion of Intergroup Harmony', in R.J. Brown and D. Capozza (eds) *Social Identities: Motivational, Emotional, Cultural Influences*, Hove: Psychology Press.

Hick, J. (2010) *The New Frontier of Religion and Science: Religion, Neuroscience and the Transcendent*, 2nd Edition, Harmondsworth: Palgrave Macmillan.

Hicks, S. (2003) 'The Christian Right and Homophobic Discourse: A Response to "Evidence" That Lesbian and Gay Parenting Damages Children', *Sociological Research Online*, 8 (4). www.socresonline.org.uk

Hilsdon, A.-M. and Rozario, S. (2006) Special Issue on Islam, Gender and Human Rights, *Women's Studies International Forum*, 29 (4): 331–8.

Hindu Forum of Britain (2008). www.hinduforum.org

Hirsi Ali, A. (2006) *The Caged Virgin: A Muslim Woman's Cry for Reason*, London: The Free Press.

Hirsi Ali, A. (2007) *Infidel*, London: Simon and Schuster (The Free Press).

Hitchens, C. (2007) *The Portable Atheist: Essential Readings for the Nonbeliever*, London: Da Capo Press.

Hjerm, M. (2000) 'Multiculturalism Reassessed', *Citizenship Studies*, 4 (3): 357–81.

Home Office (1981) *Racial Attacks*, London: HMSO.

Home Office (1999) *Dismantling Barriers to Reflect the Community We Serve: The Recruitment, Retention and Progression of Minority Ethnic Officers*, London: Home Office.

Home Office (2004) *Working Together: Co-operation between Government and Communities,* London: Home Office Faith Communities Unit.

Home Office (2006) *Tackling Hate Crime: Homophobic Hate Crime,* London: Home Office.

Honneth, A. (1997) *The Struggle for Recognition: The Moral Grammar of Social Conflict,* Oxford: Polity Press.

Hoodfar, H. (1993) 'The Veil in Their Minds and on Our Heads: The Persistence of Colonial Images of Muslim Women', *Resources for Feminist Research,* 22 (3/4): 5–18.

Hopkins, N. and Khani-Hopkins, V. (2004) 'The Antecedents of Identification: A Rhetorical Analysis of British Muslim Activists' Constructions of Community and Identity', *British Journal of Social Psychology,* 43: 31–57.

Hopkins, P.E. (2006) 'Youthful Muslim Masculinities: Gender and Generational Relations', *Transnational Institute of British Geographers,* 31 (3): 337–52.

Horowitz, D.L. (2002) *The Deadly Ethnic Riot,* Berkeley: University of California Press.

House of Commons Education and Skills Committee (2007) *Bullying,* London: The Stationery Office.

House of Commons Home Affairs Committee (2008) *Domestic Violence, Forced Marriage and 'Honour'-Based Violence,* Sixth Report of Session 2007–08, London: The Stationery Office.

Housing Corporation (2007) *Shared Places: Community Cohesion Strategy,* London: Housing Corporation.

Hunt, R. and Jensen, J. (2006) *The School Report: The Experiences of Young Gay People in Britain's Schools,* Survey by the Schools Health Education Unit, London: Stonewall.

Hunt, S. (2002) 'Neither Here nor There: The Construction of Identities and Boundary Maintenance of West African Pentecostals', *Sociology,* 36 (1): 147–69.

Hunt, S. and Lightly, N. (2001) 'The British Black Pentecostal "Revival": Identity and Belief in the "New" Nigerian Churches', *Ethnic and Racial Studies,* 24 (1): 104–24.

Huntington, S.P. (1996) *The Clash of Civilizations and the Remaking of World Order,* London: Simon and Schuster.

Hussain, F. and Cochrane, R. (2003) 'Living with Depression: Coping Strategies used by South Asian Women Living in the UK Suffering from Depression', *Mental Health, Religion and Culture,* 6 (1): 21–44.

Hussain, R. and Bittles, A.H. (2004) 'Assessment of Association between Consanguinity and Fertility in Asian Populations', *Journal of Health, Population and Nutrition,* 22: 1–12.

Hussain, Y. (2005) 'South Asian Disabled Women: Negotiating Identities', *The Sociological Review,* 53 (3): 522–38.

Hyder, R.M. (1993) *Mixed-Race People in British Society: A Study of Ethnicity and Identity,* MSc Dissertation, Bradford: University of Bradford.

Idrus, N. and Bennett, L. (2003) 'Presumed Consent: Marital Violence in Bugis Society', in L. Manderson and L. Bennett (eds) *Violence against Women in Asian Societies,* London: Routledge Curzon.

Iganski, P. (2002) *The Hate Debate: The Problem of Hate Crimes and Hate Crimes Laws,* London: Institute for Jewish Policy Research.

Iganski, P. (2008) *Hate Crime and the City,* Bristol: The Policy Press.

In-Service Training and Educational Development (2007) *The Search for Common Ground – Muslims, Non-Muslims and the UK Media*, London: INSTED.

Institute of Race Relations (2008) *Racially Motivated Murders on the Rise*, IRR Press Release, January. www.irr.org.uk

Institute of Race Relations (2009) *Racially Motivated Murders (Known or Suspected) 2000 Onwards*. www.irr.org.uk

Islamic Human Rights Commission (2008) *Online Incident Reporting*. www.ihr.org

Jacobsen, J. (1998) *Islam in Transition: Religion and Identity among British Pakistani Youth*, London: Routledge.

Jahangir, A. (2008) *Addendum to the Report of the Special Rapporteur on Freedom of Religion or Belief Mission to the United Kingdom of Great Britain and Northern Ireland*, New York: Human Rights Council, UN.

Janes, L. and Mooney, G. (2002) 'Place, Lifestyle and Social Divisions', in P. Braham and L. Janes (eds) *Social Differences and Divisions*, London: Blackwell.

Jayaweera, H. and Choudhury, T. (2008) *Immigration, Faith and Cohesion: Evidence from Local Areas with Significant Muslim Populations*, York: Joseph Rowntree Foundation.

Jenkins, R. (1970 [1966]) *Essays and Speeches*, London: Collins.

Jochum, V., Pratten, B. and Wilding, K. (2007) *Faith and Voluntary Action: An Overview of Current Evidence and Debates*, London: NCVO.

Johal, A. (2003) 'Struggle not Submission: Domestic Violence in the 1990s', in R. Gupta (ed.) *From Home Breakers to Jail Breakers*, London: Zed Press.

Johnston, R., Forrest, J. and Poulsen, M. (2002) 'The Ethnic Geography of EthniCities: The "American Model" and Residential Concentration in London', *Ethnicities*, 2 (2): 209–35.

Johnston, R., Poulsen, M. and Forrest, J. (2005) 'On the Measurement and Meaning of Residential Segregation: A Response to Simpson', *Urban Studies*, 42 (7): 1221–7.

Johnston, R., Burgess, S., Harris, R. and Wilson, D. (2006a) *School and Residential Ethnic Segregation: An Analysis of Variations across England's Local Education Authorities*. Working Paper 06/145, Bristol: Centre for Market and Public Organisation. www.bris.ac.uk

Johnston, R., Burgess, S., Harris, R. and Wilson, D. (2006b) *Sleep-Walking towards Segregation? The Changing Ethnic Composition of English Schools, 1997–2003: An Entry Cohort Analysis*. Working Paper 06/155, Bristol: Centre for Market and Public Organisation. www.bris.ac.uk

Jones, A. and Singer, L. (2008) *Statistics on Race and the Criminal Justice System, 2006*, London: Ministry of Justice.

Joppke, C. (2004) 'The Retreat of Multiculturalism in the Liberal State: Theory and Policy', *British Journal of Sociology*, 55 (2): 237–57.

Judge, H. (2001) 'Faith-Based Schools and State Funding: A Partial Argument Against', *Oxford Review of Education*, 27 (4): 463–74.

Judge, H. (2002) 'Religion and the State: The Case of Faith-Based Schools', *The Political Quarterly*, 73 (1): 422–30.

Kalev, H.D. (2004) 'Cultural Rights or Human Rights: The Case of Female Genital Mutilation', *Sex Roles*, 51 (5/6): 339–48.

Kapoor, R. and Crossman, B. (1996) *Subversive Sites: Feminist Engagements with Law in India*, New Delhi: Sage.

Katbamna, S., Bhakta, P. and Ahmad W. (2002) 'Supporting South Asian Carers and Those They Care For: The Role of the Primary Care Team', *British Journal of General Practice*, 52: 300–5.

Kaufmann, E. (2007a) *A Dying Creed? The Demographic Contradictions of Liberal Capitalism*, End of Award Report, R163250013, Swindon: ESRC.

Kaufmann, E. (2007b) *Sacralization by Stealth: Demography, Religion and Politics in Europe*, JPR Policy Debate, July, London: Institute for Jewish Policy Research.

Kaufmann, E. and Voas, D. (2007) *The Impact of Religion on Europe's Future – A Debate*, JPR News Release, 16 July, London: Institute for Jewish Policy Research.

Keighley Domestic Violence Forum (1998) *Domestic Violence in Asian Communities*, Bradford: KDVF/University of Bradford.

Kelly, P. (2002) 'Introduction: Between Culture and Equality', in P. Kelly (ed.) *Multiculturalism Reconsidered*, Cambridge: Polity Press.

Kemp, D. (2003) 'NA Law: A Legal Approach to New Age', *Culture and Religion*, 4 (1): 141–58.

Kepel, G. (1994) *The Revenge of God: The Resurgence of Islam, Christianity and Judaism in the Modern World*, Cambridge: Polity Press.

Kepel, G. (2004) *The War for Muslim Minds: Islam and the West*, Cambridge, MA: The Belknap Press of Harvard University Press.

Khan, A. (1997) *An Examination of Drug Use within the 'Pakistani' Community in Bradford*, BA Dissertation, Bradford: University of Bradford.

Khan, O. (2006) *Why Preferential Policies Can Be Fair: Achieving Equality for Members of Disadvantaged Groups*, London: The Runnymede Trust.

Khanum, N. (2008) *Forced Marriage, Family Cohesion and Community Engagement: National Learning through a Case Study of Luton*, Luton: Equality in Diversity.

Khanum, S. (1992) 'Education and the Muslim Girl', in G. Sahgal and N. Yuval-Davis (eds) *Refusing Holy Orders: Women and Fundamentalism in Britain*, London: Virago.

Khattab, N. (2009) 'Ethnicity, Religion and "Colour" as Determinants of Educational and Occupational Attainment in Britain', Mimeo.

Kidwai, Q.J. and Huda, S. (2007) *Women in Qur'an*, Mumbai: Institute of Islamic Studies.

King, M., Weich, S. Nazroo, J. and Blizard, B. (2006) 'Religion, Mental Health and Ethnicity: EMPIRIC – A National Survey of England', *Journal of Mental Health*, 15 (2): 153–62.

Kitchen, S., Michaelson, J. and Wood, N. (2006) *2005 Citizenship Survey – Community Cohesion Topic Report*, London: DCLG.

Kitchin, K. (2008) *Commission on Integration and Cohesion: The Government Response (Local Government Information Unit)*, London: Communities and Local Government. www.communities.gov.uk

Koenig, H.G. (1998) *Handbook of Religion and Mental Health*, San Diego, CA: Academic Press.

Koenig, H.G., McCullough, M.E. and Larson, D.E. (eds) (2001) *Handbook of Religion and Health*, Oxford: Oxford University Press.

Kollontai, P. (2004) 'Messianic Jews and Jewish Identity', *Journal of Modern Jewish Studies*, 3 (2): 195–205.

Korecki, N. (2010) 'Guilty of Terrorism', *Chicago Sunday Times*, 19 March.

Kukathas, C. (1986) 'Liberalism and Its Critics', *Humane Studies Review,* Winter: 1–110.

Kukathas, C. (1992) 'Are There Any Cultural Rights?' *Political Theory,* 20 (1): 105–39.

Kukathas, C. (1997) 'Cultural Toleration', in W. Kymlicka and I. Shapiro (eds) *Ethnicity and Group Rights,* New York: New York University Press.

Kukathas, C. (2001) 'Is Feminism Bad for Multiculturalism?' *Public Affairs Quarterly,* 15 (2): 83–98.

Kymlicka, W. (1995) *Multicultural Citizenship,* New York: Oxford University Press.

Kymlicka, W. (1998) 'Introduction: An Emerging Consensus?' *Ethical Theory and Moral Practice,* 1: 143–57.

Kymlicka, W. (2001a) *Politics in the Vernacular: Nationalism, Multiculturalism and Citizenship,* New York: Oxford University Press.

Kymlicka, W. (2001b) 'Western Political Theory and Ethnic Relations in Eastern Europe', in W. Kymlicka and M. Opalski (eds) *Can Liberal Pluralism Be Exported?* New York: Oxford University Press.

Kymlicka, W. (2007) *Multicultural Odysseys: Navigating the New International Politics of Diversity,* Oxford: Oxford University Press.

Lakhani, N. (2009) 'UK Fails to Halt Female Genital Mutilation', *The Independent,* 20 December.

Law, I. (2010) *Racism and Ethnicity: Global Debates, Dilemmas, Directions,* Harlow: Pearson Education.

Leavey, G., Loewenthal, K. and King, M. (2007) 'Challenges to Sanctuary: The Clergy As a Resource for Mental Health Care in the Community', *Social Science and Medicine,* 65 (3): 548–59.

Lerner, G. (1993) *The Creation of Feminist Consciousness: From the Middle Ages to Eighteen Seventy,* New York: Oxford University Press.

Levison, C. (2005) 'Partners in Care', *Nursing Management,* 12 (6): 18–21.

Levitt, H. and Ware, K. (2006) 'Anything with Two Heads Is a Monster: Religious Leaders' Perspectives on Marital Equality and Domestic Violence', *Violence Against Women,* 12 (2): 1169–90.

Lewis, P. (2002) *Islamic Britain: Religion, Politics and Identity among British Muslims,* 2nd Edition, London: I.B. Tauris.

Lewis, P. (2006) 'Imams, Ulema and Sufis: Providers of Bridging Social Capital for British Pakistanis?' *Contemporary South Asia,* 15 (3): 273–87.

Leye, E. et al. (2006) 'Health Care in Europe for Women with Genital Mutilation', *Health Care for Women International,* 27 (4).

Leye, E. and Deblonde, J. (2004) *A Comparative Analysis of the Different Legal Approaches towards Female Genital Mutilation in the 15 EU Member States, and the Respective Judicial Outcomes in Belgium, France, Spain, Sweden and the United Kingdom,* Ghent: International Centre for Reproductive Health.

Lindley, J. (2002) 'Race or Religion? The Impact of Religion on the Employment and Earnings of Britain's Ethnic Communities', *Journal of Ethnic and Migration Studies,* 28 (3): 427–42.

Lindsey, E. (1994) 'What's Black and White and Lives in a Political Minefield?' *The Independent,* 16 August.

Local Government Association (2002) *Guidance on Community Cohesion,* London: LGA.

London Association of Community Relations Councils (1985) *In a Critical Condition: A Survey of Equal Opportunities in Employment in London's Health Authorities*, London: LACRC.

Lutz, H. (1991) 'The Myth of the "Other": Western Representation and Images of Migrant Women of So-Called Islamic Background', *International Review of Sociology* 2: 121–38.

McAspurren, L. (2005) *Religious Discrimination & Sectarianism in Scotland: A Brief Review of Evidence [2002–2004]*, Edinburgh: Scottish Executive Social Research.

MacCulloch, D. (2003) *Reformation: Europe's House Divided, 1490–1700*, London: Penguin.

McCullough, M.E. and Larson, D.B. (1999) 'Religion and Depression: A Review of the Literature', *Twin Research*, 2: 126–36.

McDonald, I., Bhavnani, R., Khan, L. and John, G. (1989) *Murder in the Playground*, London: Longsight Press.

Macey, M. (1991) 'Christian Fundamentalism: The Growth of a Monster?' Paper presented to the Women in Society Seminar Series, Bradford: University of Bradford.

Macey, M. (1992) 'Greater Europe: Integration or Ethnic Exclusion?' Special Issue, *The Political Quarterly*, 63 (5): 139–53.

Macey, M. (1995a) ' "Same Race" Adoption Policy: Anti-racism or Racism?' *Journal of Social Policy*, 24 (4): 473–91.

Macey, M. (1995b) 'Towards Racial Justice? A Re-evaluation of Anti-racism', *Critical Social Policy*, 15 (2/3): 126–46.

Macey, M. (1996) 'In the Best Interests of the Child? Race and Ethnic Matching in Adoption and Fostering', *Representing Children*, 9 (2): 83–98.

Macey, M. (1998; 2000; 2007) *Transracial Adoption: What's the Problem?* Berkshire: People in Harmony.

Macey, M. (1999a) 'Class, Gender and Religious Influences on Changing Patterns of Pakistani Muslim Male Violence in Bradford', *Ethnic and Racial Studies*, 22 (5): 845–66.

Macey, M. (1999b) 'Religion, Male Violence and the Control of Women: Pakistani Muslim Men in Bradford', *Gender and Development*, 7 (1): 48–55.

Macey, M. (2002) 'Interpreting Islam: Young Muslim Men's Involvement in Criminal Activity in Bradford', in B. Spalek (ed.) *Islam, Crime and the Criminal Justice System*, Devon: Willan Publishing.

Macey, M. (2005) *The 2001 Bradford Riot: Some Questions and Answers*, End of Research Project Report to West Yorkshire Police, Bradford: University of Bradford.

Macey, M. (2006) 'South Asian Migrants in Britain', in Alan Carling (ed.) *Globalization and Identity: Development and Integration in a Changing World*, London: I.B. Taurus.

Macey, M. (2007a) 'Ethnicity, Gender and Boundaries of Choice in Minority Ethnic Communities', in C. Beckett, O. Heathcote and M. Macey (eds) *Negotiating Boundaries? Identities, Sexualities, Diversities*, Newcastle: Cambridge Scholars Press.

Macey, M. (2007b) 'Islamic Political Radicalism in Britain: Pakistani Men in Bradford', in T. Abbas (ed.) *Islamic Political Radicalism: A European Comparative Perspective*, Edinburgh: Edinburgh University Press.

Macey, M. (2008) 'Transcontinental Marriage between British and Pakistani Citizens: Arranged or Forced?' *Pakistan Journal of Women's Studies: Alam-e-Niswan*, 15 (2): 1–28.

Macey, M. (2009) *Multiculturalism, Religion and Women: Doing Harm by Doing Good?* Basingstoke: Palgrave Macmillan.

Macey, M., Carling, A.H. and Furness, S. (2010) *The Power of Belief? Review of the Evidence on Religion or Belief and Equalities in Great Britain,* Bradford: University of Bradford. http://hdl.handle.net/10454/4394

McGhee, D. (2005) *Intolerant Britain? Hate, Citizenship and Difference,* Berkshire: Open University Press, McGraw-Hill Education.

McGrother, C.W., Bhaumik, S., Thorp, C.F., Watson, J.M. and Taub, N.A. (2002) 'Prevalence, Morbidity and Service Need among South Asian and White Adults with Intellectual Disability in Leicestershire, UK', *Journal of Intellectual Disability Research,* 46 (4): 299–309.

Mackenzie, J. (2006) 'Stigma and Dementia: South Asian and Eastern European Family Carers: Negotiating Stigma in Two Cultures', *Dementia. The International Journal of Social Research and Practice,* 5: 233–48.

McKerl, M. (2007) 'Multiculturalism, Gender and Violence. Multiculturalism – Is It Bad for Women?' *Culture and Religion,* 8 (2): 187–217.

McKinnon, C. (2006) *Toleration: A Critical Introduction,* Abingdon: Routledge.

McLoughlin, S. (2005) 'Mosques and the Public Space: Conflict and Cooperation in Bradford', *Journal of Ethnic and Migration Studies,* 31 (6): 1045–66.

Macpherson, Sir William of Cluny (1999) *The Stephen Lawrence Inquiry,* Cmnd. 42621, London: Home Office.

McTernan, O. (2003) *Violence in God's Name: Religion in an Age of Conflict,* London: Darton, Longman and Todd.

Mahoney, M. and Taj, S. (2006) *Muslim Women Talk Wales: Saheli Project Report,* Cardiff: Welsh Assembly Government.

Malik, K. (2005a) 'Born in Bradford', *Prospect* (115, October); available at www.kenanmalik.com

Malik, K. (2005b) 'Islamophobia Myth', *Prospect* (107, February); available at www.kenanmalik.com

Malik, K. (2009) *From Fatwa to Jihad: The Rushdie Affair and Its Legacy,* London: Atlantic Books.

Maltby, J., Lewis, C.A. and Day, L. (1999) 'Religious Orientation and Psychological Well-Being: The Role of the Frequency of Personal Prayer', *British Journal of Health Psychology,* 4: 363–78.

Manji, I. (2005) *The Trouble with Islam Today: A Wake-Up Call for Honesty and Change,* Edinburgh: Mainstream Publishing Company.

Margalit, A. and Halbertal, M. (1994) 'Liberalism and the Right to Culture', *Social Research,* 61 (3): 491–510.

Marsh, A. (2002) *Discrimination in Europe,* London: Policy Studies Institute.

Marshall, C. (2007) 'Killed for Loving the Wrong Man', BBC News, 11 June. news.bbc.co.uk

Martin, D. (1997) *Does Christianity Cause War?* Oxford: Clarendon Press.

Martin, D. (2001) *Pentecostalism: The World Their Parish,* Oxford: Blackwell.

Marx, K. (1957 [1844]) *Marx and Engels on Religion,* Moscow: Progress Publishers.

Mason, D. (1990) 'A Rose by Any Other Name … ? Categorisation, Identity and Social Science', *New Community,* 17: 123–33.

Mason, D. (2000) *Race and Ethnicity in Modern Britain*, 2nd Edition, Oxford: Oxford University Press.

Mather, Y. (1998) 'Gender and Islamic Fundamentalism', Paper presented to the Gendering the Millennium Conference, Dundee: University of Dundee.

May, S. (ed.) (1999) *Critical Multiculturalism*, London: Falmer Press.

Media Diversity Institute (2002) *The Demonising of Islam*. www.media-diversity.org

Meer, N. (2007) 'Muslim Schools in Britain: Challenging Mobilisations or Logical Developments?' *Asia Pacific Journal of Education*, 27 (1): 55–71.

Meeto, V. and Mirza, H.S. (2007) 'There Is Nothing "Honourable" about Honour Killings: Gender, Violence and the Limits of Multiculturalism', *Women's Studies International Forum*, 30: 187–200.

Melotti, U. (1997) 'International Migration in Europe: Social Projects and Political Cultures', in T. Modood and P. Werbner (eds) *The Politics of Multiculturalism in the New Europe: Racism, Identity and Community*, London: Zed Books.

Meral, A. (2008) *No Place to Call Home: Experiences of Converts from Islam. Failures of the International Community,* Surrey: Christian Solidarity Worldwide. www.csw.org.uk

Metropolitan Police Authority (2004) *Report of the MPA Scrutiny on MPS Stop and Search Practice*, London: MPA.

Midgley, M. (2004) *The Myths We Live By*, London: Routledge.

Miles, R. (1989) *Racism*, London: Routledge.

Miller, H. (2001) 'Meeting the Challenge: The Jewish Schooling Phenomenon in the UK', *Oxford Review of Education*, 27 (4): 501–13.

Miller, J., Bland, N. and Quinton, P. (2000) *The Impact of Stops and Searches on Crime and the Community*, RDS Police Research Series Paper 127, London: Home Office.

Miller, M. (2004) *Responses to Female Genital Mutilation/Cutting in Europe*, Florence: UNICEF Innocenti Research Centre.

Minogue, K. (2005) 'Introduction: Multiculturalism: A Dictatorship of Virtue', in P. West (ed.) *The Poverty of Multiculturalism*, London: Civitas.

Mir, G., Nocon, A. and Ahmad, W. (2001) *Learning Difficulties and Ethnicity*, London: Department of Health.

Mirza, M., Senthilkumaran, A. and Ja'far, Z. (2007) *Living Apart Together: British Muslims and the Paradox of Multiculturalism*, London: The Policy Exchange.

Modood, T. (1988) '"Black", Racial Equality and Asian Identity', *New Community*, 14 (3): 397–404.

Modood, T. (1992) 'British Asian Muslims and the Rushdie Affair', in J. Donald and A. Rattansi (eds) *'Race', Culture and Difference*, London: Sage Publications.

Modood, T. (1997) 'Introduction: The Politics of Multiculturalism in the New Europe', in T. Modood and P. Werbner (eds) *The Politics of Multiculturalism in the New Europe: Racism, Identity and Community*, London: Zed Books.

Modood, T. (2001) 'Multiculturalism', in J. Kreiger (ed.) *The Oxford Companion to Politics in the World*, Oxford: Oxford University Press.

Modood, T. (2007) *Multiculturalism: A Civic Idea*, Cambridge: Polity Press.

Modood, T. and Werbner, P. (eds) (1997) *The Politics of Multiculturalism in the New Europe: Racism, Identity and Community*, London: Zed Books.

Modood, T., Bethoud, R., Lakey, J., Nazroo, J., Smith, P, Virdee, S. and Beishon, S. (1997) *Ethnic Minorities in Britain: Diversity and Disadvantage*, London: Policy Studies Institute.

Moghadam, V. (ed.) (1994) *Identity Politics and Women: Cultural Reassertions and Feminisms in International Perspective*, San Francisco: Westview Press.

Moghissi, H. (2000) *Populism and Feminism in Iran: Women's Struggle in a Male-Defined Revolutionary Movement*, New York: St. Martin's.

Moghissi, H. (2005) 'Neo-patriarchy and Gender Violence in Jordan: Women and Islam', *Critical Concepts in Sociology*, 2: 104–41.

Moore, K., Mason, P. and Lewis, J. (2008). *Images of Islam in the UK: The Representation of British Muslims in the National Print News Media 2000–2008*, Cardiff: Cardiff School of Journalism, Media and Cultural Studies.

MORI (2007) *Public Attitudes towards Cohesion and Integration*, Poll for the Commission on Integration and Cohesion, London: DCLG. www.integrationandcohesion. org.uk

Mornington, M. (2005) in S. Malik, 'A Community in Denial', *New Statesman*, 25 July.

Moss, P. (2006) 'The Limits to Integration', *The World Tonight, Mirpur*, BBC. www. bbc.co.uk

Muir, H., Smith, L. and Richardson, R. (2004) *Islamophobia: Issues, Challenges and Action. A Report by the Commission on British Muslims and Islamophobia*, Stoke on Trent: Trentham Books.

Mullard, C. (1982) 'Multiracial Education in Britain: From Assimilation to Cultural Pluralism', in J. Tierney (ed.) *Race, Migration and Schooling*, New York: Holt, Rinehart and Winston.

Mullard, C. (1985) *Race, Power and Resistance*, London: Routledge and Kegan Paul.

Munanie, E. (2001) *Female Genital Mutilation: Knowledge, Attitudes and Responses among Communities and Health Professionals: A Case Study*, London: FORWARD.

Muslim Arbitration Tribunal (2008) *Liberation from Forced Marriage*, London: MAT.

Muslim Parliament of Great Britain (2006) *Child Protection in a Faith-Based Environment: A Guideline Report*, London: Muslim Parliament of Great Britain.

Nadirshaw, Z. (1997) 'Cultural Issues', in J. O'Hara and A. Sperlinger (eds) *Adults with Learning Disabilities: A Practical Approach for Health Professionals*, Chichester: John Wiley & Sons.

Nasir, J.J. (1990) *The Islamic Law of Personal Status*, 2nd Edition, London: Graham and Trotman.

National Advisory Group (1999) *Breaking the Chain of Hate: A National Survey Examining Levels of Homophobic Crime and Community Confidence towards the Police Service*, London: Stonewall.

National Council of Hindu Temples (UK) (2008). www.nchtuk.org

Nazroo, J.Y. (1997) *Ethnicity and Mental Health*, London: Policy Studies Institute.

Neilsen, J.S. (1984) *Muslim Immigration and Settlement in Britain*, Birmingham: Centre for the Study of Islam and Christian-Muslim Relations.

Newnham, A. (1986) *Employment, Unemployment and Black People*, London: The Runnymede Trust.

Nietzsche, F. (1992) *Thus Spake Zarathustra*, London: Penguin Classics.

Norris, P. and Inglehart, R. (2007) 'Uneven Secularization in the United States and Western Europe', in T. Banchoff (ed.) *Democracy and the New Religious Pluralism*, New York: Oxford University Press.

Nussbaum, M. (1999) 'A Plea for Difficulty', in J. Cohen, M. Howard and M.C. Nussbaum (eds) Susan Moller Okin (with respondents) *Is Multiculturalism Bad for Women?* Princeton, NJ: Princeton University Press.

Nussbaum, M. (2000) *Women and Human Development: The Capabilities Approach*, Cambridge: Cambridge University Press.

Nye, M. (2001) *Multiculturalism and Minority Religions in Britain: Krishna Consciousness, Religious Freedom and the Politics of Location*, Richmond: Curzon Press.

O'Beirne, M. (2004) *Religion in England and Wales: Findings from the 2001 Home Office Citizenship Survey*, London: Home Office.

Office for National Statistics (2002) *Social Focus in Brief: Ethnicity*. www.statistics.gov.uk/census2001

Office for National Statistics (2003) *Census 2001: National Report for England and Wales*. www.statistics.gov.uk

Office for National Statistics (2004) *Focus on Religion*. www.statistics.gov.uk

Office for National Statistics (2006) *Focus on Ethnicity and Religion*. www.statistics.gov.uk

O'Hara, J. (2003) 'Learning Disabilities and Ethnicity: Achieving Cultural Competence', *Advances in Psychiatric Treatment*, 9: 166–76.

O'Hara, J. and Martin, H. (2003) 'Parents with Learning Disabilities: A Study of Gender and Cultural Perspectives from East London', *British Journal of Learning Disabilities*, 31, 18–24.

Okin, S. Moller (1989) *Justice, Gender and the Family*, New York: Basic Books.

Okin, S. Moller (1997) 'Is Multiculturalism Bad for Women?' *Boston Review*, 22: 25–8.

Okin, S. Moller (1998) 'Feminism and Multiculturalism: Some Tensions', *Ethics*, 108: 661–84.

Okin, S. Moller (1999) 'Is Multiculturalism Bad for Women?' in J. Cohen, M. Howard and M.C. Nussbaum (eds) *Susan Moller Okin (with respondents) Is Multiculturalism Bad for Women?* Princeton, NJ: Princeton University Press.

Okin, S. Moller (2002) 'Mistresses of Their Own Destiny: Group Rights, Gender, and Realistic Rights of Exit', *Ethics*, 112: 205–30.

Omi, M. and Winant, H. (1994) *Racial Formation in the United States: From the 1960s to the 1990s*, New York: Routledge.

O'Neill, M. and Holdaway, S. (2007) '"Window Dressing": The Views of Black Police Associations on Recruitment and Training', *Journal of Ethnic and Migration Studies*, 33 (3): 483–500.

Osler, A. (2007) *Faith Schools and Community Cohesion*, Interim Report, London: Runnymede Trust.

Ouseley, Sir H. (2001) *Community Pride Not Prejudice: Making Diversity Work in Bradford*, the *Ouseley Report*, Bradford: Bradford Vision.

Overall, A.D.J., Ahma, M. and Nichols, R.A. (2002) 'The Effect of Reproductive Compensation on Recessive Disorders within Consanguineous Human Populations', *Heredity*, 88 (6): 474–9.

Panniker, K.N. (1996) 'Is the Notion of Human Rights a Western Concept?' in H. Steiner and P. Alston (eds) *International Human Rights in Context*, New York: Oxford University Press.

Pape, R. (2005) *Dying to Win: The Strategic Logic of Suicide Bombers*, London: Random House.

Parekh, B. (1998) 'Cultural Diversity and Liberal Democracy', in G. Mahajan (ed.) *Democracy, Difference and Social Justice*, New Delhi: Oxford University Press.

Parekh, B. (2000a) *The Future of Multi-ethnic Britain*, London: Profile Books.

Parekh, B. (2000b) *Rethinking Multiculturalism,* Basingstoke: Palgrave Macmillan.

Parekh, B. (2003) 'Muslims in Britain', *Prospect,* July.

Parekh, B. (2005) 'Multiculturalism Is a Civilised Dialogue', *The Guardian,* 21 January.

Parsons, T. (1944) *The Social System,* New York: The Free Press.

Patel, P. (1998) 'Southall Black Sisters', Keynote Address to the Conference on Domestic Violence in Asian Communities, Bradford: Keighley Domestic Violence Forum/University of Bradford.

Patel, P. and Siddiqui, H. (2010) 'Shrinking Secular Spaces: Asian Women at the Intersect of Race, Religion and Gender', in R.K. Thiara and A.K. Gill (eds) *Violence against Women in South Asian Communities: Issues for Policy and Practice,* London: Jessica Kingsley Publishers.

Paterson, I. (2000) 'Salvation through Education? The Changing Social Status of Scottish Catholics', in M.T. Devine (ed.) *Scotland's Shame? Bigotry and Discrimination in Modern Scotland,* Edinburgh: Mainstream.

Paterson, I. and Iannelli, C. (2006) 'Religion, Social Mobility and Education in Scotland', *British Journal of Sociology,* 57 (3): 353–77.

Peach, C. (2006) 'Islam, Ethnicity and South Asian Religions in the London 2001 Census', *Transactions of the Institute of British Geographers,* 31 (3): 353–71.

Pell, G. (2007) *60/76, The Business Commission on Race Equality in the Workplace,* London: National Employment Panel.

Pennell, H., West, A. and Hind, A. (2007) *Religious Composition and Admission Processes of Faith Secondary Schools in London.* London: LSE.

Pew Global Attitudes Project (2008) *Unfavorable Views of Jews and Muslims on the Increase in Europe,* 17 September. www.pewglobal.org

Phillips, A. (2003) 'When Culture Means Gender: Issues of Cultural Defence in the English Courts', *The Modern Law Review,* 66 (4): 510–31.

Phillips, A. (2007) *Multiculturalism without Culture,* Princeton, NJ: Princeton University Press.

Phillips, A. and Dustin, M. (2004) 'UK Initiatives on Forced Marriage: Regulation, Dialogue and Action', *Political Studies,* 52: 531–51.

Phillips, D. (2006) 'Parallel Lives? Challenging Discourses of British Muslim Self-Segregation', *Environment and Planning D: Society and Space,* 24: 25–40.

Phillips, D., Butt, F. and Davis, C. (2002) 'The Racialisation of Space in Bradford', *The Regional Review,* July.

Phillips, T. (2006) Speech to the Royal Geographical Society Annual Conference, London, 29 August.

Phillips, T. (2007) *Fairness and Freedom: The Final Report of the Equalities Review,* London: Cabinet Office.

Phillipson, C., Ahmed, N. and Latimer, J. (2003) *Women in Transition: A Study of the Experiences of Bangladeshi Women Living in Tower Hamlets,* University of Bristol: The Policy Press.

Pilger, J. (1988) 'Foreword', in K. Tompson, *Under Siege: Racial Violence in Britain Today,* Harmondsworth: Penguin.

Pipes, D. (2003) *The Rushdie Affair: The Novel, the Ayatolla and the West,* 2nd Edition, New Brunswick, NJ: Transaction Publishers.

Pitcher, D. (2010) 'Thank God for Catholic Adoption Societies', *The Telegraph,* 17 March.

Platt, L. (2002) *Parallel Lives? Poverty among Ethnic Minority Groups in Britain,* London: CPAG.

Platt, L. (2007a) *Migration and Social Mobility: The Life Chances of Britain's Minority Ethnic Communities,* York: Joseph Rowntree Foundation.

Platt, L. (2007b) *Moving on Up? Pay Gaps: The Position of Ethnic Minority Men and Women,* Manchester: EOC.

Platt, L. (2007c) *Poverty and Ethnicity in the UK,* York: Joseph Rowntree Foundation.

Poldermans, S. (2006) *Combating Female Genital Mutilation in Europe: A Comparative Analysis of Legislative and Preventative Tools in the Netherlands, France, the United Kingdom and Austria,* MA Thesis, Austria: University of Vienna.

Poole, E. (2002) *Reporting Islam: Media Representations of British Muslims,* London: I.B. Tauris.

Pote, H.I. and Orrell, M.W. (2002) 'Perceptions of Schizophrenia in Multicultural Britain', *Ethnicity and Health,* 7 (1): 7–20.

Poulsen, M. (2005) 'The "New Geography" of Ethnicity in Britain?' Paper presented to the Royal Geographical Society, London.

Poulter, S. (1998) *Ethnicity, Law and Human Rights: The English Experience,* Oxford: Clarendon Press.

Purdam K., Afkhami R., Crockett A. and Olsen W. (2007) 'Religion in the UK: An Overview of Equality Statistics and Evidence Gaps', *Journal of Contemporary Religion,* 22 (2): 147–68.

Puri, S. (2005) 'Rhetoric v. Reality: The Effect of "Multiculturalism" on Doctors' Responses to Battered South Asian Women in the United States and Britain', *Patterns of Prejudice,* 39 (4): 416–30.

Puri, S. (2007) 'There Is No Such Thing as Too Many Daughters, but Not Too Many Sons: The Interaction of Medical Technology, Son Preference and Sex Selection among South Asian Immigrants in the United States', Paper presented to the Second National Bioethics Conference, Bangalore, India, December.

Ramadan, T. (2004) *Western Muslims and the Future of Islam,* Oxford: Oxford University Press.

Randerson, J. (2006) 'Revealed: Rise of Creationism in UK Schools', *The Guardian,* 27 November.

Rath, J., Groenendijk, K. and Penninx R. (1991) 'The Recognition and Institutionalisation of Islam in Belgium, Great Britain and the Netherlands', *New Community,* 18 (1): 104–14.

Rattansi, A. (1992) 'Changing the Subject? Racism, Culture and Education', in J. Donald and A. Rattansi (eds) *'Race', Culture and Difference,* London: Sage Publications.

Rattansi, A. (2005) 'Who's British? *Prospect* and the New Assimilationism', in *Cohesion, Community and Citizenship,* Conference Proceedings, London: The Runnymede Trust.

Raw, A. (2006) *Schools Linking Project 2005–06: Full Final Evaluation Report,* Bradford: Education Bradford.

Rawls, J. (1999) *The Law of Peoples,* Cambridge, MA: Harvard University Press.

Raz, A. (2006) *She Who Disputes: Muslim Women Shape the Debate,* London: Muslim Women's Network.

Raz, J. (1994) 'Multiculturalism: A Liberal Perspective', in *Ethics in the Public Domain: Essays in the Morality of Law and Politics,* New York: Clarendon Press.

Reder, M. and Schmidt, J. (2010) 'Habermas and Religion', in J. Habermas (ed.) *An Awareness of What Is Missing: Faith and Reason in a Post-secular Age,* Cambridge: Polity Press.

Reeves, F., Abbas, T. and Pedroso, D. (2009) 'The "Dudley Mosque Project": A Case of Islamophobia and Local Politics', *The Political Quarterly,* 80 (4): 502–16.

Rehman-Sabba, A. (1999) *Arranged Marriages in an Asian Community,* BA Dissertation, Bradford: University of Bradford.

Rex, J. (1991) 'Ethnic Mobilisation in a Multi-cultural Society', *Innovation,* 5 (3): 65–74.

Richardson, J. (2001) 'British Muslims in the Broadsheet Press: A Challenge to Cultural Hegemony?' *Journalism Studies,* 2 (2): 221–42.

Richardson, R. (2007) *'Islam' and 'the West' – Competing Narratives in the UK Media,* Budapest: European Youth Centre.

Ritchie, D. (2001) *Report of the Independent Review: One Oldham One Future,* Manchester: Government Office for the North West.

Roald, A. (2001) *Women in Islam: The Western Experience,* London: Routledge.

Robinson, D. (2005) 'The Search for Community Cohesion: Key Themes and Dominant Concepts of the Public Policy Agenda', *Urban Studies,* 42 (8): 1411–27.

Robinson, F. (1988) *Varieties of South Asian Islam,* Warwick: Centre for Research in Ethnic Relations.

Romito, P. (2008) *A Deafening Silence: Hidden Violence against Women and Children,* Bristol: The Policy Press.

Rooney, B. (1988) 'Some Obstacles to Change in Social Work and Social Work Organization', in S. Allen and M. Macey (eds) *Race and Social Policy,* London: ESRC.

Ross, A.J., Heim, D., Bakshi, N., Davies, J.B., Flatley, K.J. and Hunter, S.C. (2004) 'Drug Issues Affecting Chinese, Indian and Pakistani People Living in Greater Glasgow', *Drugs: Education, Prevention and Policy,* 1: 49–65.

Rozario, S. (2005) 'Genetics, Religion and Identity among British Bangladeshis: Some Initial Findings', *Diversity in Health and Social Care,* 2: 187–96.

Ruby, T. (2004) *Immigrant Muslim Women and the Hijab: Sites of Struggle in Crafting and Negotiating Identities in Canada,* Saskatchewan: University of Saskatchenewan.

Rushdie, S. (1988) *The Satanic Verses,* London: Viking Books.

Saharso, S. (2005) 'Sex Selective Abortion: Gender, Culture and Dutch Public Policy', *Ethnicities,* 5 (2): 248–81.

Sahgal, G. (1992) 'Secular Spaces: The Experience of Asian Women Organising', in N. Yuval-Davis and G. Sahgal (eds) *Refusing Holy Orders,* London: Virago Press.

Samad, Y. and Eade, J. (2002) *Community Perceptions of Forced Marriage,* London: FCO.

Samaroo, A. (2005) *Cultural Influences on Domestic Violence in Asian Communities in Britain: Service Providers' Perspective on the Relationship between Cultural Practices and Domestic Violence,* MPhil Thesis, Bradford: University of Bradford.

Sandercock, L. (2006) 'Spirituality and the Urban Professions: The Paradox at the Heart of Urban Planning', *Planning Theory and Practice,* 7 (1): 65–97.

Sané, P. (2007) 'Preface', in M. Koenig and P. de Guchteneire (eds) *Democracy and Human Rights in Multicultural Societies,* Aldershot: Ashgate.

Sani, F. and Reicher, S. (2000) 'Contested Identities and Schisms in Groups: Opposing the Ordination of Women as Priests in the Church of England', *The British Journal of Social Psychology*, 39 (1): 95–112.

Savage, B. (2007) *Sexual Orientation and Religion or Belief Discrimination in the Workplace*, London: ACAS.

Scarman, Rt. Hon. Lord (1982) *The Scarman Report*, Harmondsworth: Penguin.

Schain, M. (1999) 'Minorities and Immigrant Incorporation in France', in C. Joppke and S. Lukes (eds) *Multicultural Questions*, New York: Oxford University Press.

Scott, S. with Anwar, S. (2003) *The Educational Welfare of Female Students from Ethnic Minorities in the Department of Business Studies*, Bradford: Bradford College Equality Project.

Scottish Executive (2005) *Analysis of Religion in the 2001 Census: Summary Report*, Edinburgh: Scottish Executive.

Seidman, S. (1992) 'Postmodern Social Theory as Narrative with a Moral Intent', in S. Seidman and D.G. Wagner (eds) *Postmodernism and Social Theory*, Oxford: Basil Blackwell.

Sellick, M. (2004) *Muslim Housing Experiences*, Sector Study 34, London: The Housing Association.

Sen, A. (2006) *Identity and Violence: The Illusion of Destiny*, London: Allen Lane.

Shachar, A. (1998) 'Group Identity and Women's Rights in Family Law: The Perils of Multicultural Accommodation', *Journal of Political Philosophy*, 6: 285–305.

Shachar, A. (1999) 'The Paradox of Multicultural Vulnerability: Individual Rights, Identity Groups and the State', in C. Joppke and S. Lukes (eds) *Multicultural Questions*, New York: Oxford University Press.

Shachar, A. (2001) *Multicultural Jurisdictions: Cultural Differences and Women's Rights*, Cambridge: Cambridge University Press.

Shah, R. (1995) *The Silent Majority – Children with Disabilities in Asian Families*, London: The National Children's Bureau.

Shah, R. (1999) *Summary Report of the Development Work and Research Undertaken for Washwood Heath Young Disabled People's Project*, Birmingham: The Naseby Centre.

Shah-Kazemi, S.N. (2001) *Untying the Knot: Muslim Women, Divorce, and the Sharia*, London: Nuffield Foundation.

Shaw, A. (1994) 'The Pakistani Community in Oxford', in R. Ballard (ed.) *Desh Pardesh: The South Asian Presence in Britain*, London: C. Hurst.

Shaw, A. (2001) 'Kinship, Cultural Preference and Immigration: Consanguineous Marriage among British Pakistanis', *Journal of the Royal Anthropological Institute*, 7 (2): 315–34.

Sheikh, A., Gatrad, A.R., Sheikh, U., Panesar, S.S. and Shafi, S. (2004) 'The Myth of Multifaith Chaplaincy: A National Survey of Hospital Chaplaincy Departments in England and Wales', *Diversity in Health and Social Care*, 1: 93–7.

Simon, R.J. (1974) 'An Assessment of Racial Awareness, Preference, and Self-Identity among White and Adopted Non-White Children', *Social Problems*, 22 (1): 43–7.

Simon, R.J. and Alstein, H. (1987) *Transracial Adoptees and Their Families: A Study of Identity and Commitment*, New York: Praeger.

Simon, R.J., Alstein, H. and Melli, M. (1993) *The Case for Transracial Adoption*, Washington, DC: The American University Press.

Simpson, L. (2002) ' "Race" Statistics: Theirs and Ours', *Radical Statistics*, 79/80: 76–95.

Simpson, L. (2004) 'Statistics of Racial Segregation: Measures, Evidence and Policy', *Urban Studies*, 42 (3): 661–81.

Simpson, L. (2005) 'On the Measurement and Meaning of Residential Segregation: A Reply to Johnston, Poulsen and Forrest', *Urban Studies*, 42 (7): 1229–30.

Singer, P. (1991) *Animal Liberation*, London: Harper Collins.

Singh, D. (2007) *Our Shared Future*, Commission on Integration and Cohesion, London: DCLG www.integrationandcohesion.org.uk

Singh, S.P. and Burns, T. (2008) 'Race and Mental Health: There Is More to Race Than Racism', *BMJ*, 333: 648–51.

Smith, D.J. (1977) *Patterns of Discrimination*, Harmondsworth: Penguin.

Smith, G. (2000) 'Global Systems and Religious Diversity in the Inner City – Migrants in the East End of London', *International Journal on Multicultural Societies*, UNESCO, 2 (1): 16–39.

Smith, G. and Lowndes, V. (2007) 'Faith-Based Voluntary Action', *Mapping the Public Policy Landscape*, London: ESRC/NCVO Seminar Series.

Smith, H. (1994) 'A Damaging Experience: Black Disabled Children and Educational and Social Services Provision', in N. Begum, M. Hill and A. Stevens (eds) *Reflections: Views of Black People on Their Lives and Community Care*. CCETSW Paper 32.3. Cambridge: Black Rock Press.

Sniderman, P.M. and Hagendoorn, L. (2007) *When Ways of Life Collide*, Princeton, NJ: Princeton University Press.

Social Exclusion Unit (2005) *Improving Services, Improving Lives: Evidence and Key Themes*, Interim Report, London: ODPM.

Solomon, S. (2007) 'Sex Selective Abortion Comes to Canada', *National Review of Medicine*, 4 (15), 18 September.

Southall Black Sisters (2008) in HAC, *Domestic Violence, Forced Marriage and 'Honour'– Based Violence*, Sixth Report of Session 2007–08, Volume 2: Ev.302, London: The Stationery Office.

Southwark, T. (Bishop of) (2004) *Church of England Response to DTI Consultation Document Fairness for All: A New Commission for Equality and Human Rights*.

Spalek, B. and Wilson, D. (2001) 'Not Just "Visitors" to Prisons: The Experience of Imams Who Work Inside the Penal System', *The Howard Journal*, 40 (1): 3–13.

Spiegel International (2008) 'Go Ahead for Germany's Biggest Mosque', 29 August.

Spinner-Halev, J. (2001) 'Feminism, Multiculturalism, Oppression, and the State', *Ethics*, 112: 84–113.

Sproston, K. and Mindell, J. (eds) (2006) *Health Survey for England 2004, Volume 1: The Health of Minority Ethnic Groups*, Leeds: The Information Centre.

Sproston, K. and Nazroo, J. (eds) (2002) *Ethnic Minority Psychiatric Illness Rates in the Community (EMPIRIC)*, London: The Stationery Office.

Stacey, M. (1997) 'About Genetics: Aspects of Social Structure Worth Considering', in A. Clarke and E. Parsons (eds) *Culture, Kinship and Genes: Towards Cross-cultural Genetics*, Basingstoke: Palgrave Macmillan.

Stanfield, J.H. II (1993) 'Epistemological Considerations', in J.H. Stanfield and R.M. Dennis (eds) *Race and Ethnicity in Research Methods*, London: Sage Publications.

Stark, R. (1990) 'Secularization, RIP', *Sociology of Religion*, 60 (3): 270 (cited in Norris and Inglehart, 2007).

Stark, R. and Finke, R. (2000) *Acts of Faith: Explaining the Human Side of Religion,* Berkeley: University of California Press.

Steiner, H.J. and Alston, P. (1996) *International Human Rights in Context: Law, Politics, Morals,* Oxford: Clarendon Press.

Stewart, D.E. (1998) *Female Genital Mutilation: The Midwifery Case,* MA Dissertation, Bradford: University of Bradford.

Stonewall (2010) *Stonewall Statement on Exemptions for Religious Employers. 3 February 2010,* London: Stonewall. www.stonewall.org.uk

Stonewall/DfCSF (2007) *Safe to Learn: Embedding Anti-bullying Work in Schools,* London: DfCSF.

Suleman, A. (2009) 'Genetics', Presentation to a day conference on Consanguineous Marriage and Inherited Disorders, Bradford: Bradford and Airedale NHS Teaching Primary Care Trust.

Taguieff, P.-A. and Camiller, P. (2004) *Rising from the Muck: The New Anti-semitism in Europe,* Chicago: Ivan R. Dee.

Taher, A. (2008) 'Revealed: UK's First Official Sharia Courts', *The Sunday Times,* 14 September.

Tajfel, H. (1970) 'Experiments in Intergroup Discrimination', *Scientific American* (223): 96–102.

Taylor, C. (1991) *The Ethics of Authenticity,* Cambridge, MA: Harvard University Press.

Taylor, C. (1994) 'The Politics of Recognition', in A. Gutmann (ed.) *Multiculturalism: Examining the Politics of Recognition,* Princeton, NJ: Princeton University Press.

Tompson, K. (1989) *Under Siege: Racial Violence in Britain Today,* Harmondsworth: Penguin.

Towler, R. and Coxon, A.P.M. (1979) *The Fate of the Anglican Clergy: A Sociological Study,* London: Macmillan.

Troyna, B. (1993) *Racism and Education,* Buckingham: Open University Press.

Troyna, B. and Williams, J. (1986) *Racism, Education and the State,* Beckenham: Croom Helm.

Tully, J. (1995) *Strange Multiplicity: Constitutionalism in an Age of Diversity,* Cambridge: Cambridge University Press.

Turner, B.S. (1991) *Religion and Social Theory,* 2nd Edition, London: Sage Publications.

Tutu, D. [Archbishop] (2007) *Williams Should Tackle Anglican Homophobia, says Desmond Tutu,* Ekklesia, 19 November. www.ekklesia.co.uk

Uddin (Baroness of Bethnal Green) and Ahmed (Lord of Rotherham) (2000) *A Choice by Right: The Report of the Working Group on Forced Marriage,* London: Home Office.

UK Border Agency (2007) *Marriage Visas: Pre-entry English Requirements for Spouses: Consultation Paper,* London: UK Border Agency.

Utti, N. [Sister] (2006) *Religion, Gender and Ministry: An Analysis of Catholic Principles versus Practice in the Formation of Priests and Religious in Nigeria,* PhD Thesis, Bradford: University of Bradford.

Valins, O. (2003) 'Defending Identities or Segregating Communities? Faith-Based Schooling and the UK Jewish Community', *Geoforum,* 34: 235–47.

Vertovek, S. and Peach, C. (eds) (1997) *Muslims in Europe,* Basingstoke: Palgrave Macmillan.

Voas, D. and Bruce, S. (2004) 'The 2001 Census and Christian Identification in Britain, *Journal of Contemporary Religion*, 19 (1): 23–8.

Voas, D. and Bruce, S. (2006) 'Is Religion Giving Way to Spirituality?' *Sociology Review*, 15(4): 14–16.

Vulliamy, E. (2006) 'Welcome to the New Holy Land', *The Observer (Review)*, 17 December, 4–6.

Waldby, C. (2003) *Literature Review and Annotated Bibliography: Social and Ethical Aspects of Sex Selection*, London: Human Fertilisation and Embryology Authority.

Walji, M. (2008) 'Cousin Marriage: A Cause for Concern?' *BioNews*, 10 June.

Wallman, S. (1986) 'Ethnicity and the Boundary Process in Context', in J. Rex and D. Mason (eds) *Theories of Race and Ethnic Relations*, Cambridge: Cambridge University Press.

Walls, P. and Williams, R. (2003) 'Sectarianism at Work: Accounts of Employment Discrimination against Irish Catholics in Scotland', *Ethnic and Racial Studies*, 26 (4): 632–62.

Waterfield, B. (2010) 'Defamation Case over Prophet Mohammed Cartoons "To Be Held" in Britain', *The Telegraph*, 16 March.

Watson, C.W. (2000) *Multiculturalism*, Buckingham: Open University Press.

Weber, M. (1961) *From Max Weber, Essays in Sociology*, ed. H. Gerth and C. Wright Mills, London: Routledge and Kegan Paul.

Weber, M. (1963) *The Sociology of Religion*, trans. E. Fischoff, Boston: Beacon Press.

Weil-Curiel, L. (2002) *Combating Sexual Mutilation in France through the Application of the Law*, Campaign Against Sexual Mutilation (CAMS). www.cams-fgm.org

Weiss, S. (2004) *Religion and Faith in Focus: Statistics on Employment, Unemployment, Qualifications and Religion*. www.walthamforest.gov.uk

Welchman, L. and Hossain, S. (eds) (2005) *Honour: Crimes, Paradigms and Violence against Women*, London: Zed Books.

Weller, P. (2003) *Religions in the UK: A Multi-faith Directory*, Derby: The Multi-faith Centre.

Weller, P. (2004) 'Identity, Politics, and the Future(s) of Religion in the UK: The Case of the Religion Questions in the 2001 Decennial Census', *Journal of Contemporary Religion*, 19 (1): 3–21.

Weller, P. (2006) 'Addressing Religious Discrimination and Islamophobia: Muslims and Liberal Democracies: The Case of the United Kingdom', *Journal of Islamic Studies*, 17 (3): 295–325.

Weller, P. (2008) *Religious Diversity in the UK: Contours and Issues*, London: Continuum.

Weller, P., Feldman, A. and Purdham, K. (2001) *Religious Discrimination in England and Wales*, Home Office Research Study 220, London: Home Office.

Welsh Assembly (2005) *Housing Research Summary: A Profile of the Housing and Socio-economic Circumstances of Black and Minority Ethnic People in Wales in 2001*, Cardiff: Welsh Assembly Government.

Whitfield, J. (2004) *Unhappy Dialogue: The Metropolitan Police and Black Londoners in Post-war Britain*, Devon: Willan Publishing.

Willett, C. (ed.) (1998) *Theorizing Multiculturalism: A Guide to the Current Debate*, Malden, MA: Blackwell Publishers.

Wilson, B.R. (1966) *Religion in a Secular Society: A Sociological Comment*, London: Watts.

Wilson, B. (1982) *Religion in Sociological Perspective,* Oxford: Oxford University Press.

Wirsing, R.G. (1981) *Protection of Ethnic Minorities: Comparative Perspectives,* New York: Pergamon Press.

Wistrich, R.S. (1992) *The Longest Hatred,* London: Mandarin Publishers.

Woodhead, L. (2009) *'Religion or Belief': Identifying Issues and Priorities,* Manchester: EHRC.

Woolaston, H. (2008) *Realising Our Potential: Promoting the Talents of Muslim Women,* North West Regional Assembly.

Wright Mills, C. (1959) *The Sociological Imagination,* Oxford: Oxford University Press.

Wynne-Jones, J. (2008) 'Multiple Wives Will Mean Multiple Benefits', *The Telegraph,* 18 April.

Yalçin-Heckman, L. (1997) 'The Perils of Ethnic Associational Life in Europe: Turkish Migrants in Germany and France', in T. Modood and P. Werbner (eds) *The Politics of Multiculturalism in the New Europe: Racism, Identity and Community,* London: Zed Books.

Yip, A.K.T. (2002a) *A Minority within s Minority: British Non-heterosexual Muslims,* End of Award Report, R000223530, Swindon: ESRC.

Yip, A.K.T. (2002b) 'The Persistence of Faith among Non-heterosexual Christians', *Journal for the Scientific Study of Religion,* 41 (2): 199–212.

Yip, A.K.T. (2004) 'Negotiating Space with Family and Kin in Identity Construction: The Narratives of British Non-heterosexual Muslims', *Sociological Review,* 2 (3): 336–50.

Yip, A.K.T. and Keenan, M. (2004) 'By Name United, by Sex Divided: A Brief Analysis of the Current Crisis Facing the Anglican Communion', *Sociological Research Online,* 9 (1).

Yorkshire Churches (2002) *Angels and Advocates: Church Social Action in Yorkshire and the Humber,* Leeds: Churches Regional Commission for Yorkshire & the Humber.

Young, I.M. (1990) *Justice and the Politics of Difference,* Princeton, NJ: Princeton University Press.

Yuval-Davis, N. (1991) 'Fundamentalism, Multiculturalism and Women in Britain', *International Review of Sociology,* 2: 139–73.

Zaidi, A. and Shuraydi, M. (2002) 'Perceptions of Arranged Marriage by Young Pakistani Muslim Women Living in a Western Society', *Journal of Comparative Family Studies,* 33 (4): 465–514.

Zolberg, A. and Long, I.W. (1999) 'Why Islam Is Like Spanish', *Politics and Society,* 27 (1): 5–38.

Zubaida, S. (2004) 'Islam and Nationalism: Continuities and Contradictions', *Nations and Nationalism,* 10 (4): 407–20.

Index

Note: Page numbers in *italics* refer to figures and tables.

Pell, G., 29
60/76 report, 38–42, 55, 64, 87
Pennell, H., 136
Pentecostalism
revival, 23, 148
Pew Global Attitudes Project, 20, 72–3
phenomenological approach to religion, 119
Phillips, A., 130
definition of multiculturalism, 91, 92
Phillips, D., 97
on religious self-separation, 45, 55–6
Phillips, N. [Lord Justice], 140
Phillips, T., 30, 54, 57, 135
Phillipson, C., 52
Pilger, J., 28
Pipes, D., 126
Pitcher, D., 145
Platt, L., 29, 142
Poldermans, S., 104, 105
Police Federation of England and Wales, 63
police service
positive discrimination, 63
religious discrimination perception and experiences, 71
stop and search statistics, 71, 87
Poole, E., 81
postmodernist approach to religion, 119–20
Pote, H.I., 51
Poulsen, M., 44
Poulter, S., 108
prejudice, 72–6, 95
priesthood
gender discrimination, 139
prisons
religious provisions, 31–2
Prohibition of Female Circumcision Act 1985 (UK), 105
Protestantism/Protestants
Scotland, 66
public protests, 126–9
public services
promotion of cohesion, 97–8
promotion of religious equality, 63

religious discrimination perception and experiences, 70–1
Pulling out of the Nosedive (Christian Research), 14
Purdam, K., 69
definition of religion, 1
definition of religious practice, 9, 13
on social dimensions of religion, 8
Puri, S., 100, 106, 111

Quakerism, 2
Qur'an
on domestic violence, 141
textual arrangement, 12
on women's rights and obligations, 138

Race Relations Acts (UK), 28, 60
Racial and Religious Hatred Act 2006 (RRHA) (England and Wales), 58, 59, 75
racial identity, 10
employment achievement and, 53
ethnic identity *v.*, 10
religious groups and, 10–11
racial inequality, 28–30
racialisation, 110–12
Ramadan, T., 125
Randerson, J., 135
Rastafarianism/Rastafarians
need for legal recognition, 60
UK 2001 Census, 3
Rath, J., 3–4
Rattansi, A., 98
criticism of cultural pluralism, 95
Raw, A., 45
Rawls, J., 6
Raz, A., 77, 106, 108, 109, 111, 138, 141
Raz, J., 113–14, 155
Reder, M., 123
Reeves, F., 47
Rehman-Sabba, A., 109
Reicher, S., 139
religion
behavioural and emotional aspects, 6–7
community separation and, 43–6
'death of religion', 14–15